SELF-PORTRAIT OF THE OTHER

by Heberto Padilla

HEROES ARE GRAZING IN MY GARDEN

LEGACIES: SELECTED POEMS

Heberto Padilla

SELF-PORTRAIT OF THE OTHER

Translated by Alexander Coleman

FARRAR · STRAUS · GIROUX

NEW YORK

English translation copyright © 1990 by Farrar, Straus and Giroux, Inc.
Originally published in Spanish as *La mala memoria*, © 1989 by Heberto Padilla
All rights reserved
Printed in the United States of America
Published simultaneously in Canada by Harper & Collins, Toronto
Designed by Jack Harrison
First edition, 1990

Library of Congress Cataloging-in-Publication Data
Padilla, Heberto.
    [La mala memoria. English]
    Self-portrait of the other / Heberto Padilla ; translated from the
Spanish by Alexander Coleman.
    Translation of: La mala memoria.
    1. Padilla, Heberto—Biography.
    2. Cuba—Politics and government—1959–
    3. Politics and literature—Cuba.
    4. Authors, Cuban—20th century—Biography. I. Title.
  PQ7390.P3Z46413 1990   861—dc19   [B]   89-1263

You see them rounding the faded corners of the page of paper,
Disappearing as we turn it.
They are living on a tropical island at war,
An island where all the glasses are broken,
An island on horseback.
They slip into the suburbs of the evening
And short-time hotels,
They set off on a bed with white sails
While he sings and she is just one more noise,
A wave under the bed.
Best be still and leave them alone to sleep
  And leave them alone to live
  And leave them alone to die.
At the bottom of the snapshot a few lines
testify to the fact:
No one is sure of anyone.
But they sail on,
They sail their island over all the seas of the world.

—BELKIS CUZA MALÉ
Translated by Alastair Reid

SELF-PORTRAIT OF THE OTHER

1

ON THE EVENING of December 31, 1958, I went home early. My friend Florence planned to celebrate the arrival of the New Year with her family. They were punctual people, and Florence and I barely had a few moments together. At around nine I left her in front of her building in what was then a tranquil Washington Heights and returned quickly to my own apartment. I felt a complete stranger in this great city where everyone was preparing to celebrate at midnight, but I had not thought about an invitation for any of the usual parties. Though I had been away from my wife and daughter in Cuba for six months, I was hardly the classic Cuban single gentleman that evening. Florence's eyes were welling with tears when I left her.

I was expert in reading her reactions as they were reflected in her eyes, which were huge, though often seemingly impassive. Of course, it is not easy to measure the worth of relations people have when they are young. In the specific case of a young man looking at a woman, this goes without saying, and it is only after we reach the age of thirty that we uncover the terror of living with someone else who is the same and yet different. Any intelligent woman should view any man with unease, and I could see in Florence's eyes, in the way she moved her hands in the air and said what she was thinking (thoughts that had seemed to resemble my own), that I was looking at a woman who was on the alert, almost on the defensive.

I am no longer the person I was. The naïveté of my adolescence did not vanish when my youth did. I remember crossing Hyde Park many years ago with a young English girl; she was surprised when I started yelling at a taxi driver who had taken the wrong turn. She said, "Heberto, you're foolish, you have to be fair." I had the impression that my childish outburst made her treat me with more caution. That night, looking out the window at the falling snow, I started reading aloud, like one hypnotized, from Robert Lowell's "Man and Wife": "Oh my *Petite*, / clearest of all God's creatures, still all air and nerve . . ." I fell asleep suddenly, as I would do later in prison, a habit which means, as an ex-prisoner once told me, that you haven't really suffered.

That New Year's Eve in New York, I missed Florence as never before, and when I heard the telephone clanging in my small echo-filled apartment, I included it in the action of a dream. Who could be calling? The phone rang on and on, and I eventually realized the call was real. I answered foggily: it was Florence's voice, telling me that something had happened in Cuba. But since nothing could happen in my country, I went back to sleep. A little while later, Florence appeared at the foot of my bed, still showing signs of exhaustion. She lay down and hugged me, wet and shivering: "You've been drinking, wake up . . ."

It was not a dream; my friends were clambering up the stairs and bursting through the door. Batista had fled Cuba, the revolution had triumphed. I leapt out of bed, threw some cold water on my face, and opened the windows. As the biting air filled the room, suddenly I felt a joy I had never felt before.

Practically all my Cuban friends lived in Washington Heights or close by. A group of us went from apartment to apartment, lighthearted and happy; or so I imagine, looking back on that night. Right now I am reconstructing the event from memory. I thought about it again for the first time nine years ago, when I landed in New York in March of 1980 and began to meet my old friends in the city. Months later, the Peruvian writer Mario Vargas Llosa would ask me about those days, when we saw each other at the Wilson Center in Washington, D.C. And ever since, I keep on remembering details as I sit in my house in Princeton.

New Year's Day itself became one long party. I had been teaching Spanish at the Rockefeller Center branch of the Berlitz School of Languages, and the next day my colleagues greeted me effusively. The director, Señor Vargas, and his deputy, Señor Manso, were Spanish exiles from Franco's Spain. Perhaps for that reason, they were less than euphoric. Señor Vargas gestured at the morning paper with its photograph of Fidel Castro and said, "People who don't shave every morning get no respect from me." The truth was that he was worried about my future. He had already asked me to be the director of another branch, which would have permitted me to be in the company's profit-sharing plan. At the time, I was busy preparing for Berlitz a reply to objections that other teachers had made about the vocabulary we used in our lessons. The direction of my life seemed set.

A few weeks later, however, the Cuban writer Humberto Arenal, who was then also living in New York, asked me to work with him on the recently created Cuban news agency, Prensa Latina, which he was about to take over. By then my only desire was to go back to Cuba, and I agreed.

2

~~~~~~

THIS WAS THE END of what Robert Lowell had called "the tranquilized Fifties." I was translating as well as teaching. When the Cuban Revolution triumphed, I was translating *Anabasis* and other poems of St.-John Perse from French into Spanish. I had always wanted to visit Washington again to show him some portion of my work, and I called him at his home and left a message, without expecting a reply. A few days later, the poet returned my call; he wanted to know exactly when I would be coming to Washington, informing me that his friend Archibald MacLeish was anxious to know more details about this sudden uprising in Cuba. All Washington had were garbled and contradictory stories.

I went to Washington a few days later. Perse's face was extraordinary, a fine parchment barely touched by the years. He wore a neat cardigan underneath his jacket and, when he received me, spoke in a measured voice. He hardly took any notice of my translations. I had done a Spanish version of the poem I admired the most, "Pictures for Crusoe," from the volume *Eloges*. But Perse wanted to ask me about Castro. Something was happening in the colonial world, he said, but to me his words sounded prehistoric. What did Cuba have to do with that colonial world (exemplified, say, by Algeria)? Surely this had all ended long ago, in 1898, when the Spaniards were driven out of Cuba.

Perse had just written *Amers*, though he still cherished his earlier work such as *Exile*. Like Claudel, he worked within and finally ended by preferring, above all, grand poetic structures. In the world of St.-John Perse, however, all the gods were dead. His hero was human enterprise, and his technique an infinite accumulation of ever-changing deeds, suitable to describe peace or war with equal intensity. Perse's home in Washington was an arsenal of bizarre objects which well could have formed the basis for some of the long poems in erratic free verse that André Breton had welcomed as the precursors of Surrealist poetry.

My impression is that in France today the poems which are still esteemed are precisely the ones I had the least interest in. I am still in love with Perse's first books, the ones that come out of the Antillean world of his birth. They are poems of a pristine enchantment whose like I have never again encountered. They remain intact in my memory, and I still think of them with the fervor of an adolescent's first reading.

Perse took me to a café on M Street where he liked to go, and we sat there for a long time, talking. He had no intention of returning to France, he told me. He was happy at the Library of Congress and was working on another poem, yes, another long love poem, but this time a work whose theme was physical and carnal love.

I should say that I had first met him in the spring of 1958, in Washington, D.C. In the city on a visit, I looked him up in the telephone book and, taking my courage in my hands, called him. He said he would be delighted to see me, and he asked for my Washington address. He would be out of town for a few days, and would send me a telegram stating where and when we might meet, he explained. During my stay, Ezra Pound was released from Saint Elisabeths, where he had been a patient since the war. I was able to see him close up, as he walked along, followed by photographers, through a crowd of people who were looking at him with curiosity though they hadn't the slightest idea who he was. On that chill spring day, Pound wore a dark felt hat and a black cape. He seemed to look around aimlessly, smiling as if on cue. He walked on for a long time through the streets, and the newspapers published his photograph. I wanted to speak to him, but I couldn't bring myself to approach this man who had been vanquished by his own contradictions and afflictions.

I would later speak of Pound with Perse. He, along with MacLeish, Robert Frost, and Ernest Hemingway, had made it a cause to free the great poet from the asylum. Confinement in Saint Elisabeths had been the only solution the American authorities could come up with to avoid imposing a harsher penalty on the old anti-Semite whose involvement with the values of Europe as he saw them had drawn him inexorably to militant Fascism. Perse wanted Pound freed, for him to be the responsible moral agent of his own case, to judge himself. At that time, of course, I knew far more about Ezra Pound than I did about Fidel Castro, but Perse was interested far more in talking to me about Castro. Who was this audacious young man? What could I tell him about his life, his background?

Fidel Castro had never explicitly stated a political ideology. St.-John Perse, who had lived through the Fascist persecution in Vichy France (he had been secretary to the liberal Foreign Minister Aristide Briand, and he told me that after the French defeat in 1940 Gestapo agents had stormed into his house and confiscated many of his possessions, including some of his best poems), asked me the same questions over and over again. What kind of internal support did Castro have? Was it a national uprising or a more deep-seated revolution? Did the 26th of July Movement mark the institutional transformation of Cuba?

I didn't know how to answer Perse's questions. I had supported Fidel Castro as a way of opposing the government of Fulgencio Batista, whom I blamed for having put an end to the democratic political framework that his predecessors, Ramón Grau and Carlos Prío, had respected. Of course these governments were corrupt, but the period saw the birth of a Social Democratic wing led by two of the most popular politicians in Cuban political history, Eduardo Chibás and José Pardo Llada. This movement, had Batista not come to power, might well have institutionalized democracy in Cuba.

Pardo was the most influential journalist of his generation. All of Cuba would listen to his afternoon radio commentaries. In 1950, he became a representative at age twenty-four; he could not aspire to the Senate, since the Constitution decreed a minimum age of thirty-five. He won his first election by the greatest majority obtained by any candidate in the forty-eight-year history of the Cuban Republic. He soon joined Senator Chibás's Orthodox Cuban People's Party and the two of them became gigantic battering rams against corruption in government and against the gangsterish groups which thrived in the shadow of power. Though not the government's only critics, Chibás and Pardo had the most electoral support and the broadest popular recognition.

Fidel Castro was also a member of the Orthodox Party (as everyone used to call the group founded by Chibás), but he carried no weight within the party. Even as a student leader, he was unable to win the presidency of the University Student

Federation (FEU), which at that time wielded great influence on Cuban political life, far beyond the hilltop campus of the University of Havana. To be sure, Fidel did not take part in all the activities of the federation, but he was among the student leaders. It was a brutal era.

In 1940, 1941, and 1942, the most important groups were the student branches of the Revolutionary Socialist Movement, led by Manolo Castro (a veteran of the Spanish Civil War who had been national director of athletics in the Grau government) and Rolando Masferrer (a rash and capable politician, veteran also of the Spanish war, and a former member of the Communist Party), and the Revolutionary Insurrectionist Union, run by Emilio Tró, a U.S. Army veteran. This latter was the group which Fidel Castro joined.

The leaders of these organizations died in violent confrontations with the police or with rival groups. For many years the assassination of Manolo was attributed to Fidel. Although this could never be proven, the possibility became part of Fidel's legend. At the time, however, Fidel stood out less as a youth fighting corruption in Cuban life than as the Gallego, ready to face off even his most intrepid rivals with a pistol. The student body as a whole took little interest in Fidel, voting instead for people like Enrique Ovares, Justo Fuentes, Enrique Huertas, and Álvaro Barba, whom students recognized as their true spokesmen. Fidel was never able to do more than exhibit his love for violence and his recklessness. He was physically prepossessing, a sturdy six feet, with the hoarse voice of a child that reminded many of us of President Prío's.

It was during one of the demonstrations of the FEU commemorating the 27th of November (the date in 1871 when the Spanish colonial government had executed eight medical students) that Fidel finally persuaded the student leaders to let him speak. "The fatherland must be looked upon as an altar before which we offer our lives," he said, "and not a pedestal for us to stand on." Although Castro, then beardless, did everything he could to imitate the tone and style of José

Pardo Llada's radio broadcasts, what the peroration seemed to show was an extraordinary capacity for improvising, and without any hesitation. But gradually, as the speech wound on, the unmistakable source of what he was saying hit me—a famous speech by José Martí. I noted this fact with Carlos Miguel Díaz, a schoolmate who was standing next to me.

"He's another Pierre Menard," he said with a smile. (In those days Díaz was fanatically reading the stories of Borges; Pierre Menard is that Borgesian character who attempts to write *Don Quixote* all over again, and produces a text identical to the original without having copied it.) Castro was repeating, word for word, an entire speech of Martí's. Naturally, it won the loudest applause and the highest praise. Lucky the speaker, whose audience did not know or remember the words of Martí.

Now, I do not think that Castro would have cared if his plagiarism had been revealed: he was determined to insert himself in history in whatever way possible. The audacity which brought him to appropriate a text of José Martí's was an early foreshadowing of his ability to make use of any means in politics—perhaps in the same sense that brought Mirabeau, in the solitude of prison, to write letters to his mistress in which he included, as if they were his, any newspaper articles that he thought worthy of consideration.

This tendency of Fidel to take other people's words led him to take as his own ideas, sentences, and slogans from writers who did not by any means have the moral and intellectual fiber of Martí. These included Benito Mussolini and Adolf Hitler. The fact is that both these men were among Castro's favorite writers well after the Second World War, when both Fascist and Nazi crimes were known to the world. Castro treasured his twelve-volume set of Mussolini's *Discourses and Writings*, and *Mein Kampf* was, by his own admission, among his favorite reading in the nineteen-forties.

Just recently I heard some old recordings of Mussolini attacking "British imperialism," and I had the feeling that I was listening to Fidel Castro attacking "Yankee imperialism,"

surrounded by the raucous approval of his inflamed supporters. Fidel has been faithful to this long-standing admiration
through the years—to cite only one example, the slogan
"Venceremos" ("We shall triumph"), with which he always
ended his speeches, was also Mussolini's. The textual imitation
of Hitler is more dramatic. Fidel ended his renowned defense
of the Moncada Barracks assault with the same sentence that
the Nazi leader used in the Munich courtroom: "Condemn me
. . . History will absolve me." The unabashed manipulation of
historical memory is one of the most recurrent traits in Castro's
personality.

The first time I was able to have a long talk with him was
in 1951, in the attractive Havana apartment, decorated in
colonial style, of a politician from Matanzas Province, Yuyo
del Valle, and his wife, Maruca, who was so beautiful that no
one dared look at her face. It was very early in the morning,
just before sunrise. I had been traveling with Juan Amador
Rodríguez, a journalist who was then a candidate for the
Senate from the province of Pinar del Río. Around eight
o'clock that morning we met with Mario Rivadulla and Omar
Borges. Fidel arrived a bit later. He was wearing baggy pants
and a rumpled shirt, and it was clear that he had just gotten
out of bed. Maruca offered us coffee, and when a cup was
passed to Fidel, she couldn't resist asking him if he had slept
with his clothes on. "Not only that, your socks aren't the same
color." Fidel looked at his socks in consternation, but eventually
joined in our laughter.

"The people don't dress any better," he retorted.

"The people are neater than you think," she said, "and they
don't miss a thing. They won't understand why you have on
different-colored socks. They'll think you are crazy."

"*That*, never. Me crazy? Never."

"I'll give you a pair of Yuyo's socks," she said. Fidel promised
to return them after the trip and then asked if they could
spare a shirt.

"How in the name of God is that body going to get into one

of my shirts?" asked Yuyo. He was not very tall and a bit fat.

Someone went to iron a shirt, and after a little while we left. Later, our small campaign caravan made its way to the province of Matanzas. It was a long trip. We stopped at the towns which would be the most important in the election, and in each a good number of people were waiting. As we arrived, we could see the grandstand from which Borges, Rivadulla, Amador, and Fidel Castro would make their speeches. Each speaker enthusiastically praised "the soon-to-be Senator Yuyo del Valle, unquestionably the candidate of the people from Matanzas." Yuyo would make the last speech. The style and logic of the speech was the same as that of the others: the government party was evil; the opposition (represented by us) was good.

It was a strange trip. Fidel Castro wanted to be a member of the House of Representatives from Havana, Amador a senator representing Pinar del Río, and Yuyo one for Matanzas Province. Mario Rivadulla and Omar Borges were national directors of the Cuban People's Party. Another man accompanied us, enigmatic because of his silence, and attached to his big felt hat, which he never took off; he paid for the meals and the drinks, and he seemed content. It was José Manuel Gutiérrez, the provincial chief of the party.

At the town of Amarillas, Juan Amador asked me "to say a few words." It was the first time I spoke in public. I was eighteen years old, didn't yet have the right to vote, but I shared the same moral concerns as my friends on the trip. I was on their side. Like them, I dreamed of a kind of liberty where corruption was not the price the country had to pay to enjoy that liberty. We went from one town to another; in the stifling heat we were like actors declaiming the roles of a political action which was consuming itself with the passing hours.

Finally we arrived at Varadero, and went to the old Hotel San Carlos, where Gutiérrez had reserved us rooms for the night. We went down to the beach and swam for an hour, until we couldn't take any more. After supper, Rivadulla, Fidel, and I sat down to talk on an abandoned dock. My vocation was literature; Fidel, Borges, Rivadulla, a few years older than I, represented a new generation of Cubans in political campaigns, fighting for honesty in government. I really wanted to comprehend them, to get something out of their experiences, ideas which would help me define that fleeting, inexplicable, multifarious thing that was Cuban reality—a mixture of intractable history and geography which I could neither decode nor reflect in my own work. The tropical landscape had the same effect on me as it did on our Cuban painters; it became a flocking of light into the retina, a blackness or splendor without nuance. Suddenly Fidel said, "The writer I like best is Romain Rolland."

"Careful, this man is a writer too," said Rivadulla.

"Really?" asked Fidel.

"Don't mind him. In Cuba, everybody is a writer."

"Do you like Romain Rolland?"

"I read him long ago."

"Well, I don't read him often."

"He was a moralist." Fidel looked at me happily. "Yes, that's what I like about him. He didn't write just to write. He was concerned with social problems."

"So was Victor Hugo."

"But Victor Hugo is old hat, from another era."

"So is Rolland. His real time was before World War I, and he stayed there. The war he wanted finished him off somehow. Can you still read *Jean-Christophe?*"

"Maybe, but now I am reading other things. I like Malaparte's *Kaputt* and his *Technique of the Coup d'Etat*."

Mario Rivadulla agreed enthusiastically. Malaparte was the one he liked the most. More than Rolland.

Then Fidel began to speak of Dostoevsky, and his familiarity surprised me. Yet, how could he admire both a naïve philanthropist and an explorer of the depths of the human spirit?

What kind of *vases communicants* did this young politician establish between Rolland and Dostoevsky?

French was my second language. I forced myself to learn it while still an unhappy adolescent. The daily classes started at eight o'clock in the morning. After the hour was up, my aged professor, Robert Rest, who still dressed à la fin du siècle, threw open his arms like someone who had just completed a grand undertaking—"*Et bien, nous avons fini, cher ami. C'est à vous le travail de continuer.*" He gave me books. The first was *Noces* by Albert Camus. Whatever Rest's empathy for the book, I do not think he could begin to share my admiration for its verbal power. Camus's prose rose before my eyes, glittering patches from the sea and earth of Algeria, out of which flowed his meditations on life, love, death, and, of course, history.

I found a spiritual home in Camus's tempered lucidity and in his celebration of the flesh. His work made me feel that I was the raging prophet of an elect. Poets and painters seemed to me a barbarous lot. I believed that their genius was a kind of primary, animal secretion, and I would gladly have exchanged the most attractive metaphor of the century for a formulation that was as close as possible to exactitude itself. My heroes had the obligation to find out why they loved or hated, why they exalted themselves or scoffed at themselves. What moved me to tears was intelligence. My favorite novelist was Kafka, for precisely the reasons that some Hispanic writers disdained him. His language did not derive from literature, rather from manuals of engineering, physics, and botany. As Nabokov noted, Kafka was brother to Flaubert, but all those who attempted to repeat the desperate search of the French novelist for *le mot juste* had not the slightest notion of the cleansing effect afforded by the escape from vagueness and generality.

Cuban literary life in the fifties was utterly impoverished. Alejo Carpentier had fled to Venezuela, where he eked out a meager living. The fine writer Lino Novás Calvo ruminated morosely on his disenchantment in the editorial offices of the weekly magazine *Bohemia*, translating American detective stories, for which the magazine paid no royalties. Enrique Serpa wrote lengthy political reportage, as did the talented essayists Jorge Mañach and Francisco Ichazo. José Lezama Lima, erratic and tenacious, argued for a paradisiacal insularity. He stated that the essence of a Cuban sense of things was only the spirit at the margin of history. "A country which is frustrated in its political essence has to find its expression in other realms of greater nobility."

A polemic broke out in 1948 between Mañach and Lezama Lima which has not been given enough attention by Lezama's faithful adherents on the international scene. Mañach began it all in the pages of *Bohemia* when he reviewed two books of poetry by Lezama Lima and Cintio Vitier. Mañach criticized both writers for insisting on an outdated, hermetic poetics, and suggested that they communicate experience on a level that the common reader might understand. Lezama had always walked the highroad, prevailing because of his total dedication to literature as a virtue in itself, as against those who had traded away *la fede por la sede*, the discipline of a working writer for the easy money of the immediate situation. Even in the realm of the selfless high priests of culture, politics reared its head as a synonym of corruption and lucre.

In spite of their differences, all political parties in Cuba had a similar leadership in which one intellectual and one black man were indispensable as window dressing. Women were no factor at all then. After all, Hegel had decreed in his *Philosophy of Right* that all women had to obey men, and hard as it is to believe now, Hegel was an indispensable authority for Cuban intellectuals. That is the way things were at the beginning of the second half of this century. Cuba was a country for sale, a parody of a country.

Eight years mean much in the history of a generation. Ours began to acquire its identity during the government of Prío Socarrás. The fifties had erased the dreadful memory of the earlier tyrannies in the history of the Republic—even Batista in 1944 had been a knowledgeable politician who had not hesitated to hand over the power of government to Professor Ramón Grau San Martín, his electoral opponent. For us, democracy was inexorable.

The books we had talked about that evening in 1951, as dissimilar as they were, were a way for us to talk about morality in public life. Of the friends of that evening on the dock, I never saw Yuyo del Valle or José Manuel Gutiérrez again. Just before leaving Cuba once and for all in 1980, I saw the ex-director of the Orthodox Youth Party, Omar Borges, a few times. I have been told that Mario Rivadulla spent time in prison and now lives in Santo Domingo, but I have not even seen a photo of Rivadulla as he is today. I imagine him as he was thirty years ago—tall, thin, blond, with bright eyes and a vibrant voice which reminded me of Chibás. I have seen Juan Amador Rodríguez in Miami, and he is the same as always, jovial and surprisingly youthful. He remembers those days with astonishing precision.

At that time I lived in Havana. I didn't have a cent. The novelist Enrique Labrador Ruiz arranged it so I could sleep in the editorial offices of *Crónica*, a short-lived literary review. Every night, after the employees had left, I would set up a canvas cot between the desks. I was tormented by a small white dog, owned by two old ladies who lived in the back of the building, who would get into the offices through a broken pane on the back door and sniff at me. Resistance was futile, and for a few months we shared a bed.

In fact, I was luckier than most. My friend Rolando Escardó slept on the cobblestones of the Plaza del Vapor, now long gone, and Fayad Jamís in a shabby attic. With two or three exceptions, this is the way my generation grew up. The thought that possessed us was how to engineer a leap aboard one of those big steamers anchored in the harbor and take off for anywhere. Our ordinary living situation was misery itself, but there was also a passion for art and a hatred of the loudmouthed politicians who represented the only image we had of our country.

Juan Amador also came from a poor family. In my most desperate moments, I would visit him in the offices of Radio Progreso, always fearing that he might not be there. As I would enter, an object of a now almost archaeological nature announced the fact that he was in—a gigantic tape recorder, which he carried with him from one place to another, interviewing criminals in jails or hospitals. Juan Amador took a special interest in hospitals, believing that there the greatest diversity of human situations could be found—survivors of crimes of passion, victims of assassination attempts, criminals caught red-handed by the police. Amador would portray them accurately, though he had a special talent for bringing out the dramatic aspect of these incidents and of turning them into appealing anecdotes for the listener. This technique humanized the person involved, and even ennobled the journalist to a degree. Amador wanted to help me and suggested that I make a selection of his most intriguing interviews, transcribe them, add a short introduction, and offer the result to *Bohemia*. The magazine accepted the manuscript: Amador passed on the fifty dollars to me without keeping anything for himself.

So what was I doing in 1951, discussing things with Fidel Castro and Mario Rivadulla, militant members of the most important political party of the opposition? It is true that we were talking about literature, but we were on a political campaign, and I was as hoarse from speechmaking as they were, using the same arguments as they. No question, I enjoyed their company more than that of my melancholy, desperate litterateurs who worshipped the god of culture.

I was attracted to Juan Amador, Fidel, Borges, and Rivadulla because they were not attempting to "transform" life in the Rimbaudian sense, but rather trying to change the political and economic life of Cuba, without which it would not be possible to obtain results "in other realms of greater nobility," as Lezama Lima would have it.

Of the members of the group, Fidel Castro was for me the least appealing. His importance derived from the thrust of his personality, which had already been confirmed by a few daring political acts in which his physical recklessness was evident. I was interested more in the sober intelligence of Rivadulla, whose oratorical talents were on the same level as Pardo Llada's and Chibás's. You could get to know those people; they were accessible. In contrast, Fidel gave off an air of a lack of concentration, an inexplicable abandonment of self. He talked without ever looking at the face of the person he was addressing, a trait which we attributed to his nearsightedness, a defect he could not resign himself to. Altogether, there was a human quality missing in him which he attempted to hide behind an aggressive and unpredictable petulance. I recall his talking about Enrique José Varona, perhaps the last of our great thinkers and the only Cuban who took no interest in adjectives. Fidel told me: "His inconsequence is disagreeable to me. He fought against Spain, and then wrote a long poem of repentance, 'The Prodigal Daughter,' which would make even an Uruguayan burst out laughing; his philosophical positivism doesn't mean a thing. I hate him because he was too much a realist. Politics has to carry with it a good dose of improvisation and delirium. If I were in power, I would toss him aside, and make sure that no one remembered him. But he was right in one thing, something uglier and less attractive to the masses, and that is, he never believed in either democracy or elections, or in rule by the majority. True political changes are carried out by vanguards; the politician who gets the most votes is the worst. The assent of the majority is always spurious. Applause always brings compromise. New ideas get imposed by fists."

"Don't let Chibás hear you," said Rivadulla.

Fidel laughed. In Cuba, laughter puts an end to even the most serious conversations. I want to record his words just as he said them, with the same vehemence. I believe that I am being accurate.

Chibás had a radio program that came on every Sunday at eight o'clock on CMQ, the station with the largest audience in Cuba. In effect, it was the most important political forum in the history of the Republic. At that time, Fidel was an insignificant figure. The dominant political personality of the opposition was Chibás. But Chibás's political campaign eventually became too egocentric. When he accused the Minister of Education, Aureliano Sánchez Arango, of having bought land in Central America with public funds and then could not prove it (I remember well the broadcast, during which he pounded on a suitcase which he said contained the documents proving the minister's guilt), the collapse of his reputation was so severe that he never recovered. During the Sunday program, as Pardo Llada spoke of the pervasive political corruption, Chibás grabbed the microphone and gave a short and impressive speech, a call to the consciences of all Cubans so that they might not be deceived yet again. "This," he said, "is my last bell clap." He then pulled out a pistol and shot himself, surrounded by his closest friends.

Always at the margin of things, Fidel, ashen-faced but efficient, was waiting at the entrance of the radio station to take Chibás to the hospital. That pistol shot on the night of the first of August 1951 changed the face of Cuba. With the elections imminent, the Cuban People's Party had only the corpse of their leader. Chibás's popularity could only have been equaled by that of Pardo Llada, but he was too young; the Constitution called for a minimum age of forty-four for the presidency. The party of Chibás had no choice but to nominate Roberto Agromonte, a professor of sociology lacking in charisma, possessor of a crepuscular vocabulary, as when he referred to the late Chibás as "our champion."

The death of "our champion" gave Fulgencio Batista high hopes for a comeback. On the morning of the 10th of March 1952, the general and his followers entered his old base of operations—the military encampment of Columbia. It was a coup d'état with no resistance whatsoever. President Prío and the most important ministers of his government went into exile.

I will never forget the lengthy silence on the radio and at the television stations. Around ten that morning, a voice dryly announced that General Batista had taken charge of the government. It was the voice of Ernesto de la Fe, recently named to a ministry heretofore unheard of—the Ministry of Information. I saw Juan Amador and Álvaro Barba all the time. An atmosphere of tense expectation reigned everywhere. People remembered the grim times of the first Batista dictatorship. Nothing indicated that things would be any better now. Politicians, artists, and writers maintained a prudent distance from risks. Two weeks later, while I was in the studios of Radio Progreso, where Juan Amador was continuing his series of "Detective Interviews" with all the due caution that the moment indicated, we received news of Fidel Castro.

On the 24th of March 1952, Fidel appeared before the Supreme Court of Justice with a document which began: "I, Fidel Castro Ruiz, in my status as lawyer with offices on 57 Tejado Street, hereby accuse Fulgencio Batista Zaldívar of sixteen crimes committed against the Constitution . . . and I ask for a sentence against the usurper President of 100 *years in prison!!!*"

This document, which enumerated each and every crime against the Constitution, was one which the General Batista of the thirties would have taken as an infamous libel. But in 1952 it circulated freely throughout the University of Havana and the newspaper offices as "another lunacy of Fidel's." For Batista, it was an indication to the people that his return to power did not exclude political free expression, within certain limits. The one thing he was not willing to tolerate was armed opposition.

The Supreme Court threw out Fidel Castro's petition, ruling (cowardly enough) that a coup d'état automatically annuls a prior valid constitution. I do not know if Fidel Castro realized that his denunciation made Batista show his cards, but Batista did so without taking reprisals against Castro, who, after all, was the brother-in-law of Rafael Díaz Balart, one of Batista's closest friends and collaborators. In fact, I think that part of Fidel's strategy was to assure Batista that he was in opposition, yes, but as a means of taking part in the political process of the nation. Pardo Llada told me that, just before Fidel decided to join the Orthodox Party, he had gone to see Senator Batista accompanied by his brother-in-law, Balart, to discuss the possibility of joining Batista's PAU party. The Balart family served as Castro's protectors. They would tolerate his dreams of power as long as those dreams did not conflict with the general's own power. But they were mistaken. The recent graduate of the Havana School of Law had the same ambitions as Batista—absolute power over the largest island in the Antilles chain. Fidel countered Batista's cunning with his own. He abandoned electoral politics to the old-time politicians, since the process had never brought him any satisfactory results in any case. He had no further interest in the declarations of representatives or senators. What interested him was the power to institute his own political program.

What was that program? Whatever it was, he was certain that in order to carry it out he had to annul all electoral machinery and make use of a "good dose of improvisation and delirium." I believe that at that time Fidel felt that he embodied the vanguard, destined to carry out radical political changes. In other words, the "new ideas" would require force and "fists" to be imposed. On the 26th of July 1953, no one could entertain any doubts about what road Fidel meant to take. With the raid on the Moncada Barracks, Fidel drove his method home. Breaching all political routines with one act of violence, the politician whose face had long gone unrecognized suddenly, overnight, made the front pages of all the newspapers.

The Popular Socialist Party (Communist) condemned the attack on the Moncada Barracks. After all, the action was not to be found in the methodology of orthodox Marxism–Leninism, but since the party could count on only ten thousand or so members, its objections were taken as a kind of aesthetic irritant. Cuban history seemed to be deviating grossly from classic revolutionary models. The Moncada attack, carried out at the height of carnival time in Santiago, could have been the end of Fidel Castro. It wasn't. Fidel disguised himself as an officer in the army, convinced that in this uniform he would prevail. Haydée Santamaría has described on one occasion the scene in which Fidel, dressed in a general's uniform, looked at himself in the mirror like an actor, asking his closest comrades if he looked "like a general or not." He certainly did look like one: a general should have a proper carriage, a firm gaze, and be always ready to give an order. When Fidel and his men burst into the barracks, there was a gun battle in which a good number died. Just when the Cuban Army was about to win the engagement, he and his men escaped from the surrounded building and took refuge in the green depths of the Cuban jungle.

With this exploit, Fidel reclaimed his brand of militancy. But the action also conferred upon him the reputation of a revolutionary with a political program. Never again would he be taken as a "man with an itchy trigger finger," but rather as a member of those borderline groups which make up the ethical zealotry of a society. After a while, he was finally taken prisoner, his life saved by the generosity of Lieutenant Pedro Sarriá, the officer in charge of the chase, and by the intervention of Monsignor Enrique Pérez Serantes, Archbishop of Santiago de Cuba. Fidel was out of danger; indeed, the affair made him the leader of the political opposition to Batista. For Fidel, the fundamental obligation of a politician was survival.

The survivor could count on a comfortable prison cell, the same one which he occupied on the Isle of Pines, which is today shown to tourists as a chamber of horrors. (It would be good if they were to visit the Cuban prison cells of today, without air or light, the grim buildings where Fidel systematically locks up his prisoners.) Before two years of the sentence had been served, pressure from Fidel's family and realist politicians secured an amnesty for the commander of the Moncada attack. In the newspapers, there were photos of Fidel and his men leaving prison, greeting the photographers with hands held high.

A few days later I ran into Fidel by accident. He was climbing the stairs to Radio COCO to see Pardo Llada and Juan Amador Rodríguez. He greeted me effusively. He was thin and pale, hair cut very short and mustache neatly trimmed. "I'm off to Mexico. It's hard to keep going here. I'm going to say goodbye to Pardo and Juan." There was the implication that he had given up the fight. "You'll hear from me soon."

Just a little over a year later, everyone heard from him. "Before the 31st of December 1956, we will be heroes or martyrs." This declaration from Mexico was published in Cuba by the magazine *Alerta*. And, in fact, he landed that month with eighty-four men on the southern coast of Oriente Province.

I did not see him again until he came to the United States, now the leader of a triumphant revolution, answering questions in English at a press conference in New York. Seemingly, Fidel had decided to take another image. The resplendent olive-green Comandante's uniform was no less impressive than the apocryphal general's he made use of during the Moncada attack. Every effort had been made to eliminate that air of a "Dr. Castro," the form of address the reporters were using. No, from now on, he would be Fidel, plain and simple.

Around that time, one event disturbed me, and I brought the matter up a few times with Alberto Martínez Herrera. Why had Raúl Castro, Fidel's brother, let himself be photographed just as he administered the coup de grâce to a notorious traitor? Why was he bringing the nation together under the banner of unity with this savage spilling of blood? Why should violence be the distinctive marker in a campaign for peace and justice? As I say, these matters caused me much anguish, but I did not bring them to the attention of St.-John Perse. I limited myself to telling him what I knew of the life of the revolutionary commander whose name was now on the lips of everyone. We young people were ready to return to Cuba. We were prepared to put our enthusiasm and talent at his service.

3

~~~~~~

THERE WERE ONLY TWO employees in the offices of Prensa
Latina in New York—Humberto Arenal and myself. The main
bureau of the service was located in Washington, D.C., headed
by Ángel Boan, with whom Arenal did not get along. Boan
was a professional without ideology, an able reporter whom I
had known in Havana before the Revolution. Beneath his
modest friendliness, there was cunning in him, though. I
remember lunching with him in New York and speaking about
returning to Cuba. He told me that I was needed in New York.
With my knowledge of English and the North American scene,
the best place to start my career as a journalist would be Prensa

Latina in New York City. I was told that it was an independent enterprise backed by Cuban and Venezuelan money. What would I do in the Havana main office, where the competition would be so much rougher?

I admitted that I was probably making a mistake by returning to Cuba, but since all signs pointed to the fact that a splendid political transformation toward good government had begun, I wanted to be part of it in any way I could. You had to do away with what was bad and then start all over again.

"Have you read the newspapers and the cables?"

"Why are you asking?"

"Doing away with what was bad, as you put it, is beginning to cost us some negative reactions."

"But everyone supports us."

"We haven't lost a bit of support yet."

"So?"

"Heberto, in Cuba a revolution has begun."

I burst out laughing.

"You are a younger man than I," Boan added. "And there are problems with the United States government. They want to impose certain unacceptable conditions."

"What are these conditions?"

"Don't ask me. Just now, something important has happened. Eisenhower has refused to see Fidel. There was tough talk between Fidel and Nixon. Fidel told him that he had questions that he could discuss only with the President. Certain matters are not dealt with by talking to Vice Presidents. Nixon said he was sorry but the President was playing golf. That's the way things are. When do you want to leave?"

"Just as soon as I can," I said.

"Tell all this to Masetti" (then the general director of the agency). "Tell him what I told you. Try to see him around ten in the evening—that's the best time to get him."

I did not pay much attention to the conversation. Fidel was not the President of Cuba, and from the standpoint of protocol,

Nixon was right. Nonetheless, the encounter with Nixon gave some idea of the personal style of the Comandante—protocol, institutional mediation were all meaningless to him. Chiefs speak to chiefs. From the vantage point of thirty years later, when neither Eisenhower nor Nixon determines American policy, it seems obvious that those matters which the Cuban comandante wanted to take up with the veteran of the Second World War were well worth postponing a golf game for.

Once Boan had ratified my decision to return to Cuba, New York rose before my eyes, that early spring of 1959, as an unreal spectacle which I would be able to enjoy as few harried office workers might. Art seemed embarked on a new phase. The publication of Robert Lowell's *Life Studies* was a revelation for me. This young poet had brought back to American poetry a vigor of language that had dissipated—he was different from Eliot, Auden, Stevens, and William Carlos Williams. He was a product of the university but paid no attention to the dictates of Allen Tate or Yvor Winters. He distanced himself also from the Beat poets, headed by Allen Ginsberg, who had made a strident and self-pitying formula out of personal experience. For me, the chaotic enumerations of the early Ginsberg were just too close to the late poetry of García Lorca. Without the Spanish poet's book *Poet in New York*, without his extraordinary "Ode to Walt Whitman," many of the most significant American poems of the fifties would be inconceivable. But Robert Lowell was far superior to them.

Along with *Life Studies* I read *The Hawk in the Rain* by the English poet Ted Hughes, who at that time was living in the United States. Both poets helped sustain my notion that poetry does not inevitably have to be subjected to abstraction and the systematic chain of metaphors which have tyrannized poetics in the Spanish language over the centuries. I believe that the premises of the baroque Spanish poet Luis de Góngora and the ongoing Gongorism with which our poetry is plagued embody an error for which we are paying dearly today.

Gongorism is a totalitarian discourse that was imposed by the Spanish Generation of 1927 as a delayed reply from Spain to the French Surrealist movement.

I felt free in New York, and used to shout out this fact with my habitual insolence. My dear friend Eugenio Florit, a great poet in any language, would always greet me in his office at Barnard College and then argue against whatever I was saying, smiling all the while. He gave me his translations of American poets to read; they stand on their own in Spanish.

Every morning I would buy all the available newspapers, just as we used to do in Havana. I would bring my white shirts to one of those laundry chains called Peter Prompt and pick them up the next day—immaculate, with a paper band around them printed with the logo of the firm, a smiling boy with a blue cap. I did not mind the work I did as a teacher of Spanish with Berlitz at their Rockefeller Center branch. There I met a broad cross section of artists and writers from all over the world, all the same age, more or less. Between classes we would discuss intensely the work we were doing on our own. All of them had been in the States for only a short time—French, Germans, Russians, Italians, Japanese, Chinese. Many of them had little English. I found my best friends among the French.

I had met Florence at the school. She was young and pretty, and spoke a number of languages, including Spanish. Depending on the circumstances, we would speak either French or Spanish, and our friendship flourished because each was able to speak the language of the other. Florence used to intone some relatively unknown poems of Antonio Machado, and she introduced me to one of the great women poets of France, Louise Labé: *"Et si jamais ma pauvre âme amoreuse . . ."* Florence would insist on my pronouncing correctly certain other poems, of Ronsard, for example, which she also adored. Years later, no matter where I am in the world, I say aloud poems that I learned from her: *"Mignone, allons voir si la rose . . ."* or *"Quand tu serais bien vielle . . ."* Both of us despised the final, exhausted vestiges of Surrealism that were coming over from Paris. We found it pompous and learned in the worst sense. Rimbaud was always an innovation for us; when we sought out the verbal music which "newspaper prose" had not destroyed, we would recite "La chanson du mal aimée" or "Sous le pont Mirabeau" of Apollinaire.

Nevertheless, I was seeking something different in poetry. As with the novelists and poets I admired, I did not want to describe but rather to construct, following the dictum of Pound—the best symbol is the object itself. New York was the exact archetype of a construction, a profusion of precise beauty where no one, or practically no one, felt a stranger. After forty years in the United States, Auden had said, "I do not know if I have become an American, but I am convinced that I am a New Yorker." But I wasn't.

The real citizen of a great city becomes one only after an inevitable maturing process which time gradually affords us. I could never be seized by the city as it looked twenty years later; it seemed to me a malodorous site in ruins, with streets and façades looking as if they had just undergone a bombardment. *This* New York City reminded me of those lines of St.-John Perse from his poem "Pictures for Crusoe": "Grease! / Odour of men in crowds, like the stale smell of a slaughterhouse! sour bodies of women under their skirts / O City against the sky! / Grease! breaths rebreathed, and the smoke of a very dubious people—for every city encompasses filth . . ."*

I said goodbye to my friends at Berlitz. Florence wanted to talk about something personal before I left. We went to the elegant café we frequented after work. Sometimes she tried to describe all the opportunities her parents had to get out of Paris when the German troops were but a few kilometers away. She was three years old at the time, and could never forget the desperation and the panic of the people. When I reminded her that it was impossible for her to have such a clear memory

* St.-John Perse, *Collected Poems* (Princeton: Princeton University Press, 1971), trans. Louise Varèse.

of something that happened at that age, she took pencil and paper and imitated her father tracing out routes to safe places in case he were to disappear. Since he did die at the hands of the Gestapo, I suggested that maybe she was repeating the stories told her by her mother.

"What is it that you want to talk about?"

"As long as you're on my side," she said, smiling.

I nodded, and she went on: "With my four languages and typing abilities, couldn't I go away to work in Cuba, in your press agency, or someplace? I would love to get out of this routine for a while."

I thought it was a fine idea, and we agreed that as soon as I arrived in Havana I would look for something and get in touch with her right away. "Study the terrain, and above all, don't hide the truth from me," she said. After two weeks in Cuba, I was not only incapable of studying the terrain; I kept on oscillating between two worlds without knowing where the truth was.

I met with my old friends again. I spoke with Masetti and passed along the message from Ángel Boan, but Masetti, an Argentinian, smiled wanly and said nothing. We agreed that I would start work the next day.

I woke up with the light, which in Cuba is penetrating even at six in the morning. On the way to the offices of Prensa Latina, I was barely able to move through the tumultuous street crowds. But there was something even more powerful and overwhelming than the agitation of the people in the streets; it was an atmosphere that I had never been able to become reconciled to—the climate of Cuba.

I left New York at the beginning of June, when there is still a cool breeze at sunset. I took the midnight plane, which was to make a stop in Miami in the early morning. After three years, it was my first encounter with a climate identical to Cuba's. I stayed in a downtown hotel, no air-conditioning, and I could not sleep. In the morning I had a glass of iced tea in a cool cafeteria, killing time until the hour of departure. To leap from a cloud-covered New York in the month of June to this enslaving luminosity makes for an impact in which things lose their perspective and profile, converted into a multicolored ensemble where each color struggles to dominate what we see. Strong yellows, whites, blues. Like Havana, Miami is an orgy of blues. Every object seems larger than when it is clouded over by the Northern winter. The people seem older, clothes are dirty and greasy; after a bath we see the silt from our bodies whirling down the drain. You have to change clothes constantly if you do not want to look wilted. Our bodies undergo a sudden transformation; heartbeat rises, breathing becomes more rapid. You get the impression that your lungs are filling up with an oily substance—the air breathed in seemed a leftover from my own memories of asphyxiation.

When I was in grade school, this sense of being suffocated turned into an adolescent neurosis. After even a short walk under that brutal sun, I would be exhausted. My hometown, Pinar del Río, is not near the sea, and during the school holidays I would take a bus to Las Canas, a small beach on the southern shore, twenty minutes away, or to Santa Fe, a ghost town on the northern shore. At sunset, it was pleasant to swim at Santa Fe, facing north toward the frontier of another universe that I imagined to be suffused with a delicate half-light and the accompanying changes of seasons so well described by William Blake in his early poems. These idyllic moments had their bad side—in my stifling room back home, I suffered all the more keenly.

Although I wasn't yet twenty, I felt I could shout out, as did Paul Nizan, "I was twenty. I will let no one say it was the best time of my life" ("Aden, Arabie"). Since I was so poor, I went off to school early every morning wearing my father's pants and his *guayabera*, that loose shirt of the tropics. He would go off to his office at ten o'clock, after I had returned from my first two classes. I would hang up my father's clothes where he wanted, and then put my own clothes on, the ones my friends saw me in. My father's pants were too big, and I used to hitch them up to hide that; the *guayabera* was supposed to cover the bulky pants, or at least I thought it did. One of my cousins once said to me, "Sometimes I think you're a quick-change artist who gets up fat and goes to bed thin." She thought I wanted to appear in public as heavier than I was. Then I was as thin as my sons Carlos and Ernesto are today. In the end, I do not feel that anguish belongs particularly to any social class. Many of my rich friends suffered just as much as I did, but with a more neurotic and complex intensity.

My despair was such that I attributed all the evils of my world to the climate. I was so stuck on these excesses that I turned them into dogma. If there is a landscape that truly repels me, it is the one on the cover of the first Spanish edition of my novel *Heroes Are Grazing in My Garden*—you see a dreamy beach with palm trees and a deluxe sun, a scene from a tourist's postcard to be sent back home, stimulation directed at an attraction felt by Northerners which I cannot bear. For me, the beach, the palm trees, and the pounding light are a snare and a delusion beneath a vengeful sun.

I know some Cuban writers who are quite taken with that landscape and that sticky climate. The Siboney poets thought they were the inheritors of the first inhabitants of the island and claimed that Cuba was a lost paradise that even now could be revitalized. José Lezama Lima, who saw "invisible gardens in the island night," and who was killed off by the climate, wheezed with asthma at every hour in his small home with its dank rooms, which he left only to die. On the other hand, the poet Julián del Casal thought that the tropical landscape was an abomination; for me, his descriptions of the Cuban countryside are exactly right.

Another writer enamored of Cuba's climate, particularly Havana's, is Guillermo Cabrera Infante. Guillermo arrived in Havana in his teens from Gibara, in Oriente Province, the entrance hall to hell. People from there never sweat. Neither Cabrera Infante, Pablo Armando Fernández, César López, nor my wife, Belkis Cuza, all of them from there, has been seen to sweat one drop. They tremble with chills amid the flames; in the Cuban winter, they would wrap themselves up as if on the North Pole.

Martin Green, an English literary critic, once came to see me. He was writing a book on the topic of the city in contemporary literature. He wanted me to show him the Havana of Guillermo Cabrera Infante, the city/protagonist of his works. I accompanied him and pointed out what was still left of Guillermo's Havana. He reacted enthusiastically to what I was able to show him, and was sweating profusely. But he kept up a quickstep as we walked through decrepit scenes, spying through boarded-up doors the leftover debris of taverns long ago closed, trying all the while to uncover beneath the boards of the Tropicana Club the hidden image, barely discernible now, of the defunct Havana. When I asked him his feelings about what he had seen, he said, "I adore these neglected cities."

4

~~~~~~

IN THE OFFICES of Prensa Latina, I began to realize that the public clamor was by no means unanimous. There were considerable differences between the various revolutionary organizations. I had friends in all of them, but the ones closest to me were Alberto Mora, a member of the Revolutionary Directory; Carlos Franqui, of the 26th of July Movement; and Juan Marinello from the Communists.

I had met Marinello in my early teens, when politics and literature were for me inseparable. I still have the snapshot with me standing next to him: I am young and thin, he graying and middle-aged (this was in 1949). I was interviewing him for the newspaper *Vocero Occidental* of Pinar del Río. This man had practically everything: sensibility, talent, prestige. He came from an old Cuban family, landowners of the highest rank in Cuba or anywhere—a Cuban blueblood, if you will. Having earned recognition as a writer, he entered politics. Still, he really was neither a writer nor a politician. Reading him after all these years, I ask myself: How is it that this bombastic spokesman for leftist clichés got to be a political leader?

Marinello was always held up as an example of probity and genius, but in his most representative moments he would write things like this: "No matter where we touch the firm and fevered orb that gave birth to his manuscripts, we will feel his throbbing and intense avidity and the pulsations in his veins." This was his reaction to reading Martí. He was terribly inept, a man who blithely moved in that stylistic circle so dominant in the thirties. Gabriela Mistral adored him. She thought of him as the spiritual son of Martí, with whom, many noted, he shared even the initials of his first and last names. He was, in fact, a fin de siècle aesthete, a Hispanic *post-modernista* sensibility who stopped being a litterateur to dedicate himself to political militancy as if he were the high priest of a clerical order. I saw him frequently, and we spent many hours talking about Spanish literature. He used to boast of his Catalonian roots, and I always thought of him as caught between Castile and his own ignorance. He loved to speak Catalan. As was the case with many Cubans who were children of Spanish immigrants, he was the kind of perfect hybrid which in another era the Spanish colonial troops would have shot without hesitation. But I do not want to be unfair; the man imposed upon himself the apostolate of social justice. I went with him on a few occasions to the political meetings of the Popular Socialist Party—sparsely attended, it might be added. Dressed in white, he would advance toward the speaker's lectern. The public—blacks, mestizos, oddballs—felt gratified by the presence of this refined gentleman whose speeches they could only half understand. His oratory was similar to his prose—a patchwork out of Martí.

He himself said that Martí was a "sterile writer" in the sense that he had not fostered disciples, but Marinello was unable to avoid a heavy-handed imitation of the master.

Like Martí, he was a grave man, distant and untypical of a Cuban. Martí, too, was humorless, had no interest in satire and even less in parody. And he was consumed by an ethical fervor and did not approve of the frivolous idiosyncrasies of the Cuban temperament. As he was wont to say: "We must expunge from our blood all traces of farcical Madrid." Marinello could recite Martí from memory, and by the hour. In 1930, he collected the poetry of Martí in a volume, and had it published with a prologue in a series of Cuban books edited by the ethnologist Fernando Ortiz. I remember hearing him explaining a new plan for university reform to a group of foreign academics. It left them nonplussed; he was paying attention only to himself. As rector of the University of Havana, he was an honorable figure utterly unsuited for the job. Each time a particular visitor would press him for some facts, the aged rhetorician would slip away from any specifics. He incarnated the moral aura of the *magister*. In the meanwhile, matters technical and concrete were in the hands of Vice Rector Altshuler, one of the keenest scientific minds in the country, and by the way, Marinello was the only Cuban I saw who burst into tears like a child on hearing of Stalin's death.

One evening, Marinello said to me, "The best thing for you would be to go to the Soviet Union on a scholarship. These are very confused and dangerous times." I consulted with Manuel Navarro Luna, a Communist poet, friend and admirer of Marinello. He was of the same opinion: "The only alternative that man is leaving us is a counterrevolution." That man was Fidel Castro. These conflicts would result in the 1962 trial of Aníbal Escalante, the old militant of the CP. Marinello had no power to influence the future direction of the party. He was the president; that is, no one—a statue.

Early on in the Revolution, he had set himself up in an office of the World Congress for Peace, that convocation sponsored by the Soviet Union as a Cold War offensive. His was a strategic location (on the mezzanine of the Havana Hilton, now the Havana Libre). This office gave him the opportunity to cultivate his international connections and keep open the possibility of trips abroad. I saw him there on many occasions. He seemed enthusiastic, but there was a serious mien to him, too—his gestures seemed both tense and amiable.

I do not think that he was expecting any compensation for his impeccable stewardship, but he did hope for a minimum of recognition, and even that was a long time coming. He had too many enemies, and the worst of them seemed to have no grounds for their enmity. For example, the family of Celia Sánchez, the close friend of Fidel, hardly disguised the contempt which they thought he deserved. Her father, a physician from Manzanillo, was one of those patriots from the interior who venerated José Martí. For him, it was an intolerable mockery that anyone should cultivate the memory of the man in so exorbitant a fashion. Her brother Orlando, whose liberal ideas, carousing, and public admission of his family's secret *santería* masses were passed over in silence, was also a determined opponent of Marinello. Orlando Sánchez was the type that felt it his duty to advertise the phobias and passionate secrets of the family. Navarro Luna once said to me, "Poor Marinello has the worst enemies imaginable—not the bourgeoisie, but that bewitched lineage represented by the provincial adulators of Martí."

Carlos Franqui is the victim of chronic hope. He was a militant member of the Popular Socialist Party, perhaps its poorest adherent. He was born into a peasant family and attained a secondary education against enormous odds. From childhood he knew the coarseness of life that accompanies the children of misfortune. The social injustice of which he was victim and witness led him, while still young, to identify with Marxism. After much effort, he won a scholarship to study in the town of Santa Clara in Las Villas Province. He was a voracious reader even then, and he kept up his studies without interruption while taking part in union and peasant campaigns. When he finished secondary school, his political orientation prevented him from obtaining a university scholarship; he went to Havana anyway, but the party sent him back to Las Villas as an activist organizer.

When he returned to Havana, Franqui found a job as proofreader for the newspaper *Hoy*, the official organ of the Cuban Communist Party. At that time, the party was headed by Aníbal Escalante, who even then was clearly a "despot," in Franqui's word. Franqui was the sort of person members of the party describe as "a man of fundamentals"—never to be corrupted by bourgeois temptation, a product of too much pain and misery, a true "class consciousness." At any rate, Franqui had some words with Escalante, left the employ of the paper, and a year later enrolled in the ill-fated Santo Domingo expedition to topple the dictator Trujillo. There he met Fidel Castro and many of the others who were to come together in the struggle against Batista.

Franqui was always a radical, and although bitter experience has led him to make a clean break with his political executioners, he has not totally abandoned his faith in "the midwife of history." It should be said that the Franqui I met in the fifties showed few qualifications for conversion to the revolutionary of a few years later. At that time his passion was art: literature, painting, music. He was a member of the cultural society Our Time, which the Communist Party first infiltrated and then took over, though the group was supposedly open to anyone in the cultural avant-garde. Our Time held lectures, concerts, recitals, expositions; its well-known director was Harold Gramatges, a talented composer, a militant Communist, and later ambassador of the revolutionary government to France. The group also put out a modest literary review, to which Franqui contributed. His first piece was a poem dedicated to the rose. In Cuba, the rose is more than a flower—it is a reminder of the verses of Martí the revolutionary.

Franqui believed, following Martí, that ethical questions must take precedence over political exigencies; for that reason, he was unable to accept the iron discipline of the Communist Party. He refused to conform, and so he had to seek out other revolutionary organizations to fulfill his social vocation. For him, this was the 26th of July Movement—the one most worthy of his allegiance.

Officially, Franqui was a journalist who worked for Channel 2 in Havana; behind the scenes, he was organizing the urban opposition to Batista. He took charge of propaganda and information and created the clandestine *Revolución*, which became the official organ of the 26th of July Movement after the fall of Batista.

When I arrived in Cuba, I joined the staff of *Revolución*. I contributed to the international page and to the literary supplement *Lunes de Revolución*, edited by Guillermo Cabrera Infante. Never before in Cuba had there been a literary supplement that was part of a mass-circulation newspaper. This was Franqui's doing, as was the founding of Ediciones R, a small publishing house directed by Virgilio Piñera which took up the cause of writers who had no access to larger houses. Piñera's active participation, coming as he did from the *Orígenes* group, which was well known for its indifference to political matters, was also the work of Carlos Franqui.

Franqui's deadly enemies (manipulated at a distance by the secret police) lived with him and all around him. His most notable character trait was the extravagant combination of, on the one hand, an impassioned advocacy of literature, music, and painting and, on the other hand, a militancy amply demonstrated by his daring and courage under Batista's repression. Fidel Castro was the first to see danger in Franqui's penchants. Undoubtedly, Fidel was responsible for keeping Franqui off cultural matters in general, above all as they might relate to the younger generation. Official culture was put under the watchful eye of the old-time orthodox Communists, for whom the artist should be the "engineer of souls," as advocated by Joseph Stalin. They also set forth the doctrine of Socialist Realism, thereby gilding the latrines of political repression.

When the new ministries of the Revolution were at the planning stage, Fidel asked Franqui which he wanted. "Culture," he answered. Fidel offered him posts of greater responsibility, but never Culture. Franqui turned down the other offers and continued as director of the journal *Revolución*. Perhaps his enemies did not realize that if ever there was a polemical paper in Cuba to which powerful people were hostile, it was *Revolución*. Fidel stopped by daily, dictated a few headlines, but he never considered the newspaper his own, rather one more thing to make use of, to manipulate.

Franqui was the spokesman of the antisectarian, democratic spirit which the world outside saw in the Cuban Revolution in its initial stage. Against the blind opposition of the hard-line pro-Soviets, Franqui convinced Jean-Paul Sartre and Simone de Beauvoir to visit Cuba, after which they became active and convincing allies. On the subject of Cuba, Sartre both wrote and said what he desired and what he imagined. He was deeply moved as an artist and as a philosopher to see history in action, in the process of forging, transforming, and expressing itself in a dialectic which before the Revolution he had only envisioned at his desk. Just as Franqui was the personal manager of the democratic club of Fidel Castro, the other line was taken up by Edith García Buchaca—a tenacious promoter of unswerving Stalinism. As I mentioned, Carlos Franqui participated in the campaigns against Rafael Trujillo first and then Fulgencio Batista. In both cases, he was governed by a kind of primordial ethos which Fidel could not entirely guard against. Revolution and poetry were synonymous for Franqui. I cannot imagine that being so for Castro. Yet we must recognize the fact that—one of the many ironies of history—they were close at two crucial moments in their lives. The peasant from a squalid background and the well-to-do law student reacted in the same way in face of the political panorama of Cuba at this particular time and both chose an extreme revolutionary solution.

Alberto Mora was different. He was younger than I and had always been interested in politics. His father, Menelao Mora, was a member of the House of Representatives until Batista's coup d'état. Alberto joined the Revolutionary Student Directorate before the armed attack on the Presidential Palace, during which an attempt was made to assassinate Batista. Months before the attack, Alberto was arrested and accused of conspiracy against the dictator. While he was in prison, his father died, and the government permitted him to attend the funeral services. The newspaper photographs taken at the graveside show him young, very thin, his head bowed.

We saw each other in Miami a few years later, in 1956. We were peddling the *Diario de las Américas* from door to door. After the triumph of the Revolution, he drew apart from his old writer friends. He had become radicalized and had decided that his friends had not responded properly to the demands of the moment. In the existing rivalry between the 26th of July Movement and the Student Directorate, he joined the former. This choice brought about his opprobrium and the final break with his old comrades-in-arms—above all, Faure Chaumón, head of the Student Directorate and later Minister of Transport; Mora was named Minister of Foreign Commerce.

Alberto Mora was genuinely an intellectual politician. I have met few Cubans to equal his in-depth knowledge of literature, philosophy, and music. In his last years at the ministry, he traveled frequently to Europe and sought out his old friends. He was concerned about approaching Guillermo Cabrera Infante, once one of his closest friends. He feared that Guillermo wouldn't talk with him, but it did not turn out that way at all. During one of his missions, Guillermo, Pablo Armando Fernández, and I happened to meet in Paris. He was deliriously happy at being with us. We talked, read poems aloud, listened to jazz; Guillermo made up a list of records to buy, to be brought up to date. Pablo Armando was commissioned to make the purchases in London, where he was cultural attaché. We all wanted to meet again in London, but Guillermo had to return to Brussels, where he, too, was cultural attaché.

In London I was able to have a long talk with Alberto. I had just come from Moscow, and what news I had about Cuba had come to me after a sifting process—either affable or malevolent. Alberto told me everything, without twists or editorializing. Pablo Armando was also present during that conversation. The man was overwrought and tense; he drank too much, and as his monologue proceeded apace, Pablo and I could see that he was on the verge of tears. This was 1965, when Cubans in important posts could still permit themselves the luxury of confession.

That night in London, Alberto Mora seemed a man torn apart. Suddenly he stood up and went out into the street. Pablo and I ran after him, vainly trying to hail a taxi, until he finally fell down, exhausted. We took him back to the hotel and he collapsed on the rug, where he cried like a child.

He was the youngest minister in the revolutionary government, and one of the most capable. He spoke English and French, had a rich but select library, and had trained himself in economics. After four years in the post, he could deal with assurance with any economic problem. He was the first to call attention to the currency drain that was taking place at all levels of the Cuban economy. The alarm reached right to the top, and Ernesto "Ché" Guevara was appointed president of the National Bank. Ché did the job with his accustomed discipline—every bank transfer had to be approved by him personally. He set up a military ambush to halt the flight of cash; the National Planning Group, along with the recently created Ministry of Foreign Commerce, in Alberto's hands, began a massive campaign to control the outward flow of money. At that time Mora felt less preoccupied; he worked late, and I would drop by his office often, but he was irritated about the dearth of economic technicians for the posts of commercial representatives for the twenty or so enterprises of the ministry. As if that were not enough, State Security and the Counterintelligence Service were attempting to place more and more of their agents in his offices. At first, they were only code people; later they attempted to expand their activities into the economic realm. Mora discussed the matter on many occasions with Ramiro Valdés, the Minister of the Interior, who insisted on the necessity of strengthening vigilance over the technocrats, most of whom had no ideological foundation whatever and were therefore open to bribes from the enemy.

Valdés was right about their lack of ideological foundation, but this lack was evident not only in the commercial-representative corps. One of the branches of the Foreign Commerce Ministry received a letter that had been returned from England in which a State Security agent stationed in London had been informed that the *santería* shamans of his hometown of Regla, who had been protecting him, had carried out all necessary esoteric exercises to guarantee his staying on permanently in Europe. I read the letter. Alberto laughed hysterically, then was silent. He was also disturbed by the special commissions that were traveling around the world making purchases with convertible exchange outside his authority. They would buy costly installations and the many products called for in Fidel Castro's plans. None of this took into account the priorities established by the Central Planning Group. Payment for these purchases affected the budget lines assigned to Foreign Commerce by Planning, but it was approved by an untouchable authority: Fidel Castro.

5

~~~~~~

IN 1959 the Cuban Communist Party still functioned in the shadows. The year before, with the success of the Revolution already assured, one of the prominent leaders of the Cuban CP, Carlos Rafael Rodríguez, ex-minister without portfolio of the earlier Batista government of the mid-forties, was received by Fidel in the Sierra Maestra. Rodríguez's visit marked the entry of the Communists into the armed struggle. This was a remarkable shift. At the time of the attack on the Moncada Barracks, the party had denounced Fidel, and indeed the most benign of their adjectives had been "putschist."

The party, in fact, was Marxist only in the sense that it relied on the same arsenal of invective with which Marx adjudged his contemporaries. Neither Juan Marinello nor Carlos Rafael Rodríguez ever wrote a line which can properly be called Marxist. None of them felt the need for a scientific analysis of Cuban reality, and for them politics was really a substitute for a poetic or an artistic impulse. Read today, their speeches are a stale catalogue of the people's sufferings and a list of statistics illustrating the exploitation of Latin America by imperialism. They preached redemption, with similes drawn from mountain ranges such as the Sierra Maestra. Fidel permitted the party to enjoy the benefit of its clandestine status. The ministers in Fidel's cabinet were all members of the 26th of July Movement, but in every ministry there was an "advisor" who, by the very fact of his militant Communism, was accorded an infallibility which not even the most ludicrous idiocy could bring into question. One of these gems was a man named León Torrás, an amateur economist who contributed commentaries to the party newspaper. If this man had not died in good time, he would have turned Cuba into a warehouse of Chinese furniture imported from Peking. The commercial exchange agreements which he signed were later used as case studies in the training program for the Foreign Ministry, as examples of what not to do.

I was never active in the Popular Socialist Party, but several of its militants were good friends of mine. Navarro Luna, the official poet of the party, even asked me to write a prologue to an anthology of his verse; I *did* write the piece, and the book was published by the Writers' Union. Even so, the motives behind the cordial treatment accorded me by Navarro Luna and Marinello were a mystery to me; even today I cannot explain them. Surely it was not intellectual admiration, for that was wholly secondary in a complex political process dominated by values which all but excluded literature. Nicolás Guillén showed the same deference in 1952, when he mentioned me as one of Cuba's significant younger poets.

Navarro Luna published a perceptive essay on my poetry in

Verde Olivo, the official organ of the Revolutionary Armed Forces. The old man affirmed that I was one of the great poets of our time, and his statement gained legitimacy with *Verde Olivo*'s sanction. Navarro told me that Ché Guevara personally approved the publication of the laudatory essay over the objections of the director of the magazine, Luis Pavón Tamayo, a recently arrived versifier from the town of Holguín. Tamayo ran *Verde Olivo* until Fidel Castro handed over the direction of cultural matters to the army, much the same way the leaders of China had done during the Cultural Revolution. When he was dismissed from his post, Pavón floundered around aimlessly and began to drink. These days he is described officially as the force behind innumerable unpunished treacheries committed in the name of the Revolution and the working class.

Pavón did have a mellifluous voice, the tidy look of a country orphan, and that reverential and abject mien needed for moments when the *caudillo* demands unconditional loyalty. He could count on the close collaboration of State Security, who in turn were the originators of that particular word with which he justified so many purges in matters artistic—*parameters*. The parameters were or were not fulfilled. The National Board of Culture created groups of political commissars to judge (parametize) each member of the artistic and cultural associations of the country. The decision-makers were more interested in the reports of the police informants than in the works of art under consideration.

Sexual conduct was a determinant factor. What could one expect from a fag or a lesbian but political disaffection? The homosexual was not a problem for the new society. Quite the contrary, it was a leftover aberration of the *ancien régime* which undermined the Revolution. Pavón thought he was adding inches to his stature every time he deflated the reputation of a poverty-stricken ballet dancer or an ill-paid actor. He gave more stipends to bad poets and novelists with writer's block than in the worst years under Batista.

Still, senior officials insisted that the government, for fear of arousing international protest, was not suppressing with sufficient force those "touchy" and dangerous elements lurking in the country. Pavón was the point man for this view. From his post as director of *Verde Olivo* he articulated this campaign in collaboration with mediocre academics, pretentious types who incarnated that "resentment" in ethical matters of which Max Scheler has written. The basic component of Pavón's revolutionary ethos was ineptitude, a faith solely in art that was accessible and obvious to the people, even those who had just learned to read. Originality and verbal inventiveness were terms of abuse to him. It was a grotesque and tragic time. People who knew nothing of art or of history trumpeted their theories. Symmetries between the October Revolution and the Cuban Revolution were insisted upon. Each phase in our revolution had its equivalent in theirs. For instance, Roberto Fernández Retamar denied that Nicolás Guillén was the poet of the Revolution; the most he could aspire to was the role of an Aleksandr Blok; the Cuban Mayakovsky was about to be born. Of course, Fidel was Lenin; Pavón was Zhdanov. After a while there was talk of a first revolutionary generation, a second: generations were counted in weeks. The habit continued in exile, where one speaks of the Mariel generation, even though it represented, in fact, a highly diverse sampling of the Cuban people.

The years between 1959 and 1962 were crucial ones. Although in reality the country was splitting apart, with ever-increasing numbers choosing exile during the first two years, this meant nothing to us. We believed that they were simply members of the privileged classes who naïvely expected to return in the near future. The North Americans would take care of them. With the passing years, individuals representing the most antagonistic ideologies have come to meet in exile. Fidel Castro eradicated seemingly insuperable differences. No dictatorship from Cuba's past bettered him in insanity and arbitrariness, but no political organization has achieved the necessary unity to oppose him.

6

~~~~~~

YOUNG PEOPLE from all over the country were welcomed by the Revolution. Yellowed manuscripts by poets and novelists found their way into print. In 1961 the First Congress of Cuban Writers and Artists took place; its motto was "To Defend the Revolution Is to Defend Culture." The congress ended its sessions by giving unanimous approval to the new government; unanimous applause also greeted the new relations between society and its artists. Thousands of delegates gathered in the Havana Libre Hotel, but at the end it was quite clear that membership in the newly organized Writers' Union was to be granted only after approval from the National Board of

Culture. Reluctant to create a Ministry of Culture, Fidel had placed all literary and artistic activity under the guidance of a board that was dependent upon the Ministry of Education. He was already worried about the danger that culture represented in Communist societies abroad. The political directorate wanted no repetition of the Pasternak affair.

Boris Pasternak was of the same generation as Mayakovsky and had shared the same innovative literary experience. Thirty years later he submitted for publication the manuscript of *Doctor Zhivago*, the most impassioned literary witness to that political process which has transformed the face of our times so completely. The suicide of Mayakovsky was implicit in the moving pages of Pasternak's novel, and the novel was eventually suppressed. Nonetheless, for Pablo Neruda, Pasternak did not deserve the intellectual respect accorded him in Russia. In his memoirs, Neruda complained that, while everybody spoke of Pasternak in secret, they did so with reverence. Neruda preferred Mayakovsky as endorsed by Stalin. Not the poet's suicide, of course, but his reputation as the author of poems of political exaltation and conformity, which the Chilean poet attempted to imitate without success.

In fact, Fidel's worries were prompted less by any possible replication of the Pasternak case than by a modest incident which the old Cuban CP blew up out of all proportion. Orlando Jiménez Leal and Sabá Cabrera Infante had made a documentary film of barely twenty minutes' length which they titled *P.M.* The filmmakers wanted to take a look at certain aspects of Havana nightlife. They did it on their own, ignoring the recently created National Film Institute (ICAIC), which had at its head an old, wily political adversary of Fidel Castro's, Alfredo Guevara. Alfredo was a consummate politician, a militant of solid Marxist formation. However, this barely cloaked his homosexuality and his many lovers. Understandably, he did not want any of this used as blackmail. But if he was to dominate Cuban culture, he could allow nothing to slip out of his hands. *P.M.*, though of little importance, was an exercise in free cinema. It was made with a hidden camera, and it sought to capture the spontaneity of customers having a good time in the clubs. Guevara used the film as a pretext to gain control of the cultural sector. He claimed that the documentary expressed the political alienation of its creators. Where was the Revolution in the portrait of drunkards having fun at the expense of the working class? No, Cuban nightlife deserved a different kind of treatment. It was not enough to place a hidden camera in a bar where people on the fringes of society danced and sang. The techniques through which those people were observed by the camera were ultimately a reflection of a nascent cultural policy, and in this respect reality should be observed in the most positive way possible. Film needed militant artists.

P.M. was shown to hundreds of artists and writers in one of the studios of the Casa de las Américas, the cultural center of the Revolution. We were too unaware to discern the intentions of Alfredo Guevara. He had organized his radical shock troops in order to confront the liberals, who had gathered there under the auspices of Carlos Franqui. This group, in charge of the weekly literary and artistic review *Lunes de Revolución*, represented a brand of irrational spontaneity that was synonymous with right-wing reaction. The literary critic Mirta Aguirre, lesbian and Communist as it happens, led the attack on the *Lunes* group with the words: "That's the way it all started in Hungary!" We were perplexed when we heard her making the Hungarian intellectuals responsible for the brutal intervention "which the Soviet Union saw itself obliged to carry out," as she put it. In the long debate that followed, there were no contributions to equal Mirta's, but when I arrived back at the offices of *Lunes*, I saw that Franqui had already been apprised of everything. "Don't speak to anyone," he said. "Try to keep the debate from widening any more than it has already."

But the debate had not only widened. It led to the first

meeting between Cuban writers and the revolutionary government. This encounter took place in the auditorium of the National Library. Fidel presided, with the instigators of the meeting at his side: Alfredo Guevara, Edith García Buchaca, and Carlos Rafael Rodríguez. The young Russian poet Yevgeny Yevtushenko attended the meeting. I had met him a few days before, when the *Pravda* correspondent in Havana, Vitali Borovski, introduced us in the offices of the daily, *Revolución*. We hit it off instantly. Together, we sat at the Gato Tuerto bar, trying to put Yevtushenko's poems into Spanish. It was extraordinary to begin to penetrate a poetry so distant from my own. For me, that had far more import than any meeting in the National Library. I didn't care about history at all. On the other hand, Yevgeny, I think, sensed its importance to a much greater degree than any of us who participated in it.

The fact is that the debates between the *Lunes de Revolución* group and its adversaries didn't worry me. I thought it natural that everyone express himself freely. But those in charge were not of the same opinion, and in retrospect I can see that we were pushing the two groups into conflict. As people used to say at the time, when things are on the line, freedom is a figure of rhetoric.

Yevtushenko sat next to me during the National Library meeting, with Borovski on the other side, translating for him. In one corner of the auditorium there were tape recorders and technicians. In order to be heard, participants had to go up to a microphone placed just under the table of those presiding, who also included President Dorticós, Minister of Education Armando Hart, then president of the National Board of Culture Vicentina Antuña, and Edith García Buchaca, who was vice president of the National Board. Shortly we learned that, in the interest of the unity of writers and artists with the Revolution, the literary supplement *Lunes de Revolución* would be eliminated, and two new weekly publications assigned to the recently created Writers' Union would replace it, publications which would group together artists in their respective sections—literature, music, plastic arts, film. The president of this new entity would be Nicolás Guillén.

In a sense, the meeting was a response to the malaise caused by the pronouncements of Mirta Aguirre after the showing of *P.M.*, opinions which did not differ at all from those of Edith García Buchaca in her pamphlet outlining the aesthetic and political paradigms of Cuban revolutionary culture. Those implementing this policy were all members of the old guard of the Cuban CP, whose orthodoxy guaranteed to Fidel that culture would remain under control, avoiding such scandals as the Petőfi group's in Hungary and Pasternak's in the Soviet Union.

P.M. represented a threat which Fidel took note of instantly. The film was an independent achievement, made without the use of government money. At the meeting in the library, Fidel asked everyone present to speak his mind. Virgilio Piñera, who had been arrested a few months before during the infamous Operation 3P—a roundup of prostitutes, pimps, and pederasts—went to the microphone. He said that he could not hide the fact that he "felt afraid." Mario Parajón asked whether it was possible for a Catholic writer to coexist in complete freedom within the revolutionary process.

Carlos Rafael Rodríguez, at that time editor in chief of the Communist daily *Hoy*, then spoke up. He insisted on ideological rigor in a literature now directed toward a public which had just learned to read. For instance: was Ezra Pound a fine poet? Yes, but a Fascist. T. S. Eliot was a reactionary who would never find a place in the pages of *Hoy*. I objected, noting that such prejudicial zeal against T. S. Eliot was excessive; Rodríguez answered back, clearly irritated. I then reminded him that on the occasion of a visit to Pinar del Río we had a long conversation about literature. He nodded in the affirmative, agreeably.

"Don't you remember," I argued, "that one of your future projects was to be a comparative study of the works of T. S.

Eliot and Pablo Neruda, which would point out their affinities and their differences?"

"Yes," he replied, "but that study was to highlight the differences, not the similarities. The footnotes for each of Eliot's poems took up half the book."

"Eliot is most generous with you," I noted, "but we can enjoy his poems without any footnotes."

Rodríguez looked at me angrily and pushed the microphone aside. President Dorticós whispered something to him; he pulled the microphone back. "I just want to say that I have not gone on speaking because I have said everything that I am going to say on this matter."

We then took a short break. I went off to the men's room, and at the urinals I found myself next to Fidel.

"Wow, it looks as if Carlos Rafael got all heated up," he said.

He laughed aloud, entertaining himself by tracing successively expanding circles of piss against the marble slabs along the wall.

In those early days, Fidel was everywhere. Every day he spoke on television, and the speeches could last up to nine hours. Toward the end of 1959 he appeared one night at the offices of *Revolución*, where many of us used to work until dawn. Present were Guillermo Cabrera Infante, Pablo Armando Fernández, Jaime Miller, José Álvarez Baragaño, Natividad González Freire, Walterio Carbonell, and, of course, Carlos Franqui, always the last man to leave the premises. Fidel summoned us to the editor in chief's office.

"I've got an idea. Now that we are setting up popular militias, you people should create one that is different, a militia which would demonstrate the intellectual's support of the Revolution. It should be named after a writer."

Carbonell suggested Rubén.

"That's it—Rubén Martínez Villena, the man who gave up literature and dedicated his life to the revolutionary struggle."

Just then Tirso, the photographer from the paper, appeared and took a few photos. In the edition of December 31, 1959, *Revolución* published a photograph of Fidel, Walterio, Natividad, Álvarez Baragaño, Jaime Miller, and me. The caption: "Newly Organized Militia of Revolutionary Intellectuals Named for Rubén Martínez Villena." The article added many more names; they were included without the individuals' consent, as usual. At three in the morning we went off to the Pekín Restaurant.

As we ate our fried rice, Fidel suddenly said to me: "You know what happened to me in a Mexican bookstore? I found a novel by Dostoevsky with the title *The Sepulcher of the Living* and I bought it; I thought it was the only book of his which I hadn't read, but it turned out that it was really *The House of the Dead*. I got cheated." He laughed, and added, "Well, you people can't complain anymore. The Imprenta Nacional is there so you can publish everything you write, with unrestricted freedom. This is a fact. As I said, 'Within the Revolution, everything; outside the Revolution, nothing.' We all have to be in agreement on this." Of course, everyone at the table agreed.

Even then, we knew that acceptance or rejection was up to Fidel. I do believe, however, that his criteria at that time embraced both the obese José Lezama Lima and the lean, angular Virgilio Piñera. Their writing didn't get in Fidel's way. Lezama's work was labeled as baroque, a style which Spain had exported to America as a peninsular model, while Virgilio's, too direct, had never found any readers to speak of in Spain. For all of us, Spain was the baroque, a noisy, idiotic homage paid to the bullfighter, the man who dies in his "suit of lights." Tossed into the air by a thrust of the bull's horns, these men seem flashy suicides who might die yet are hooted by the crowd because the bull wasn't brought to kneel at the torero's feet with sufficient grace and aplomb. A friend said to me, "Don't get the idea that Spain is open to you because they understand you or because you speak the same language. Spain is one of those tough university courses which not everyone passes."

The Cuban intellectual circles which I found on my return in 1959 were not led by Nicolás Guillén but by José Lezama Lima, the poet and critic who was final arbiter of the worth of any new work—poetry, novel, play, or essay. When an authority establishes itself in this way, there are only two roads to take—submission or revolt. I chose the latter. I remember saying to Cabrera Infante that I wanted to blow up the baroque bastion that was the Trocadero home where Lezama lay wheezing. My hostility to him in matters aesthetic eventually reached such a point that I wrote an article against Lezama called "Poetry in Its Place," which appeared only after a few prudent cuts executed by Pablo Armando Fernández. It appeared in *Lunes de Revolución*; the changes were in the interest of fairness; it was an effort by Pablo Armando to remove mere resentment from my argument.

Texts of Camus and Lezama had recently been published in the *Revista Mexicana de Literatura*, edited by Carlos Fuentes and Emmanuel Carballo. In my article I compared the well-defined position of Albert Camus in favor of a literature which rejected "latter-day tyrannies brought to their last perfection." For this reason, I argued, we had to be for or against the noble defense which Lezama had made of literature itself. For him, Social Reality could only be expressed "by evaporation and image." Just before my article appeared, the Ministry of Education accused me of unjustly attacking Lezama, the poet the Revolution paid homage to and published under state sponsorship. But *Paradiso*, Lezama's novelistic masterpiece, had already been condemned by the commissars of Cuban culture. Moreover, Fayad Jamís, who oversaw production of the text and did the cover, was severely criticized for the almost intolerable negligence of not having read the manuscript—"the monument to the fag," the term used by officials to refer to the book.

Both the commissars and I were in agreement, then, that José Lezama Lima might be considered the symbol of an evasionist aesthetic, hermetic and elitist. But I wanted to make very clear that my disagreement with him would never bring me to attack the man—the destitute Lezama, the Lezama who had consecrated himself to literature amid such economic privation. In Cuba, our literary generations have always been cannibalistic, it must be said. Antón Arrufat used to say that any book published in Cuba was more a pistol than a book. But Lezama was no less exigent with his own contemporaries.

"I am perturbed by those debates in the National Library," Yevtushenko said to me, "even though no one is about to be shot. During Stalin's time in my country, you would all have died in a concentration camp. Lezama would have been the first to go." Yevtushenko counseled extreme prudence. The most important thing in a revolution is the saving of one's own head. "You are drunk with literature, but I am aware that people are getting their heads blown off every day. Violence is the real question. Though I am younger than most of you, I am actually your grandfather. I was born twice—once in Zima, Siberia, in 1933, and then again nine years ago, after the death of Stalin. This Cuban Revolution of yours is like the infancy of ours."

Yevtushenko spoke with compelling ardor, more with body language than anything else—his lips, of course, but also his keen blue eyes and an endless movement of head and arms. The diehards of the Cuban CP hated him, but, as Vitali Borovski quipped, "when a young poet gets published in *Pravda*, he obtains the only credentials worth having in the Soviet Union." Yevtushenko and Borovski recommended that I try to obtain a scholarship for study in the U.S.S.R. But how? Juan Arcocha, the *Revolución* correspondent in Moscow, would find a way. It was worth a try.

Juan Marinello and Navarro Luna had already put me on the alert. "You've got to get out of this fishbowl just as soon as possible," Navarro said. Marinello agreed: "Yes, this country continues being what it was"—meaning that the new Marxist order had not been able to do away with the intrigues and deals which Marinello formerly considered the exclusive property of the *ancien régime*.

I left Cuba shortly after giving a poetry reading in which I was joined by the poets of my generation. It was early September. The next day, Roger Garaudy gave a lecture in which he spoke of "Realism without Frontiers." We were packed into the main room of the Writers' Union. The French philosopher dominated everyone with his formulations. He was there to bring a message of solidarity from the French Communists, who were hoping that a pernicious revisionism could be prevented from taking root in our country.

Before Garaudy finished his lecture, José Álvarez Baragaño told me he felt ill, and left the hall. He fainted in the taxi on his way home and died on the way to the hospital, victim of a brain hemorrhage. Baragaño had been an enthusiastic partisan of the Revolution; he had just published a "Hymn to the Militias," and Fidel had taken a liking to him. Everyone in the Writers' Union attended his funeral. He had been a powerful force in the Union; his literary and political positions were highly polemical, as were his overheated contributions to *Lunes de Revolución*. His poetry is now forgotten, but I think he was among the most talented from that era. His first book took its title from a verse by Rimbaud, "To change life," and he had been the friend of André Breton, Benjamin Péret, and Wilfredo Lam, the last a true Surrealist. He had carried that experience to its limits. He was only thirty when he died. Alejo Carpentier, who had been a frequent target of Baragaño's attacks (he considered him a deserter from Surrealism), approached the casket in silence and looked down at the pale face of the poet. "One less," said the novelist, casting his eyes on Cabrera Infante and me.

Nicolás Guillén gathered us together afterwards. Baragaño had been his adversary as well. As we drank coffee in a corner café, Guillén entertained us by telling us about a book he had read a long time before, a description in excruciating detail of what its author termed the "fauna of death"; that is, a complete catalogue of each of the worms which invade the body after burial. We had stayed by the coffin until dawn; we were all a little high. The end of *Lunes de Revolución* and of many of our hopes had taken its effect. Nonconformist poets and writers began to find work abroad with the Ministry of Foreign Relations. *Lunes* became a memory. Nicolás Guillén took charge of what turned out to be a flimsy successor to *Lunes, Gaceta de Cuba*, to whose first issue I contributed a piece.

"Everything is going fine," said Yevtushenko as we bid each other goodbye. "I have a contract to do a film script here in Cuba, but we will see each other in Moscow in a month."

7

I SHOULD MENTION that on my way to Russia I stopped in London at the invitation of the British government. I was accompanied by José Aníbal Maestri, the dean of the Cuban press; Enrique Labrador Ruiz, representing the *Diario Nacional*; and Enrique Grau Esteban of the conservative *Diario de la Marina*. Throughout London, the effects of the German bombardment were still visible. On the day we spent visiting Coventry, we received news of the first significant act of sabotage in Cuba. As we were walking by the statue of Lady Godiva, we saw a newspaper with banner headlines. Something had happened in America. *La Couvre*, a French ship, had been blown up in the port of Havana. Our ambassador in London could not hide his concern. There was total confusion in the embassy regarding events in Cuba. What were the plans of the Cuban government? The ambassador could clarify nothing and only lamented the lack of official information.

Ironically, during my short stay in Britain I became the first chief correspondent of Prensa Latina in a European capital. The articles I had sent from London (Great Britain was about to purchase enormous quantities of Cuban grapefruit; it had not permitted counterrevolutionaries to use British possessions in the Antilles for attacks against Cuba) were published on the front page of Cuban newspapers. There was euphoria back in the Havana offices of Prensa Latina. Masetti told me: "Ché Guevara has authorized thirty thousand dollars for you to open a London office. The dollars are being sent to you now." In fact, I didn't have much to do in London after setting up the office. I did meet with a delegation of Cuban journalists— among them Guillermo Cabrera Infante. He said to me, "There's a man in this delegation named Pastor Vega who says that you opened the Prensa Latina office in the same building as AP and UPI." What I had done was rent a small office on Farringdon Street, near the British Press Association, the internal news agency; they were helpful to me on more than one occasion. But Masetti was disturbed. He was being pressured by the hard-liners of the CP—they insisted on giving Prensa Latina official status, much like that of Tass in the Soviet Union. Rodolfo Walsh, the chief of Special Services, with whom I had always been on cordial terms, advised me that, given the confusion caused by Pastor Vega's allegations, I should return to Cuba. So once again I went to Heathrow with my wife and children.

Unlike my temporary sojourn in England, which was more accidental than anything else, I had chosen Moscow with forethought. I was convinced at the time that in this far-off land I would be able to glimpse the outlines of Cuba's future.

We were all on the move. Cabrera Infante went to Brussels as cultural attaché; Pablo Armando Fernández was posted to London. I had been offered a job in the Cuban embassy of either Mexico City or London; there was also a Soviet invitation to work as a rewrite man on the weekly *Moscow News*, which just that year had begun to be published in Spanish.

I had no illusions about working as a diplomatic functionary in an embassy abroad. The various Cuban embassies I had become acquainted with during the time I was chief correspondent in Great Britain were closed rooms full of brawling cats. In each and every one, the ambassador and the commercial attaché were constantly feuding. This was so because each had been appointed by a separate ministry—Foreign Relations and Foreign Commerce—and each chief of mission received orders and directives from a different superior in Havana. There was, indeed, no coherent policy. To be sure, the omnipotent Ministry of the Interior had infiltrated both branches within each embassy. At least thirty percent of the posts were held by employees of Interior; that is, Security people.

With that in mind, it was not difficult to choose the opportunity available in Moscow. And I would be able to keep my hand in as a journalist. I liked the city. I was overwhelmed by the singular magic by which totalitarian countries conceal the clash of differing opinions within the fabric of their societies, that ease with which deep divergencies are papered over into an apparent meeting of minds. In these countries, even shadows are under surveillance; the name of the woman whom you love and the place where you meet have a spot in the police files, all the more so if you are a foreigner. Of course, I am speaking now of the Iron Curtain countries as I saw them at the time.

The bureaucracy always viewed culture as if it were an opposition party; a poet begins to feel like a cabinet minister representing a hypothetical enemy power. Every word spoken is listened to and analyzed as if it were a decree about to be enacted. And there is a certain satisfaction in being observed by the powers that be. It is easy to identify agents and informers, because they listen so impassively as we compromise ourselves in public. You can also detect their true nature because of the eager and self-satisfied way in which they chart our moods and humors. Almost all the informers I met in Moscow were short, well turned out, and quite ceremonious. Almost all of them spoke Spanish, but of a peculiar and memorable brand. I recall once that when Marinello was dropped off at his hotel his interpreter took leave of him saying, in Spanish, "Well, your excellency, I shall bring about my return at eventide." This was too much even for the Communist rhetorician: "I have the impression that the man is living out of a chapter from Cervantes."

A genuine attraction of totalitarian countries lies in the intensity with which friendships thrive and flourish there. Since there really are no bars, all social life takes place in small family apartments. These are places of refuge in which the enjoyment of a friend's presence can never be excessive, because it is always tempered or threatened by danger from the outside. At the time, informers would arrange to get invited to such encounters, above all when foreigners were present, and I have no doubt that they were openly invited by the hosts in order to guarantee the safety of the occasion. We would drink and eat a lot at those parties, listening to popular music, not on ordinary vinyl long-playing records, but dubbed onto the strangest disks I have ever seen—discarded X-ray plastic sheets. After seeing those trimmed sheets in circular form on a Moscow record player, I have never been able to separate the shadow of a hipbone from the sound of "I Want to Hold Your Hand" or any other song of the Beatles. It might be said that the unfortunate victims of Moscow traffic accidents contributed to the spread of American and British rock and roll, the music that young Russians of the early sixties loved the most.

As I clambered down the steps of the plane that had brought me and my family to Moscow, a Russian journalist who had come to meet me shouted out, "You are a bear!" I did not know if he was praising my courage in coming or had discerned my long-standing passion for snow and freezing temperatures. But it was not snowing in Moscow when I arrived there in 1962; it was raining hard, and it kept on raining until the real Russian winter arrived. I was put up first at the Hotel Moscow, just a short distance from Red Square. We had a large set of rooms, almost a suite, with a dining room, and a grand piano in the foyer. The hotel was full of Russians from the various republics, called to the capital for one reason or another, and they all dressed in suits of Prussian blue, very much out of style even for 1962. The hotel was huge, typically Russian I thought, with heavy carpets, gilded staircases, broad chandeliers, and furniture of carefully sculptured birchwood, upholstered in dark red velvet. It was another world. After we dropped off our suitcases, we went out into the street—fog, rain, and cold, of course—but there were glints of light coming off the Spasskaya tower, lighted red in the darkness over the arch which opened into the Kremlin.

The scene belonged more to literature than to life. There was nothing in Moscow that did not seem transfigured by my own bookish dreams—the stuff of my daydreams back in Cuba. The Cathedral of St. Basil, topped by Byzantine domes, stood surrounded by the dark streets of old Moscow, and Lenin's tomb and the marble tribune above, the only elements which seemed out of place with their false modernity in such an ancient setting.

At the Moscow airport I had been met not only by the Russian journalist (who turned out to be Yuri Poporov) in charge of the Spanish-language edition of *Moscow News*, but also by a man from the Cuban embassy and two Spanish–Russian translators. One of them, Pedro Cepeda, was born in Málaga, Spain, and became a dear friend. As happened to so many children from Republican families during the Spanish Civil War, Pedro had been sent off to Russia. He had only a vague memory of his homeland. With time he had magnified

Spain in his imagination and had taken it upon himself to try to return, by whatever means. He befriended some clerk in the Argentine embassy in Moscow, who helped him escape from Russia in a trunk, which was duly loaded onto a plane as freight. Unfortunately, he began to moan and vomit as the cargo was being unloaded at whatever foreign airport it was, and he was sent back to Moscow. He was, of course, jailed as an "enemy of the people" and sent off to a concentration camp for over ten years. After the 20th Party Congress and Khrushchev's revelations and condemnation of Stalin's crimes, his sentence was cut in half; he was "rehabilitated," and given employ in the newly established *Moscow News* as a translator. He was a gifted writer and had a magnificent voice. His sufferings had not affected his huge, contagious smile, or his long-standing plan to return someday to the land of his birth.

When he eventually told me of his longing to leave Russia for Spain, I said I would do everything in my power to help him. During one of my visits to Spain, I mentioned my friend's secret ambition to the poet and publisher Carlos Barral, and it was he who was able to arrange Pedro Cepeda's return to Spain. I received a letter from him, written in Madrid. "I hope we may be able to see each other soon. I am here in my own country, reunited with my family." But it was not until 1981 that we finally saw each other again. He was rejuvenated, happy. We went out to eat with Svetlana, his wife, who now spoke fluent Spanish, and we made a date for me to see his baby daughter, just born in Madrid. He had greeted me with his habitual enthusiasm; the bad times were over for him. But when I first saw him on that rainy Moscow autumn of 1962 he was a bony creature, chain-smoking Bulgarian cigarettes, dressed in a greasy overcoat and with a gray hat pulled down over his ears.

My journalist colleague Poporov had told me that "Aníbal Escalante is here in Moscow."

"I knew that back in Cuba," I said. "He was sent here by

Fidel Castro himself when they removed him as secretary of the ORI. I want nothing to do with him."

"But he will be working in the offices of *Moscow News* with us, right next to you, as a matter of fact. It is known here that he was one of the worst enemies of *Lunes de Revolución* and of Carlos Franqui, of all of you."

"What are you afraid of, Yuri? Do you think that he is in any position to make trouble? As far as I am concerned, he can work wherever he wants. He is here just as I am here, but for different reasons."

Poporov laughed and clapped me on the shoulder affectionately. "It was decided that it would be good for you to know before your first day at the office. We wanted to save you from any embarrassment."

Later I saw the defeated ex-official of the Cuban Communist Party often. He seemed a very ordinary person to me. Fidel Castro's attack on him had performed the feat of turning a nonentity into a figure of renown. It was undeniable that Aníbal Escalante had high hopes of continuing to control things in Cuba from his post as First Secretary of the Cuban CP, using the same strategy that Stalin had brought to bear immediately after Lenin's death. When Fidel decided to create his own political structure, he would pigeonhole all those he called members of the "First Communist Party of Cuba" into a separate entity, distinct from his own grouping—the "true" Communist Party, born with Fidel Castro.

Moscow News had in its employ a heterogeneous group of workers—Hispano–Soviets, Russians, and others from the various republics who had a good command of Spanish. Old Escalante was a fish out of water not only in the office but in Moscow itself. Beginning in September, he would dress for winter, which contrasted sharply with how the rest of us dressed. Everyone laughed at him behind his back as he would arrive at the office exhausted after climbing the long flight of stairs. And this laughter was of a particular kind, somewhere between scorn and pity; it should be said that he always arrived on time and worked hard at correcting the rough translations put before him.

In the late afternoon he would look out, with a notably melancholic expression, from the thick windows overlooking Pushkin Square. He was a creature of the Caribbean and gradually spent himself as the winter grew more intense. When snow covered Moscow, he seemed to cringe inside his black overcoat, like a turtle in his shell, as he crossed the square on the way to the *Izvestia* building, where a car was waiting to take him home. The bundled-up body bending past the open car door had an eerie look, poised between the white shroud of snow and the doleful black of the limousine—his last link to power. Fidel Castro had decreed his extinction, and he was never able to bring himself back to life.

An early-morning routine was quickly established in the offices of *Moscow News*. Each day, Pedro Cepeda drew up an exhaustive itinerary of cultural apprenticeship, clipping the most important articles from the daily newspapers. He would indicate to me the general direction of the literature and criticism then in vogue—scrutiny of Stalin's methods—but these critiques were watered down with such prudence that my friend was convinced the so-called de-Stalinization was being brought to a halt by the same authorities who had put it into motion.

Just then, the first novel by a rehabilitated victim of Stalin was published. It was the work of a mathematics professor with no known literary reputation, and Khrushchev himself had authorized the publication in the literary review *Novy Mir*, edited by the respected poet Tvardovsky. *One Day in the Life of Ivan Denisovich* caused a sensation in Moscow. Pedro Cepeda was swept away by that taut, moving, tragic testimony of a man who had undergone the experience of the forced labor camps—the Gulag. Those "members of the opposition who had gotten off the track," those who lacked "class consciousness," those "objective enemies of the people" were given voice in Aleksandr Solzhenitsyn's novel. Pedro read the entire book to me aloud; two days later I showed him an article which I had just sent to Cuba, and he approved. "Cubans deserve to know that the Soviet people have suffered this political experience as has no other, and they should avoid the repetition in Cuba of the errors of those times." This was when many critical poems and essays were being published; and, too, *Pravda* was publishing Yevtushenko's poems exalting the progress of the Cuban Revolution. Near the Smolenskaya Naberezhnaya, where I lived, there was a small café where Pedro and I would sit after work in the waning afternoons of September. I used to order "solianka," a soup with lots of sausage, the favorite dish of black marketeers.

"Listen," Pedro inquired, "about that old Cuban in the office—is he important? I think that he has some power here. He has a limousine. What happened to Escalante in Cuba?"

I told him the story.

"It's a strange situation; it could be dangerous."

"Why?"

"Because if the man wanted to run the machinery of power in the same way as did Stalin, he is no fool. Did he have a friend of Fidel's shot?"

I laughed.

"When you are in power, people kill each other off just like that," he went on. "Haven't you seen what has happened here? Anything in one country can happen in another."

This constant discovery of parallels between different histories and nations was typical of the Soviet mind then. For my part, I did not give it much weight.

All Moscow was inundated with Cuban cigars, which I used to buy in great quantities in the small shops along the Arbat. On one occasion Pedro and I bought cigars to give to Ilya Ehrenburg. We phoned him from the lobby of the National

Hotel, which occupied the lower floors of his building. He invited us up. We rang the bell and he eagerly opened the door, accepting our gift with a connoisseur's relish.

"Lucky you can still find them," he said. "One of these days they will stop coming. Moscow is full of strange people who can corner an entire shipment in a few hours."

He looked at us out of exhausted blue eyes. His smile, too, was a bit wan, his pale and expressive face barely visible behind disheveled hair. Ehrenburg was proud of his skill in translating the rhythms of classic Spanish verse into Russian. We spoke in French, but he read us some of his versions of poems by Antonio Machado, and as he did, I recalled the rhythms and meter of the originals, which in his translations had been completely obliterated. What Ehrenburg was most interested in was poetry itself, all of it. He was a laconic prose stylist. His works of fiction did not attract Soviet critics, but his essays and newspaper articles made a deep impression. The old man was the possessor of a style which only Chekhov and Isaac Babel before him could command. At the time of our visit, he was writing his memoirs.

"Such works can only be written by old people. Boris Pasternak wrote his at age thirty. What kind of an age is that for such a task? His *Safe Conduct* is not a memoir at all."

For him, all memoirs should be *livres fleuves*, books that grow with the years. Only in old age can one remember the way people looked, he said, their traits and characters, the flavor of the times.

Pedro Cepeda considered Ehrenburg one of the Soviet intellectuals who had compromised the least and achieved the most.

Afterwards, as we walked down Gorky Street, he asked me: "Do you want to write a book of memoirs someday?"

"What about you?" I asked.

"Perhaps I need old age, just as Ehrenburg says."

"But you are not lacking in personal experiences," I pointed out.

"Would you want to do such a book?"

"I don't know."

"Keep a diary of everything you see. You are in the privileged position of witnessing a revolution in Cuba."

"Books on revolutions should be written by foreigners."

"But," Pedro said, "my book could not be as precise in its chronology as Ehrenburg would want. How would you begin your memoir?"

"I would begin, 'I was born in Pinar del Río, Cuba . . .' "

"But you're reading out a birth certificate," he protested. "Your memoir should give the *real* date of your birth, the most crucial moment of your existence. You would remember it well, and then continue in the style of a tapestry from Central Asia—you mount panels helter-skelter, piling up people, train stations, horses, trees, roads, houses, and castles. In reality, genuine discourse is not lineal but is made up of an endless number of forking paths, just like life."

He laughed sadly. Trembling, he grew pale behind his antiquated glasses. He had the wrinkles of a much older man.

"You are much younger than I," he said. "I advise you to think in terms of experience. Literature is an evaluation of experience."

I repeated my idea that such an evaluation is not best carried out by its protagonists, but rather by those who are witness to the "experience," but from a distance.

"Take the Spanish Civil War as an example. Baroja was incapable of recounting what he lived through, nor could Unamuno or younger writers. There are no Spanish novels of the Civil War of any note, but there are books by André Malraux and Ernest Hemingway."

"I'm not interested in Malraux, but I do like Hemingway. *For Whom the Bell Tolls* hasn't been published in Russian because the Spanish Communist Party considers it a libel against its leaders, but the translation is complete. We're only waiting for Dolores Ibárruri, La Pasionaria, to die; she has been opposing its publication with great determination. *For Whom the Bell Tolls* is the only book by Hemingway that has not been published here. He is very popular. Did you ever meet him?"

Pedro was continually astonished at the number of people I had happened to meet in a short period of time. Yes, I knew him; in the forties and fifties he was a familiar figure in the bars of Havana. I had seen him for the last time when he returned to Cuba accompanied by the bullfighter Antonio Ordóñez, just after the Revolution triumphed. I still have a photo of the three of us, taken on his arrival. Hemingway was all fired up to live in a revolution. At the airport, he kissed the Cuban flag, and when the photographer asked him to do it again, he said he was offended by such a request—the repetition of a sincere act. All this went into the interview with him which I wrote up for Prensa Latina.

Pedro was intrigued and asked me about other writers I had met. I spoke of Pablo Neruda, who had been in Cuba many times, but whom I had first met in Paris.

"Here all of Neruda is available, but the translators have rhymed everything."

I tried for a moment to imagine the unthinkable—the Chilean Communist poet frenetically trying to rhyme his exultant poem to Stalin, called in English "Let the Railsplitter Awake," a work which surely won him a place in hell. But my imagination quickly balked at such an absurdity. Instead, I asked Pedro what Neruda sounded like in Russian.

"Like that claptrap Spanish romantic Zorrilla, but much more pompous."

On occasion, Pedro invited me to venture farther out into the outskirts of Moscow. We went through sections of the city well away from the center—twisting, barely lit streets. I never felt the human presence more intensely than among anonymous Russians along those icy thoroughfares. They would stop in front of small stores called "Gastronom," indicating with hand signals that they wanted a bottle of vodka to share, and drinking it right there—comrades in payment and enjoyment.

Afterwards, there would be a quick embrace before they staggered down the street.

One day, as we were walking through Red Square, Pedro pointed out the sights. "There you have some of the greatest monuments in the city."

He motioned toward Lenin's tomb first and then toward Lubyanka prison, where the KGB was imposing the exigencies of a true Communist education upon individuals.

"It is one of the last pyramids in the world, created by a Pharaoh of the working class. It is the temple where his guardians are given their education. My second birth took place in that temple. My first was in Málaga, as you know. My book will begin in Lubyanka."

He did start his book. I wonder if his widow has those manuscript pages, which brought together the multiple threads that made up his world, similar in montage to those Central Asian tapestries he admired so extravagantly.

8

~~~~~~

In October 1962, Juan Arcocha telephoned from Havana to say that he was coming to Moscow. I went to meet him at the airport; he had startling news. "In Cuba, things are at the point of no return. Everyone is saying that there are Soviet nuclear rocket installations on the island. Photographs from U-2s have been published in American newspapers, but in Havana we pretend to know nothing about it. The accusations from Washington are categorically denied."

Two days later Moscow Radio announced that President Kennedy had ordered a naval blockade which would stay in place until the Soviet Union dismantled and retired the missiles.

In Moscow, people would stop in the street to listen to any portable radio. After a period of almost unbearable tension, the agreement between the two governments was announced—the missiles would be brought back to the Soviet Union. In the offices of *Moscow News*, Aníbal Escalante followed the developments with the same anxiety as the rest of us. When he heard the announcement of the accord between Kennedy and Khrushchev, he raised his head: "That's politics. The humiliation doesn't count. What counts is that Cuba is still there."

The news we were getting was disjointed in the extreme. Our embassy knew nothing of any specifically Cuban response to what was happening, and even less about the agreement between the two superpowers. Just then we attended a festive reception on the anniversary of the October Revolution, a resplendent occasion which took place as planned before the crisis. Arcocha and I were accompanied by friends, including the Italian journalists Augusto Pancaldi and Paolo Pardo. We all awaited expectantly the toast by the Soviet leader. When it came, Khrushchev made only a laconic reference to Cuba: ". . . The Cubans don't want to believe in the word given by the President of the United States, but one must believe in his word." Kennedy kept his pledge.

After the October crisis, I began to keep a lower profile in Moscow. The cordial and affable Cuban military attaché, Eddy Suñol, a man given to sharing with me many of his most private thoughts, suddenly fell into an inscrutable silence. The embassy became a bunker inhabited by survivors. The sense of failure which Ortega y Gasset has placed at the center of human existence began to take hold of us—that sudden fear that one morning when we opened the front door we would find *the street wasn't there*. It was like the painful discovery that in moments of great passion the honest intellectual must remain silent or lie.

When Yevtushenko came back from Havana, he brought news and many heroic poems. He asked me to write something quickly. "I will translate it myself and have it published in

Pravda." I was about to leave for Helsinki for the Christmas holidays; I wanted to talk to Cuban friends in the West about what was happening. Yevtushenko tried to calm me down. "Nothing has happened. Cuba is there. If I were a Cuban, I would write a poem in support of the five basic points the Cuban government used as the basis for any negotiation. I would write, 'They are five points, five points on high,' and he began to recite the possible poem in the declamatory fashion so dear to Russians. I did dash off the requested poem and then took the train for Helsinki. Yevtushenko, who had huge feet, had begged me to buy him a pair of shoes, the biggest I might find in the Finnish capital. I did as requested; they were two thin black sharks which took up half my suitcase, but it was no use—they were too small. When I returned, my poem, as translated by Yevgeny, had been published in the December 31 issue of *Pravda*, but the poet had disappeared from the Moscow scene. Since we had been seen in public together and had given joint poetry readings, people recognized me on the street and asked about him. I decided to go to his apartment. Without first ringing the buzzer, I climbed the stairs and knocked on the door. He was stretched out on a bed. His wife, Gala, explained that the publication in France of his *Precocious Autobiography* had enraged the bureaucrats. He had been summoned to a meeting at the Writers' Union and subjected to a blistering dressing-down.

I must say that Yevgeny Yevtushenko treated me with a degree of friendship which I will never forget. When my difficulties in Cuba were just beginning, he sent me a cable congratulating me on receiving the prize of the Cuban Writers' Union, without paying the slightest attention to the scandal the award had provoked. "Yours are bitter truths, but bitter truths are also truths. Your Russian brother embraces you. Signed, Eugenio Yevtushenko." After I was arrested and acted out the classic rite of self-degradation, which gave Fidel Castro a few hours' solace, he was one of the friends who gave me moral support. He wrote me a long letter: "Wounded isn't dead. People tell me that you are working on a farm or on a cooperative, but I want to tell you that I have always admired your poetry, and I want to hear again the clang of horseshoes coming from the horses of your poetry . . ." And he went on in that vein.

In Moscow, he would show me what he considered to be great contemporary poems in the Russian language, but they seemed to me anecdotal and descriptive. The images were primitive, and almost all the poems rested too easily on rudimentary similes and analogies. Metaphor was nonexistent. But from him I learned to distrust what he called Orientalism, the abundance of abstractions which exhausts a poem's power. Yevgeny loved rhymed poetry, and believed it a Western error not to have kept it up. In his opinion, musicality was an essential attribute of all poetry. And it was during the brief period of his own difficulties in Russia that we shared an experience difficult to forget—the visit of Fidel Castro to the Soviet Union.

Yevtushenko had been accused of claiming a friendship with Fidel which did not exist. With this in mind, we thought that an effusive public encounter with the Comandante would persuade people that Yevgeny was telling the truth. After all, the omnipresent bureaucrats of the Communist Party would send the news on up to their superiors if such a positive meeting took place.

We went to the hotel where Fidel was staying on his official visit, on a corner of the Arbat, near my apartment. Fidel was seated on a sofa in the main reception room, surrounded by Cuban and Soviet functionaries. We approached the group.

Fidel's voice seemed hoarser than usual. "Is it true that Harry Winston is living in this hotel?"

One of Fidel's aides went over to inquire at the desk and quickly returned. "Yes, Comandante, but he is asleep. Because of his age and ill health, he can barely leave his room. He takes his meals there and is tended to by a nurse."

Winston, the aged militant of the CP/USA, was now almost

blind, and at the hotel an official authorization enabled him to obtain all necessary services without charge. Fidel attempted to decline respectfully a toast which an Armenian admirer was offering, a toast "to the health of the Cuban Comandante." Fidel tried to tell him in Spanish that his health would be undermined if he drank up the contents of the gigantic goblet of cognac that was being handed him; while the befuddled Armenian pretended not to understand the nature of Fidel's refusal, Fidel asked again for Harry Winston.

A few minutes later, after Fidel asked yet again, Winston appeared in his pajamas, with an unsteady gait. "Fidel, it's a great honor, it's a great honor."

After a few minutes of the usual inquiries, and without paying much attention to Winston's answers, Fidel lost interest in the old man in pajamas seated on the edge of a chair, head turned in his direction. By now Fidel had converted Winston into just one more listener, an incidental member of his entourage. And he kept on toying with the Armenian, who insisted that the toast be completed in a formal fashion. In the end, Fidel made him drink not only his own goblet but Fidel's as well. The Cuban retinue could barely conceal their glee. All the while, the Armenian kept on drinking on his own, and he started on another toast in honor of the Comandante. The laughter turned into an ongoing din, with the aides-de-camp, the followers, functionaries, and interpreters joining the chorus as if by command. Harry Winston attempted a wan smile, but the effort was too much for him. After the noise had eased a bit, he whispered, "I am tired, Fidel; I am old and ill. Permit me to leave."

The Comandante continued laughing. Two aides accompanied Winston back to his room. At that moment Fidel spotted us. Addressing Yevtushenko, he said, "Hello, poet, how are you?" We should have realized right then and there the kind of objects we were: small animals of history which someone superior knew how to make use of and then discard. I am sure that Yevgeny remembers that our suspicions after Fidel's curt words were not unfounded. Where the paths of poetry and politics cross, there is little room for reconciliation. The tyrant is the natural enemy of the poet, and not because he is superior.

It had stopped snowing and the streets were silent and white. I remember walking with Yevgeny to a nearby café, shivering in the cold. So sure was I that no danger could ever come my way that I felt a kind of superior solidarity with my troubled friend. He was the one who was suffering. Doubtless, news of the deliberate contempt which the Cuban Comandante had shown toward the young, popular Soviet poet had been passed on to the highest levels. As we walked along in that cold Moscow air, neither one of us realized that Fidel's snub was directed not so much at the poet as at the political institutions of the Soviet Union. Fidel did not consider Yevtushenko an artist in his own right, but rather a spokesman for the Soviet state. This all took place, it should be noted, just after the October missile crisis, and the Comandante had given the back of his hand to a spokesman for the "new" Soviet Union; he had accorded the same treatment to Anastas Mikoyan. Thinking along the same lines as the *Pravda* correspondent in Havana, with his memorable dictum about the "credentials" of a poet in the Soviet Union, Fidel firmly believed that publishing poems in the official organ of the Communist Party was not just a sign of distinction in the arts, but a reflection of a deeper engagement with the government. Even if this was not in fact true in the early sixties, it was the kind of Stalinist thinking that Fidel was prone to.

Around that time, the American journalist Robert Scheer arrived in Moscow bearing a letter from Pablo Armando Fernández in London, asking me to introduce Scheer to Yevtushenko. Scheer seemed many years younger than he was, dressed in an overcoat which made him look like a gnome. Behind his long hair and hirsute beard, he looked at me with the keen eyes of either an intelligent man or a hustler. I accompanied him around a Moscow swept by frigid winds.

Scheer was interested in the new condition of Soviet culture, and expressed this interest in a questionnaire so well organized that it would be hard to forget. As we talked, I gave him my uncensored opinion of the Soviet political system. He asked if I said such things with the same degree of frankness to the editor of my newspaper back in Havana. I showed him some of the letters I had written to Carlos Franqui, letters which accompanied my regular dispatches. This was an issue years later in Havana, when Scheer, now dressed like a yuppie, asked me to hand over those letters.

"What letters?"

"The ones you sent Carlos Franqui from Moscow."

I couldn't imagine that he would remember; moreover, I did not have copies of those letters. But Scheer, who had ceased to be the good-natured fellow I had met in Moscow, was now one of the editors in chief of *Ramparts* magazine, with exclusive rights to publish the diary of Ché Guevara in the United States. He had remembered the letters to Franqui with the selective memory of someone who knew how to couple moral curiosity with the prudence of an efficient executive. But Scheer was unable to meet Yevtushenko, who had gone off to the Black Sea with Gala. Just a little later I would travel to Paris; I was beginning to be concerned since I never saw in print any of the articles I regularly sent back to *Revolución*. Franqui was in France, and I wanted to find out in person what was happening.

In Paris, K. S. Karol awaited me. A Pole who had lived in the Stalinist world, he never quite believed in apparent changes which had taken place in the Soviet Union. We used to meet in the editorial offices of *Le Nouvel Observateur*, where I also had occasion to speak to its editor, Jean Daniel. At that time in France, the attacks from the left on the political ideas of Albert Camus were virulent. For Jean Daniel, friend of the author's, Camus's work was equivalent to Molière's for his time, a scrutinizer of hypocrisies. Daniel wasted a great deal of time talking to me and planning some way to support

Camus. I was ready to defend him publicly; he asked me, "Yes, but how?" I outlined my thinking, but he kept on interrupting. He was not satisfied. There was too much moral abstraction in my argument. In any case, we could do nothing. The Sartrian left and the Communists had greater resources than we did.

They described Camus as a "man who walked around with his own statue under his arm," and such primitive characterizations helped destroy a reputation a quarter of a century ago. Merleau-Ponty suffered the same fate, as did Raymond Aron.

9

~~~~~~

"WE DO NOT WANT to miss anything in our times," wrote Jean-Paul Sartre. This was by no means Sartre's only declaration of his compulsion to experience every vicissitude; and his contemporaries shared this ambition. Along with the sense of the commitment of the intellectual to history, there was also a sense of estrangement from the world. But the postwar French intellectual did not represent a clean break with the literature and the thought characteristic of France before the outbreak of the Second World War. Drieu La Rochelle, Montherlant, Céline, and Malraux—the great figures of prewar French culture—are inseparable from the central figures of the intellectual scene after the war: Sartre, Camus, Merleau-Ponty, Simone de Beauvoir, and the others. The links between Sartre's *Nausée* and Céline's *Journey to the End of Night*, between Camus's *The Stranger* and Drieu La Rochelle's *The Fire Within* exist. A similar brand of moral desperation emanates from these works, even when the political views of the writers differ. It might be said that French thought is a world of moral discriminations taken to the highest degree. Indeed, these writers represent the best of what France has produced. The rationalist will of Sartre, on occasion more apparent than real, can be contrasted with the moralism of Camus, above all in the latter's analysis of the political realities of the time, an analysis which led him to rebel against any variety of totalitarianism.

Toward the end of the fifties, it was not easy to approach either Sartre or Camus without running the risk of making an enemy of the other—and, even more dramatically, of their respective followers. This was the case at the time because, intentionally or not, both men were dependent on their faithful and jealous partisans. On every occasion when I mentioned to a friend in France that I would like to meet either Sartre or Camus, I always encountered the same cautious prevarication. One had to choose one or the other. Sartre's tribe was headed by his disciple Jeanson, whose pompous rhetoric all but drowned out the sober loyalty of Jean Daniel and the rest of Camus's adherents.

One day in 1959 I asked Juan Goytisolo to introduce me to Camus, since I knew that Juan worked with him at Gallimard; Juan declined. No, he and his wife, Monique, and Nathalie Sarraute were unconditional friends of Sartre. Sarraute had told me that, after *The Stranger*, Camus had ruined his work with such books as *The Plague* and *The Fall*. So I had to go through Cuban friends. René Álvarez Ríos introduced me to a young Algerian, who in turn arranged the interview over lunch.

Camus spoke in Spanish. Like Montherlant, he had a solid knowledge of Spanish culture, and had translated Calderón de la Barca's *The Devotion of the Cross* into French. I tried to get Camus to speak about his own writing, but he was more interested in asking about Cuba. After all, in 1959, Cuba was *the* topic in Europe. The Paris newspapers carried daily reports from Havana. Camus was worried about certain signals coming from the island, and he wanted clarification. In retrospect, I only wish that these signals he perceived had been as visible and as alarming to me as they were to him. By this time, his political activity was restricted to the columns he wrote for *Combat*. But his novels were concerned in one way or another with political and moral questions. In *The Plague* he had attempted to expound these preoccupations in an allegorical mode owing much to both Kafka and Dostoevsky, but the purport was clear, nonetheless. Camus sensed danger arising out of the new tyrannies which by then had perfected their techniques of repression. One had to take sides. In opposition to the revolutionary, he posited his rebel, and it was this pairing that occasioned the virulent attacks that were mounted against him.

In his tone of voice, in his judgments, and in his bare commentary, Camus was a man imprisoned in his moral vocation. That was precisely what his enemies considered the most vulnerable aspect of his thought. His denial of history was unacceptable to Sartre, who, after all, had founded his own philosophy on the reign of history, and Sartre was, in any case, the preeminent philosopher in the France of his time. When I spoke to Pierre Courtade, the French writer and journalist, about my interest in Camus's work, he noted ironically that one of the few times when Sartre was right was when he described the style of Camus as *pompous*. The general feeling of the time was of a simple and fraternal human being, but one now very much on the defensive. Also, my impression was that the fact that he was born in Algeria and extolled life, sun, and the sea had irritated those born in the rain and gloom of Paris. Evidently, Camus attracted people with the same intensity as he drew their hatred.

During those years, Camus was criticized for not being a professional philosopher, which really meant that he refused to function within the orbit of Marxist categories. Camus not only rejected Marx but turned his back on the neo-Hegelianism that was then fashionable in Paris. He believed that it sanctioned political crime. As for Husserl and Heidegger, Camus admired them but found their thoughts to be superfluous abstractions, bloodless and frigid. He was a follower of Nietzsche and in *The Rebel* eloquently defended the philosopher's work. Camus was one of the few at the time who exempted Nietzsche from a share in the responsibility for Fascism.

In person, he gave off a youngish, athletic impression—thin, short hair, lucid and intense eyes. There was nothing of incipient middle age in his body, his voice, in the way he walked or the way he lit a cigarette. Even the Nobel Prize seemed to have cast no shadow over his public and private life. That having been said, I must add that he did seek to make use of it in the social and political sphere. I asked him if he was interested in visiting Cuba. He was enthusiastic, but when our ambassador Manuel Grant was notified of Camus's interest and passed the request on to Havana, he received no response. Neither Ambassador Grant nor Camus meant much to Cuba that year. Grant was a well-known professor of physics at the University of Havana; his political prestige derived from his membership in the Orthodox Party. Neither this aging ambassador nor the theoretician of rebellion could offer much to a revolutionary government in crisis or to an army of rebels soon to be disciplined into rigorous order by dogmatic bureaucrats.

At the end of lunch, Camus offered me a Cuban cigar. I smoked mine down to the butt, he smoked his halfway. We went on talking for a long time, and finally did speak of Algeria in relation to his own writing, and later about Faulkner and Hemingway. He admitted that the narrative method of

The Stranger had been used before by American writers. I suggested that a certain kind of so-called secondary literature (James M. Cain, Dashiell Hammett) seemed to have had a greater influence over him than did Faulkner or Hemingway. I mentioned Drieu La Rochelle and Céline. "They will be remembered," he said. And we spoke of the younger generation of French writers, to whom he seemed open. Finally, he spoke of Kafka and the influence that this writer had had on his generation and on his time. As I went on mentioning names, he either approved or was silent; but almost always I sensed the fervor of his commitment to literature, even in the amiable way he had of not entering an acrid dissent when a particular writer was mentioned. It so happens that I did not mention Sartre to Camus, but I had the feeling that he expected me to mention him, since we had just had such a long, over-arching conversation about the Resistance, the founding of *Combat*, the Age of the Mandarins, and other such topics.

The last image I have of Camus is the photograph handed to me in the offices of Prensa Latina after his death a few months later, in January of 1960. When I later read the issue of *La Nouvelle Revue Française* dedicated to him, containing photographs from different periods of his life, I thought that the photographs summed him up best, more so than the essays on his work and his personality. Of the latter, I do remember the three pages by William Faulkner, which acutely gave the fairest possible evaluation of the work of Albert Camus.

I returned many times to Paris, to its *quartiers* and narrow streets so well described by Nathalie Sarraute in her *Tropismes*. I took great delight in sitting in the café Le Babel, facing the *cité universitaire*. Walking from Saint-Germain to Montparnasse, I went into a movie theater and saw Fellini's *8½*—Goytisolo had urged me to see it. When I left the theater, I felt that my mental and emotional life had changed. It made me happy to know that Fellini existed, and I fantasized that I was meeting him and shaking his hand, a dream which became reality in Moscow two years later. *8½* would be awarded the prize for the best film in the Moscow Film Festival, but, ironically, this did not imply any intent on the part of the Soviet cultural bureaucracy to distribute the film. Yes, I loved the Paris of the *nouvelle vague*, the Paris of the early novels of Butor and Robbe-Grillet, the Paris where Merleau-Ponty still lived.

10

~~~~~~

SINCE CHILDHOOD, I have been governed by a sentiment which I have not been able to explain to my own satisfaction—a fascination with old Saxon words, with Germanic literatures, with the Scandinavian sagas. The first Nordic country I came to know was Finland. When I lived in Moscow, I took either the train or the plane to Helsinki on various occasions. I remember once taking a plane to the Finnish capital in the company of Ilya Ehrenburg. I planned to stay in Helsinki for a few days, and he was to continue on to Sweden to take care of some details connected with the World Peace Congress. Helsinki enchanted me. Its inviting atmosphere was like something I had known before. And yet my only knowledge of Finland came from an adolescent reading of the extraordinary *Letters from Finland* (*Cartas finlandesas*) by the Spanish diplomat and essayist Ángel Ganivet, a contemporary of Miguel de Unamuno. During that period (encompassed roughly by the presidency of Urho Kekkonen), there was an atmosphere of cultural freedom difficult to imagine in a country that is really a halfway house between the Soviet Union and the West. Finnish politicians knew how to coexist with the U.S.S.R. Russia was the "giant reflected in the lake," to quote the poet Pinnti Saarikoski, an important figure in Helsinki at that time. Some of his poems, translated from his 1962 book *What Is Really Happening?* by Matti Rosi, another Finnish poet with a fluent command of Spanish, introduced me to his world. I also became familiar with the work of Paavo Haavikko. His book *Rumanian Nights*, his poems, and his novels revealed him to be a great artist. Such was the impact of the poetry I was able to read in Helsinki that I thought I had to go back to the source; I bought a copy of the Finnish national epic, *The Kalevala*—which sounded to me like an ancient poem from my own corner of the earth.

Why was I so overcome by the landscape of Lapland? Why did I think I was discovering something in my own nature as I gazed on that remote terrain? The same sensations overwhelmed me when I visited Norway, Denmark, and Sweden. Those landscapes are indelibly etched in my memory.

I unburdened myself of these bizarre impressions when I spoke to Sartre back in Moscow, sometime in 1963.

"I understand it perfectly," he said. "During a long period of our adolescence we are drawn to alien and impersonal states of mind and atmospheres. I lived for a long time in love with the idea of writing a novel full of sunlight."

"Similar to *The Stranger*?"

"Yes, I would have preferred for the characters in *Nauseé* to have had an encounter with the meridional atmosphere of North Africa. But apparently you Cubans react antagonistically toward the milieu into which you were born. You have a prenatal nostalgia for snow. Alejo Carpentier almost never alludes to the most visible element of his country, the sun, which might be the equivalent of a Russian writer never mentioning snow. Tropical storms are fascinating, as are snowstorms, don't you think?"

He looked at me, worried. I replied that I was in complete agreement.

He then went on in a professorial tone. "You have to internalize your world, your own, the one in which you were born and lived. That Scandinavian enchantment of which you speak is purely literary. Moreover, any childhood is full of ballads. Childhood is primitive and immediate. It is the age for great terrors and great emotional outbursts."

Sartre wanted a cup of strong coffee and was convinced that in the hotel where he was staying, the Metropole, they did not know how to brew it. I suggested the Hotel Moscow, where I had lived for a while and where I knew the employees in the cafeteria could make a passable cup of espresso with their shiny Italian machines.

But I had other things to talk to Sartre about. I bore a message from some of my Russian friends who were painters and considered themselves in the "abstract" school. Their work had been taken down from the walls of a gallery personally by Nikita Khrushchev, who loudly alleged that they were obscene examples of "decadent Western art." The Hotel Moscow was not far from the Metropole, and Sartre wanted me to accompany him on a stroll. As we walked, I told him that his personal influence was considered decisive by my painter friends. The furious reaction of the Soviet leader meant the possible disappearance of this group of artists. But Sartre did not know what had happened. He stopped as I described the scene, asking me for more details—had Khrushchev himself taken the paintings down?

"He himself? Khrushchev physically removed the paintings? All this in front of everybody, and in a rage?"

"Yes, in front of everybody, and in a rage."

"But this is unbelievable," he exclaimed, widening his agile but slightly uncoordinated eyes.

"It happened last night. He was taken to see the show, and I believe he even smashed one of the paintings in anger."

Sartre was astonished, almost joyful even. "Don't you see? It's magnificent. It is the presence, the provocation of culture."

This was typical of Sartre. Every event contributed to a totality. The rage of a chief of state in front of a work by a painter was an "intellectual" answer to a set of aesthetic values. The *action* was more important than the consequences. Besides, the painters had not been thrown in jail.

"Surprising country, this; have you been here for a long time? It must be fascinating to live with these passionate people."

In the Hotel Moscow, the *café bien serré* that Sartre asked for was obtained by means of a simple expedient: reducing the water by half. The waiters were gratified by our effusive compliments. Sartre asked for a second cup and lit cigarette after cigarette with the first disposable lighter I had ever seen.

"I am getting strange news from Cuba," he said. "Do you ever see Aníbal Escalante?"

"Every day," I replied. "I am an assistant on the weekly *Moscow News* published here in Spanish. We work in the same office."

Sartre was interested in the Escalante case.

"A typical party professional."

"Is there any hidden intent behind Castro's attack on Escalante and his group?"

I really didn't know and told him so, and he continued: "Enrique Oltuski is a barometer for me," he said. "I met him when he was the youngest cabinet minister in Cuba. He is a Jew, and the Jews are incapable of betraying themselves when they speak. In 1960 I found him enthusiastic about the Revolution, but the last time I saw him he was no longer minister, his enthusiasm more mechanical, and he no longer the same man. Forgive me for speaking to you so frankly. The Revolution is more important to me than you can imagine."

I never saw anyone smoke so many cigarettes in so short a time. I had the impression that Sartre lit up in part for the pleasure of using his wine-colored lighter, which each time shot up a seemingly uncontrollable flame.

"I have also heard that there are problems with homosexuals. Do you know anything about that?"

"Rumors only, but Arcocha is in Cuba and will bring news of what is going on."

"Oltuski told me that there is no anti-Semitism in Cuba, that they don't know the meaning of the word. True?"

"If Oltuski says so, it has to be true."

"That is what Simone de Beauvoir says: If you want to know if a certain society is *machista*, go and ask any woman. I believe Oltuski, but I am also convinced that a society which doesn't have any Jews will end up by inventing them. Perhaps the homosexuals are the Jews of Cuba."

Sartre wanted to walk farther; he said he didn't want to waste the bright morning hours in a city as gloomy and somber as Moscow.

"We must contradict Dostoevsky," he said with a smile. From the Hotel Moscow we walked along Gorky Street through Pushkin Square, and ended up in front of the statue dominating Mayakovsky Square, with the figure of the poet in stone, young and headstrong.

"Just as well you Cubans have been spared such tragic glories. It's not that I dislike Mayakovsky; as a matter of fact, I find him disturbing, though his poems are not meant to produce that effect. I have the impression that he is something of an operatic poet. Doubtless, he imitated Whitman, but the enthusiasm of America, the product of recent history, is not the same as his Slavic will, which found in Lenin the poet's own prophet and executioner. I am not speaking in racist terms . . . Here the word Slavic is genuinely descriptive. Ah, well . . ."

He left the explanation hanging. Since I felt under obligation to carry back a response to my abstract painters, I returned to the matter of the show.

"I will speak with Yekaterina Furtseva, the Minister of Culture, but I will do so tactfully. You can get anywhere with Russians that way. You can tell them what I have said, but tactfully. We can't be braggarts. Nothing irritates politicians more than an artist boasting of his own importance."

And, in effect, nothing terrible happened to the abstract painters. Later, when I went to Paris to see Carlos Franqui, then supervising the installation of a Cuban exposition in a gallery near the Aux Deux Magots café, I saw Sartre again. He spoke of the Cuban Revolution with the enthusiasm of a child. The room was full of young people who sat at his feet, listening with veneration. Sartre was eloquent. Each of his formulations was dazzling, and as he spoke, he never stopped playing with that wine-colored lighter, which he twiddled in his fingers as if it were a toy.

11

~~~~~~

In Paris, K. S. Karol asked me to lunch with Pierre Courtade, the French correspondent for *L'Humanité*, whom I had first met in his Moscow apartment. His wife, Nicole, was an attractive blonde who dressed in black, a fashion made popular by Juliette Greco just after the war. Courtade had published a book, *Red Square*, which had accredited him in the eyes of the French Communist Party. It is hardly remembered today. At that time he and other foreign correspondents from the Communist and Workers' Press (the official designation) enjoyed privileges for which they had to pay a price—their obligation was the spreading of "Soviet truth" throughout the world.

Their vengeance consisted in sending back verbatim, without changing a word, the press releases distributed by the Press Section of the Ministry of Foreign Relations. Over a few drinks they would loose more venom against the Soviet Union than even its worst enemies abroad. I used to meet with these correspondents, since I was the recently arrived Cuban, who needed to learn the rules of the game. In the group, Courtade sported the air of a cardinal in mourning, expounding truths with an aggrieved mien, utterly convinced that any evidence given should betray a hidden anguish.

After the famous vernissage at the abstract painters' show and Khrushchev's equally renowned reaction to the Muscovite avant-garde, Courtade threw a big party at his apartment for all those constituting the Communist and Workers' Press. The dean of the group, Max Leon, denounced the "foreign pressures trying to dominate the cultural sensibility of the country." After making this solemn declaration, he exclaimed, "Comrades, let's face it once and for all, the Russians don't like Western art." The problem at hand, Leon said, was not that Khrushchev was engaging in political repression but rather that the man was insisting on his own standards of art. It was all a false problem. "What can our Cuban tell us?" Courtade asked gravely. The Cuban didn't have much to say to those who exported their own Soviet beliefs to the entire world, the political and aesthetic influences governing their country: Social Realism and the rest. They were used to being accused of creating the rosy stereotypes for what was, in fact, an ever more contradictory and knotty society. Augusto Pancaldi, correspondent from the Italian Communist daily *L'Unità*, shouted, "I'm not taking this one more day!" But Leon responded soothingly, "Comrades we have to calm down and make a scientific study of the situation." It was a call to order, since scientific analysis was of use only to remind us that the problem of Russia was historical and not ideological. In Western Europe, history brought about other exigencies. Such primitive problems, observable in Russia, couldn't happen back there.

In any case, most of the journalists were too drunk to listen to the call to order. Alcohol was gradually devouring them; you didn't hear any conversation, but rather an intermittent barrage of words. The fact that they were exhausted gave them a look both ingenuous and diabolic. Their despair was brought on by their having lost faith in the cause. Only Courtade, I thought, had found a way to keep himself afloat. He was a man of some years and adored a lovely and sympathetic young woman in a city buried in snow.

At lunch back in Paris with Karol and Courtade at the Café de l'Alexandra, I was able to corroborate the dictum of the German poet Hans Magnus Enzensberger, who once stated that "a Communist lies with the total conviction of a man who knows he is lying." It occurred to me once again as I was recounting to Karol and Courtade what I had seen a few nights before in Moscow.

I had been standing in the wings of a Moscow theater with Yevtushenko and Dmitri Shostakovich. It was just before the second performance of the composer's Thirteenth Symphony. This was a work for orchestra, chorus, and bass soloist, with texts by Yevtushenko. Suddenly a few frightened musicians came up to us and told us that they had heard that an order had been given to cancel the concert. Later, two men from the theater administration approached Shostakovich and spoke to him in low, anxious voices. Yevgeny and I kept our distance. Shostakovich then walked toward us, nodding and mumbling, "*Eto pravda*"—it's true. He had tears in his eyes. The Thirteenth Symphony made use of five poems by Yevtushenko, including "Babi Yar" and "Humor." The music starkly dramatized the intensity of "Babi Yar," and the lighthearted, witty poem on humor was set to agile, springy rhythms. Such lines as "They tried to buy off humor, but humor cannot be bought! They tried to kill humor, but he just thumbed his nose!" were just too audacious for the old-time Stalinists, who could not tolerate the slightest expression of artistic freedom.

Courtade listened to my description of the scene in the Moscow theater with mounting indignation. Karol was scrutinizing him as I spoke, taking note of every reaction. The cardinal of French Communism kept exclaiming, "*C'est beaucoup . . . c'est beaucoup.* I go on vacation, leave Moscow, and everything goes down the drain. What you are telling me is intolerable. When do you return to Moscow?" He asked me to come with him to the offices of *Les Lettres Françaises.* Courtade did seem quite exercised, his face growing redder: "You must tell all this to Aragon. I will meet you at one at Aux Deux Magots." As we left, Karol said to me, "I don't trust people like that." I did meet Courtade at Aux Deux Magots later. In Moscow, he wore drab clothes, but in Paris he was always elegantly decked out. And as we sipped our coffee, his conversation took a surprising turn.

"Karol is an embittered man," he said, unsmiling. "There is no doubt that he works for British Intelligence."

I looked at him, astonished. He put his hand on my shoulder. "That is what they say. I mean, that is what certain segments of the party assure me."

I didn't dare say anything.

He went on: "In our world, no one makes his real opinions known in the presence of a third party, as you did in the Café de l'Alexandra." At this point he began to use the familiar *tu.* "He and I are witnesses against you. Of course this is only an example, but I advise you not to express your opinion concerning the Soviet Union to people like K. S. Karol. He is a Pole who fled Russia and writes for an anti-Communist journal. The objections that we might have to the Soviet Union—and they are many, I don't deny it—should not be shared with the enemy. If that man were to repeat tomorrow all that you said about Soviet cultural life, he could do so because I, a member of the French Communist Party, was present. Karol set a trap for you. I do not believe that he means to harm you, but if it became necessary, he wouldn't hesitate. He is a political renegade."

Smiling now, with that same treacly tone and seeming to be offering me a protective blanket, he ended the conversation by saying that, of course, nothing could be said to Louis Aragon that he did not know already. Courtade stood up and offered his hand. Paris had transformed him; it had refreshed his spirit, he said. He hoped to see me upon his return to Moscow either in his apartment or in Pancaldi's. We should see each other more often. Moscow was such a cold city.

Trembling with rage, I returned to my hotel across from the Gare Montparnasse. An icy rain began to fall. I had on one of those nylon caps which were popular in Paris at the time. The old lady behind the hotel desk raised her eyes to greet me. *"Bonsoir, monsieur, vous venez d'Afrique?"* When I told her that I was Cuban but had come from Moscow, she said, "All the guests here are fleeing from North Africa. They are *pieds noirs*," she cried in anguish. I went to the bar of the hotel and called Juan Goytisolo. His wife, Monique, answered. "Come on over," she said.

In their apartment on the rue Poisonnière I unburdened myself of all the worries and uncertainties of my life in Moscow. I described what the Communist world, the one we had given our allegiance to, was really like. "What worries me," I said finally to Goytisolo, "is that this will only exacerbate your Dostoevskian vein. Things are so complex. I suppose things have always been complex, damn them."

A few days later, Juan and Monique threw a party for some close friends—Italo Calvino and his wife Chichita, Francisco Rabal and his wife, Jean Daniel and Jorge Semprún. Once again, the inevitable topics of conversation were the Soviet world and the first years of the Cuban Revolution. We oscillated between concern and disenchantment. That evening, only Daniel and I accepted the conclusions of Albert Camus—that because of the monstrosities in the recent history of Soviet

Communism and in the other socialist countries, it was impossible to be a Communist. At the same time, you could not be anti-Communist because that would mean acquiescing in the shameful history of Western colonialism. So it was the duty of supporters of the Cuban Revolution to prevent it from repeating the same errors the Soviets made. But our criticisms should be made from within.

In Cuba, the Revolution (or those who governed in its name) had instituted the Agrarian Reform Law, had broken up the powerful sugar plantations, had embarked on a gigantic literacy program, had converted barracks into schools, established hospitals in every corner of the country, and had ended unemployment—all this as it struggled against enemies from within and without. Cuba, we thought, would never adopt the Soviet model. After all, the highest rank in the rebel army was that of comandante (major), not general or marshal. That was the tenor of our thinking.

Even as I expressed my confidence to friends, I was prey to long bouts of depression. More and more had to be explained away. The seizing of revolutionary power had encountered resistance, of course, but we glided over the reasons for this resistance, making use of scientific analysis. For instance, it was logical for a radical change of institutions to give rise to hostile reactions, and it was understandable that the Agrarian Reform Law would encounter opposition from the rich landowners. Already, by the end of 1959, the military commander of the Camagüey district, Huber Matos, was in jail for having opposed the authoritarianism of Fidel Castro. But what revolution does not create similar situations? The Catholic Church had quickly made known its opposition to revolutionary measures, but what could you expect?

My friends were ready to support the revolutionary process in face of the enemy. Jean-Paul Sartre went so far as to say that the bourgeois press had to be eliminated, that the revolutionary press would monitor the political progress of the masses. That was the language of the times. The democratic aims of the revolution should not be corrupted. All the rest was only an anecdote.

But what of us Cubans who were the anecdote? The Europeans could give or refuse their support and their world would not change in any way; that was not so for me. My allegiance sanctioned each step of the process; rejection would mean turning my back on the most ambitious transformation ever undertaken in my country. Actual practice lay somewhere between these two poles. To accept everything was like swallowing live toads with full knowledge of what we were doing, to quote the Polish poet Czeslaw Milosz. It is a repugnant image, but a vivid one nonetheless. Those of us who had to swallow live toads will have with us for the rest of our lives an inescapable sensation of nausea and a loathing of our very act of hope. That is the worst of it all—the denaturing of hope itself.

Russia arose before my eyes as an imposing stage, a construction over a primitive set of plans which had spontaneously and of necessity taken a life of their own. Facing it, I felt irredeemably alone. Others might be alien to it, completely ignorant of its meaning. But for those of us who had embarked on the path of revolution, it was a threat.

As a visitor in Paris, I was greeted effusively. People couldn't stop asking questions. One afternoon Juan Goytisolo invited me to a party impossible to imagine in the new Cuba. It took place at the offices of Gallimard, where writers of the left and right shook hands with each other, people of every political bent side by side, for whom the intellectual life was not a bloody battlefield. In a corner of the garden at the back of the building, we greeted the merry guests as they moved about the immaculately trimmed lawn. I whispered to Juan: "They don't understand a thing." "What did you say?" he asked. "They haven't the slightest idea about anything."

* * *

At last Franqui arrived in Paris. During his absence from Cuba, Raúl Castro had finally been able to persuade Fidel to have Franqui replaced as editor of *Revolución*. What they insisted on calling the radicalization of the Cuban process turned out to be the liquidation of old militants from different revolutionary organizations. In the view of the extremists, who were becoming more powerful every day, Franqui was a "liberal." He had swallowed more live toads than any of us and he physically reflected to the worst degree his repugnance and rage. Franqui's health was permanently affected, in fact, and he survived only thanks to a rigorous diet which changed him into a gaunt and trembling man with a face whose large mustache and exhausted eyes mirrored a secret misfortune.

He was living in a small apartment outside central Paris when I went to visit him. It was a long ride, but I did not have to change trains, and for some reason there were almost no passengers. As the train plunged into the suburbs, one could see the beginnings of autumn, a surge of yellow and red which brushed the train windows. Here and there I could see neat white houses with stone chimneys spouting blue smoke; a country smell made its way through the chinks in the coach, or at least I imagined it did.

In the brisk air, what I was seeing made me very happy. This was the landscape of Europe, a landscape which could be closely observed as it stretched out before me, into the middle distance. Through the train window, I could see the varied assembly of tree trunks, branches, stone walls, and paths that lost themselves in the woods. It was a landscape which reflected the presence of men who had subdued nature with such care that even the most modest shrub seemed reduced to obedience.

I was on the train between Gare Montparnasse and Franqui's station for more than an hour. I do not remember the name of the place where I got off, but since it was late afternoon, the waiters in the cafés were already setting up folding screens by the round tables to protect the habitués against the chill autumn air. That afternoon marked a milestone in my life. When I was still a good ways from the house where Franqui lived, I spied him outlined against an ocher, reddish vine which covered one side of a building. He was waiting for me at the door, dressed as he usually was in those years—corduroy pants of a dark golden color, soiled leather jacket, Italian scarf and cap.

He invited me to one of those small cafés. All the tables were occupied by workers loudly discussing a soccer game then in progress on TV. We were like two smugglers trafficking in a substance that was draining our life. He was completely up to date on what was happening in Cuba. There was discouraging news everywhere. His removal as editor of *Revolución* was more an alarming symptom than a condemnation. Fidel had approved his removal, he said, and his duties had been temporarily taken over by Enrique de la Osa, who was also in charge of *Bohemia* now that his predecessor, Miguel Ángel Quevedo, had fled to Miami.

Franqui saw in Fidel's decision the outcome of a growing conflict in which, either way, Raúl Castro would be the beneficiary. Raúl had been fascinated with the Chinese Cultural Revolution. He wanted to place the ideological direction of the country in the hands of the armed forces, as had been the case in China, because he thought the best way to impede the unruly liberalism of certain militants was through the general militarization of culture.

The mandate of Fidel became ever more authoritarian. The possibility of a collective command in which each militant might express himself without fear appeared less and less attainable. But despite the clear evidence of the despotism which Fidel and his collaborators were imposing on the revolutionary process, almost all the international left continued to support the regime, justifying the necessity of continued allegiance by citing the hostility of the U.S. government. The negative attitude of the Americans was thought to require a disciplined militancy within Cuba which would never tolerate any kind of truce. Moreover, the enemy—trained and supported by the United States—had increased its sabotage against Cuba and could even count on armed groups in the Escambray Mountains. For us, they represented the most reactionary sector of pre-revolutionary Cuba, the class that had been eliminated from the nation by the people themselves. In such circumstances, it was not possible to oppose Fidel Castro.

Franqui advised me not to return to Cuba for the moment. His closest friends—Guillermo Cabrera Infante and Pablo Armando Fernández—had been appointed to European diplomatic posts. The most convenient solution for me would be to take refuge in a socialist country with a more democratic structure. He mentioned Algeria, since he was close to Ben Bella, and the idea began to appeal to me. I had constantly defended the Algerian cause in the pages of *Lunes de Revolución*, and had been designated by *Revolución* and Prensa Latina as a war correspondent. Carlos wrote out a letter of introduction to Ben Bella, and the next day I left for Algiers.

I was impressed by the city—its agreeable climate, tree-lined streets, and imposing buildings. Algiers had been built with dedication by colonialists who were incapable of imagining that the Arabs who had lost their homeland in a war with one of the most powerful European empires would ever be able to take it back.

In the Cuban embassy I was greeted by Ambassador "Papito" Serguera. He was alarmed when I informed him that I wanted an interview with Ben Bella. "Every Cuban who passes through here wants one," he said. But when I showed him Franqui's letter, his attitude changed. He thought I should bring it personally to the president, a simple and accessible man who carried out his functions almost without a staff, and was loved and respected by all. That same day, I went to the modest house where the Algerian leader lived with his mother.

"The president is not in, but please be assured that he will receive your letter today without fail," a smiling official told me as I wrote out my telephone number. Ben Bella never answered my letter. Already Boumedienne's plot was well advanced. A few days later he seized power, placing the deposed president under house arrest in a desert town in the south, where he remained until Boumedienne died. I left the city in a melancholy mood. The evening before my departure I was invited by the correspondent of Prensa Latina to a famous restaurant located at the top of the tallest hill in the city. We sat on the floor, in the Arab manner. Around midnight a group of artists and singers arrived with tambourines in hand. Their music could have been that of Andalusia, except that at the moment when I thought it was coming to a predictable climax it went off with more elaborate musical variants.

Life had given me the opportunity to witness another fissure in the anticolonial revolutionary movement. The first was in the Congo, where the short mandate of Patrice Lumumba was cut short by the military intervention of Joseph Mobutu. I had watched Lumumba one night in 1960 at a press conference which he gave in London while I was correspondent for Prensa Latina in Great Britain. A few months later, a photograph was published showing him standing on a rough two-wheeled cart with his hands bound, his eyes looking anxiously toward the camera. Mobutu had appeared on the scene as the realistic alternative to Lumumba's revolutionary romanticism.

In the Algeria of Houari Boumedienne, many arguments against Ben Bella were being put forth. It was said that during the war of liberation Ben Bella was only a symbol of the struggle, a young patriot arrested and jailed by the French, whereas Boumedienne had earned on the battlefield his military and political credentials as head of the army of liberation. Many people viewed Ben Bella as simply a victim of history. He was thought of as weak and excessively influenced by European values. It was galling to the orthodox Muslims that he would give his speeches both in Arabic and in French. Even the most novel aspect of his regime—the coexistence of theoretical options in economic and political governance (a mélange of Chinese agrarianism, Yugoslavian individual initiative, and state control on the Soviet model)—was deemed to create confusion in government. It was alleged that his knowledge of French and Spanish, along with his sometime marriage to a Parisian journalist, alienated him from the people.

Fidel Castro did defend Ben Bella publicly when he was toppled, calling the coup a "perfidious and ignominious act." He also attacked the man considered responsible for the insurgency, Chancellor Abdelaziz Bouteflika, whom Fidel mocked with the nickname "Butterfly." The new directorate responded with aplomb, however, saying that Castro was ignorant of the internal situation in Algeria because his Cuban diplomats were under Ben Bella's sway.

Algiers didn't react with enthusiasm or with alarm to the change of leaders. The main preoccupation was the flight of capital to metropolitan France and the closing of businesses, factories, and shops. The lack of technicians was causing serious problems. The hotel on the avenue Saint-Michelle where I was staying was run by former chambermaids and busboys who had assumed the functions of the owners after they had fled to France. As I took out my wallet to pay the bill, the clerk informed me that the total due was the equivalent of five dollars. After examining the bill and doing my own addition, I handed over $150. The clerk shook my hand fervently. Let it be said, however: in spite of all the naïveté, Algerians from the very first believed in the principle of a collective directorate, and they found solutions for problems which still elude the Cubans.

I recall an incident in the plane from Algiers to Nice, one of the stops on my return to Moscow. I was sitting next to a French Army officer, who in turn was seated next to an old Arab, who was unable to decide if he should eat the lunch served him by the stewardess. He looked at the meat closely, gave it a few turns with his fork, smelled it. Finally, he asked me in French if it was beef or pork. I couldn't tell the difference, and the Arab said, "It's very serious. It is a religious problem."

Seeing that I could not be of any help, he asked the French officer next to me, in a tone of anxious inquiry. "Don't worry," the officer assured him, "it's not pork. Eat it." The Arab, newly confident, devoured the meal without a pause.

I thought it incredible that after the bloody war between the French and the Algerians, an Arab would trust the judgment of a French officer. But the war was over and it would seem that the Algerians had never really identified France with its *pieds noirs*. The Arab and the officer also had a language in common, above and beyond that quarrel, though it had lasted for over a century. It was an understanding born of living together, the simple element which goes beyond the distance and hate that political language imposes upon most of us.

12

~~~~~~

BACK IN MOSCOW, I went over to Yevtushenko's apartment
after coming in from the airport. He and his wife invited me
out to the Aragvi Restaurant for supper; they insisted that we
all order a singular and, according to him, exquisite dish.
When they brought out the platter, I could see a solid white
mass covered with almond sauce. I tasted some of the meat
buried in the sauce, but no matter how hard I tried, I could
not identify what I was eating. I wish Gala hadn't told me.
"It's cock's combs in almond sauce," she said, just when I had
a half-chewed piece in my mouth. I swallowed it as if it were
a toad. The light flavor of almond could hardly conceal the

insipid, wrinkly texture of the chicken cartilage softened up by boiling water. The dish may well have had an exotic name on the menu, a dish harking back to an ancient culinary tradition; but for me it was a proof of misery—the dreadful stuff tossed out to beggars lurking at the doors of feudal Czarist mansions. All the almonds in the world could not transform my dish into anything but what it was.

On each trip back to Moscow from Europe, I would bring with me Western books and records which Yevgeny had asked me to get for him. The couple lived in a small apartment on the outskirts of Moscow, part of an enormous residential square with a lawn in the center. Most of the people there were artists, poets, and novelists. Of course, there were lodgings for the State Security man, a colonel who did not trouble to hide his identity and whose function was to watch over the good behavior of the confraternity. He was a tall, middle-aged man with a red face who was treated by everyone, including me, with a certain deference.

After leaving the restaurant, we drove back to Yevtushenko's place and got out of the car. The colonel approached us and inquired about my trip, since I had told him that I would be away. Yevgeny showed him the records I had brought, some disks by the Beatles and other English and French pop-music groups. I had also brought a radio-cassette player for Yevtushenko's car. He pointed to the slot on the dashboard where it would be put in.

"See, Genya, now you'll be able to hear all the music you want. It's great!" Winking at us, the colonel added, "You cannot deny the truth; there are good things in the West, too." Later that night, we drank champagne as we listened to the Beatles. Gala hardly took a sip. As the evening wore on, she listened more and more intently and eventually fell asleep on the sofa. Yevgeny brought me home to my apartment by the frozen Moscow River.

I could not stay in the Soviet Union. My family had already returned to Cuba; and as Yevgeny and I made our way through the snowy streets, a bit tipsy, I recalled another turning point in my life. It was in 1961, on my way back to Havana from London. I stopped off for two days in New York.

My stay in Europe, brief as it had been, revealed another world to me. It was there, not in the Americas, that you could hear the noise of the world. The tensions of the Cold War and the collapse of the colonial regimes in Africa were analyzed in Europe from the most divergent outlooks. There was no country in Western Europe which did not have a newspaper representing each political party, and this diversity was enriching. In England, France, Italy, and Germany, in Scandinavia, all ideological options were permitted. Liberals, conservatives, Social Democrats, Christian Democrats, and Communists vied without restriction. In contrast, the United States at the beginning of the sixties was still under the residues of McCarthyism, and the press reflected a naïve and dangerous homogeneity.

I arrived in New York late in the afternoon, and I took a taxi to the Empire Hotel in Manhattan, where I would be staying. I asked the driver to pass by the Berlitz School in Rockefeller Center. When we were a short distance away, I asked him to slow down so I could take a look through the windows of the school, which were at sidewalk level. There stood my colleagues of two years before, holding the blue course book and the yellow cards on which each professor noted how far he had gotten in each lesson. "I have leapt into another dimension" was the first thought that came to me as I observed my former colleagues. I remembered the two exhausted, dull-witted students sent over to the school by Anaconda Copper, who were to be assigned to Chile as soon as possible—two engineers who patiently repeated over and over the imperfect subjunctive (which, in any case, no Anglo-Saxon can ever completely master).

From my hotel room I could see Lincoln Center and the portion of Broadway leading up the West Side to Florence's apartment. I felt so estranged and distanced from everything that had been my former reality in this city that I was afraid

Florence wouldn't recognize my voice when I called. She was out, but in her mother's voice I sensed rejection, or, at least, a veiled reproach. Florence was working in the Bronx and would be home late; she would tell her that I had called.

It was snowing; the wind whipped the flakes into swirls. Broadway was without a soul, lifeless; the lights from cafeterias and corner pharmacies gave a livid tinge of unreality to everything I looked on. I did and did not want to speak to Florence. In the two years since I had last seen her, the most radical and drastic changes in Cuban history had taken place. These events placed me on the other side of order; I was a partisan of brutal assaults, an outlaw. At two in the morning the telephone rang. Time had not changed Florence's unmistakable French accent, but her words were edgy and severe. "See *me*? That meeting should have happened two years ago," she said. "Now I have another life, and if you want to know why I'm calling you it's only because I wanted to find out if my mother had gotten the message wrong." She hung up, and though I kept calling, the phone was busy. She must have taken the receiver off the hook.

When I was leaving New York for Havana, the important newspapers carried big headlines about the recent revolutionary nationalizations in Cuba, along with the implication that the United States government had taken the first step to break off with the bothersome dictatorship of Fidel Castro. At the check-in desk of the Cuban airline at what was still Idlewild Airport, there was visible unease. For a few minutes before boarding, I looked out onto the parking lot covered by snow. There was a weak winter sun, but it was lovely. I had walked up and down in front of the ticket counter and then sat down by the enormous windows of the waiting area. I would not see them again for almost twenty years. "Nostalgia for the other side of the river," as Hegel put it. Florence felt no need to change; the alienation of the salaried work week did not disturb her. Her daily routine, the same as in the world of

Sisyphus, compensated her with simple joys. Just as Camus had done, she must have imagined Sisyphus to be happy.

I could not. I saw the world around me as a battlefield full of mines that might blow me up. I preferred *that* to the unyielding disease of routine. Between Florence and me a divide had opened up, the same that was about to split Cubans apart as no one could then have imagined. She looked forward to struggle and victory in the United States. One day, much later, I got an urgent call from the Havana morgue; they wanted me to come down and identify a drowned woman, a foreigner, who was carrying my address in the pocket of her dress. Not even then was I capable of envisioning that in the schizophrenia that was gradually dominating all our anguish, she would have found her portion and her end.

In Moscow, Yevtushenko asked me: "When we met in Cuba, did you ever imagine what Moscow would be like?"

"I had read many descriptions, I had seen hundreds of photographs and films, but I could never have imagined it as it is."

"I think the Soviet Union has disappointed you."

I denied it, but he kept probing. He said he could list for me down to the last detail the things that had disappointed me—the lack of freedom, the power of the Secret Police, the untouchable bureaucracies known as the Nomenklatura, the hegemony of the party, the stagnation of literature, the constant presence of the censor, the cynicism of most of the writers. "Is what I say true or not?" Yevgeny always expressed himself vehemently, but I had never heard him speak with quite that degree of enraged indignation.

"Besides," he continued, "that scene with Shostakovich at the canceled performance of his Thirteenth Symphony must have seemed monstrous to you. I could see the way you were looking at him when he burst into tears. I was about to cry, too, but tears don't solve anything. Khrushchev isn't Stalin, even though the nation is full of his defenders who would do anything to prevent his crimes from being exposed. The 20th Party Congress did take place, and no one can ignore that. I have to tell you that your Cuban leaders aren't interested in knowing the historical truth about Stalinism. Any time I mentioned it in Havana or in any other Cuban city or town, they listened with only half an ear. Why do you think that was?"

"Because everything Khrushchev has revealed about Stalin is what the counterrevolutionaries say, what *Reader's Digest* says."

"But the important thing is for Cuba not to repeat those errors!" he exclaimed.

"Many people think that Communism is the error."

"Communism?"

"The system itself. More people than you can imagine."

"But I saw enthusiasm in Cuba."

"Of course it exists. For example, I am an enthusiast."

He laughed. "I thought you were a chronic pessimist, but it is possible that you are an enthusiast."

"*The Highway of the Enthusiast* is the title of one of your first books," I said.

"I didn't invent a thing; there is a road with that name. But what do you think of the system here?"

"I am only aware of its deformities. Khrushchev's speech is a catalogue of horrors."

"But he was witness to the horror, and it is admirable that he found the opportune moment to denounce Stalin."

"But meanwhile, all the intellectuals who considered themselves organic to the system, to use Gramsci's term, shot themselves or took a razor to their wrists when they stood accused as victims or when they confronted their own moral tragedy. Fadeyev committed suicide two months before the 20th Congress, leaving behind three letters—one to his wife, one to the Writers' Union, and one to the Central Committee of the party."

"You might have added that the content of those letters has never been revealed. Certainly, that is part of the history of my country, my history," he said, almost shouting.

"It's the history of the entire socialist world," I interjected. "The history of the Soviet Union is its principal export."

"I think that you have been gradually acquiring an illness, and it worries me," he confided in a low tone.

"Why didn't the 20th Party Congress continue on to its logical conclusion?"

"One day it will," said Yevgeny. "I know that one day it will do it. We must not be pessimists."

"And the Pasternak affair, reviling the man as a pig all over the Soviet press—how do you explain that?"

"Justice will be done; *Doctor Zhivago* will be read throughout the country just as we now read Pasternak's poetry."

"But when?"

"For many years, official Soviet literature has been empty bombast, but there is another literature coming out of the bottom drawer. *One Day in the Life of Ivan Denisovich* is part of it. Remember what I am telling you."

He stood up, wrapped his scarf around his neck, put on his cap, and tightened the belt on his coat. "Dawn's coming," he said, looking out the window.

"I hope so."

He clapped a hand on my shoulder. "Yes, in general, dawn is coming. We have spent our lives talking about changes and openings, and now that we are living them, we refuse to believe."

As he headed toward the door, he rummaged in his pockets. "Here is my latest poem. I put it into Spanish myself. It is called 'The Deaf.' It's yours, tonight you'll tell me if you like it. Get some sleep, see if you can feed the enthusiast in you a bit."

After he left, I read the poem, written in that special calligraphy of his, the words printed out individually as separate letters. I liked the poem. Later I would read it again in English translation.

It was a long time before I could get to sleep. The champagne had excited me and I decided I needed something stronger. I grabbed a bottle of Armenian cognac and drank deeply. I went back to bed, throwing a blanket over myself—a draft of cold air was coming through the half-open kitchen window.

I thought of Cuba. In the offices of Prensa Latina back in Algiers, I had read some issues of *Bohemia* and *Revolución*. More sabotage, more arbitrary sentences, more executions. I used to look for the list of people who had been shot. I will never forget running across the name of Comandante Plinio Prieto, a young professor of English who had joined the rebel army and whom I had last seen working as a trainee in the Film Institute. He was shot for being an agent of the CIA. In every accusation that resulted in a death sentence, the CIA was said to be involved. Doubtless, the Agency was behind the open insurgency against the regime, but there existed another kind of opposition to Fidel's authoritarianism that had nothing to do with the CIA. Illegality and the cult of personality had begun to have an influence on the tactics and methods of the Cuban Revolution. Stalin, always in his marshal's uniform, continued to exercise a hypnotic fascination over the island. The 20th Party Congress had opened up a phase of rectification in the history of the Soviet Union which everyone applauded, but the applause given to Fidel legitimized the Stalinist authoritarian style under the pretext that "the enemy is ninety miles away" and it was intent on taking advantage of any crack in the unity of the Revolution. In this atmosphere, the element which flourished was the sloganeering spirit of the omnipotent political police. Decisions handed down by that body were decisive and subject to no appeal.

Whoever dared to think about the institutional structure that should characterize the new system was considered an "objective counterrevolutionary." Even the simple reading of materials from the 20th Party Congress was enough to raise suspicions. "The anti-Stalinists of today are the anti-Communists of yesterday," stated Carlos Rafael Rodríguez, and this turned out to be the official line.

I awoke at noon. Only my baggage remained in the apartment. Looking out the window, I could see a dense fog which tinged the morning an aluminum color. I brewed a strong cup of coffee and added the remaining cognac, then went back to bed to enjoy a drowsy half-sleep. The manuscript of my poems for the book *Fuera del juego* (*Out of the Game*) lay on the floor. The mixture of coffee and cognac brought a wave of warmth to my body as I let myself sink into a delicious lassitude.

Years later, when the poems in that book (written in Moscow, Budapest, and Prague) were termed, by the bureaucrats of the Cuban Writers' and Artists' Union, a "detailed assault" on the Revolution, I was finally able to understand how destructive were the opening phases of all twentieth-century tyrannies. My friend Julio Cortázar, discerning before anyone else that a symbolic guillotine was beginning to make itself felt in the Cuban Revolution, lost no time in taking up my defense in *Le Nouvel Observateur* in 1969, with an article entitled "Neither Traitor nor Martyr." Much later, in an article written in 1984 about Orwell's *1984,* he posited that "no ideological argument justifies putting the community over the individual . . . but this statement is valid only insofar as the notion of the individual does not damage the interests of the community, as is certainly the case with an egocentric kind of criticism—the kind which extrapolates the Sakharovs and the Padillas from the community of their respective compatriots and makes them into at least potential victims."

"The Sakharovs, the Padillas"—a clear judgment with a scientific appearance which would have fascinated the later Saint-Just. The plural, applied to both of us, transforms into an anonymous species all those who are "extrapolated from the community . . ." Julio Cortázar must also have felt a morbid pleasure in denying the accusation of the Chilean painter

Roberto Matta when he said, "You understand nothing of what is going on." The essay on Orwell bore the revealing subtitle "Discourse of the Idiot." But what idiots prefer are not discourses but rather a collage of aphorisms concerning matters they are ignorant of, party lines good for a sermon maybe, but parodies of common sense. At the very least, I can say that Sakharov has been more useful to the "community of his compatriots" than the mindless revolutionary slogans pronounced by those who understand nothing of what is going on, just as Matta said. No, for me, Communism, or whatever one wants to call it, can no longer be the challenge of our time. Communism remains a prisoner forever of those astonishing revelations of Nikita Khrushchev at the Party Congress. The reality I came in contact with had been subverted, poisoned; this was a nation given over to the rites of burying and exhuming bodies in an atmosphere of anguish, rage, and exorbitant hopes for the future. These were reckless times, but caution and fear prevailed in the end. Who could be sure that the public denouncement of Stalin and his methods was supported completely by those who had been his accomplices up to the day of his death? The fearless artists I felt closest to were all full of enthusiasm—Yevgeny and Gala Yevtushenko, Andrei Voznesensky, Yuri Yasakov, Vassily Aksyonov, Bella Akhmadulina, Yuri Vasiliev, Ernst Neizvestny.

I was the one who feared. I would often go to the Cuban embassy in Moscow, where the commercial attaché, Armando Morales, would pass on clippings from the Cuban press. Eddy Suñol would invite me into his office for a cup of Cuban coffee and a discussion of the latest developments. He was worried about the fate of his former comrades-in-arms—the soldiers from the original group who had been thrown out and replaced by people he never heard of. He made no complaint about his own situation, and continued to have full confidence in Fidel and Raúl, or at least that is what he said to me. But the shadow of Huber Matos's fate haunted him. After lacing his coffee with two or three shots of cognac, he would blurt out, "What they did to Huber was shit." Raúl Castro said officially that Eddy had taken ill because of his war wounds; what is for sure is that this revolutionary from Holguín, posted to Moscow in the sixties and surrounded on all sides by snow and nightmare, embodied to the nth degree the grand disorder and confusion amid which we were living. Eddy Suñol killed himself the day after I acted out my "self-criticism" at the Writers' Union. It was evident that on that "island of liberty" where Russians were saying that they had found again "the youth of the October Revolution," the same struggle of old for power was under way, the same authoritarianism had taken hold.

A few days before I was to leave Moscow, Yevgeny had told me that he wanted to throw a farewell party. "Gala has invited some friends, and we will have it at Pavel Antokolsky's dacha." As we were driving out to Peredelkino, Moscow seemed ever more somber to me. At every stoplight along the way, I peered out of Yevgeny's car and saw people rushing into the subway, anxiety on their faces.

Antokolsky's house was roomy and attractive, full of furniture and objets d'art *d'avant la révolution*. He had been a young writer under the last czar, joining the Revolution after the triumph of the Bolsheviks. Well over seventy in 1964, strong and lively, he was a respected figure not so much for the quality of his writing as for having lived in pre-revolutionary times and for having accepted with nihilistic resignation the terrible years that Khrushchev was later to denounce.

He was a short, bony man with darting eyes set in an affable and smiling face, and he went out of his way to make us feel at home. His sleeves were rolled up, and he had put on a pair of blue jeans, which he obviously wore with pride. During the entire evening, he never put down a tiny camera, and kept organizing groups for snapshots, which he took from the main staircase. In addition to two or three Georgian poets whose names I do not recall, he had invited Yuri Naguibin and Bella Akhmadulina, recently married, along with Yuri Kazakov, whose stories set in the Russian countryside were highly praised at that time.

As always happens when friends meet in such circumstances, people soon began to recite their poems. In Russian poetry, alliteration is a fundamental aspect of expression; any vocal recitation of a Russian poem is perforce full of syllabic sounds. For instance, Voznesensky's fine poem "Goya," so much admired in its many translations, is composed of innumerable guttural alliterations based on Goya's name. In any case, we ate and we drank, and one after another we declaimed our poems in what I now recognize as the emphatic Mayakovskian manner. I had written "The Firebird," a poem in rhymed tercets; composed as a rhetorical exercise, it seemed very Russian to me. But Yevtushenko preferred another poem of mine, entitled "The Street Cleaner." He knew it by heart and recited it very theatrically. I have mislaid this melodramatic poem, but I recall that it made a strong impression on everyone that night. The street cleaner was named Masha; she was one of the many old women who sweep away the snow from Moscow streets for almost no pay at all. She does her work because it gives her the authorization to reside legally in Moscow; without the job, she would have no residence permit. In general, the state prohibits ordinary citizens from moving from their place of birth, but exceptions are always made for those who want to sweep the streets. In winter, it is moving to see those old women, draped in rough clothes from head to foot, brushing away the snow with their primitive brooms.

Antokolsky stopped smiling when he heard the poem. Everyone seemed surprised that I had chosen that "tragedy," as Antokolsky called it, as a theme for a poem. The old poet put down his camera and said to me: "Young man, it will be a long time before such women are freed from that duty, but someone must sweep the streets. Meanwhile, we are the beneficiaries of what they give us. What else can we do? Consider the year 1917. The first thing any revolution creates is misery. Now I ask you. Are the Cuban people richer now?

Are they poorer? Do you know what will happen soon in your country, if it hasn't happened already? Your society will divide into fractions, and the poorest will always be the poorest. You, and all of us here, will have no difficulties. You belong to the intelligentsia, as we Russians call it. You will have your privileges, even though you do not seek them out, even if such things repel you. The only thing that will save you from desperation or cynicism is this: you must learn to suffer in resignation. If you do not, young man, you will succumb. I warn you right now. That street cleaner is a tragedy which we all see and which we all suffer, but we cannot give any space to her in our poetry. And let me tell you something else. Ours is the worst fate of all, because we are condemned to hope. Tonight, when you return to the city, you will see the sunrise and there will be men and women walking along the roads with baskets on their heads. But *I* am not able to carry those baskets and I *have* to hope for a day when our fields will be mechanized and happy citizens will live on them."

We listened to the old man in silence. He spoke with the characteristic energy of the Russian temperament, looking intently at each of us, nailing us with his blue eyes. After a pause he grabbed a glass of wine and raised it. He said he wanted to make a toast to the island of liberty, Cuba, and to its brilliant future, but his earlier fervor was no longer there. The toast did not have its expected effect. What weighed on all of us were the words uttered before the toast, the confession of a very old man who continued to be condemned to hope. As we left his dacha, he hugged and kissed me, and said that he would send the best photos of the evening to me in Cuba, but I never received them.

13

~~~~~~

WHEN I RETURNED to Havana, my friend Alberto Mora, who was still Minister of Foreign Commerce, gently reproached me for the excessively severe opinions about the nature of the Soviet Union that I had developed in Moscow. It was, he said, the result of the revisionism of the 20th Party Congress. Obviously, I could not have stayed out of the controversy when all of Europe was agonizing over Khrushchev's denunciations of Stalin. The radical left, Mora said, had contributed to the collapse of everything it had supported earlier, "but we Cubans are not part of that history," he concluded. "There are serious problems here and our struggle will continue."

He came to my house for dinner that evening. Over coffee, he began to ask me in great detail about life in the Soviet bloc. The conversation ranged over all the countries I had visited. Mora was worried about the complete centralization of economic activity and the perils of an inefficient bureaucracy. Bureaucracy in and of itself was not a problem for him—he thought that all societies were organized bureaucratically and that only the level of efficiency distinguished one system from the other. Alberto favored a market economy along the lines proposed by the French economist Charles Bettelheim. This was a pressing matter at that time, since Mora was engaged in a polemic with Ché Guevara concerning Ché's thesis that a socialist country should establish the centralized economy outlined in the work of the Belgian economist Ernst Mandel. Their polemic was couched in cordial terms, but functionaries on both sides defended their causes aggressively. As he left my house, Mora invited me to the meetings held every Thursday night in the Ministry of Foreign Commerce. Ché Guevara attended without fail. These meetings were also "study circles," and the past few months had been devoted to a reading and discussion of Marx's *Das Kapital*. Alberto was anxious for me to give Guevara my impressions of the Soviet Union and the other socialist countries of Eastern Europe.

The scheduled meeting did not take place the following Thursday, because Ché had had an attack of asthma. He asked us to stop by the following evening. When his administrative assistant ushered us into his office, we were presented with the image of a wasted and bony Ché, shirtless, stretched out on the rug next to his desk, working at bringing back the natural rhythm of his breathing.

"Alberto has already told me that you've come back pretty depressed from the world of our brothers," he said, staring at the ceiling. "I must tell you that I don't need to listen to what you have to say, because I already know that all of it is a pigsty, I saw it myself. Stalin went too far, but these guys now in power are not far behind. It's two ways of overdoing it. They've been sloppy with the whole system of education. What do you think?"

He got up and put on his undershirt. Before I could reply, he asked me if it was true that all of Mayakovsky's poems were rhymed. I replied that the entire Soviet Union was obsessed with Khrushchev's speech and that not an hour passed in which new rumors did not circulate concerning the ultimate responsibility in the party for Stalin's repression. All the supposed probity of his years in power was being undermined by new revelations of his ruthlessness. "And yes," I added, "all the poetry of Mayakovsky is rhymed, in its way."

"And your own poetry, were you writing?"

"Yes."

"Do you have enough for a book?"

"The book's all finished."

"What's the title?"

"Fuera del juego"—Out of the Game.

"Why that title?"

"Because its basic theme is history."

"For or against?" he asked me jokingly. And then suddenly: "Do you know any of the poems by heart? Let me hear one."

I recited the first poem of *Fuera del juego*, the one called "In Trying Times." He listened closely, staring at the ceiling.

"Exactly the same idea that I have about history," he said. "Many people criticize me because they say I put too much emphasis on sacrifice; but sacrifice is fundamental to a Communist education. The Chinese understand that very well, much better than the Russians do. And there is an explanation—they are two distinct traditions. Russians will never be able to understand Asiatic asceticism. The Soviet Union could only have disenchanted you. But when you go to China you will discover a genuine effort toward the realization of Communism. Theirs is the model to be studied."

Alberto and I listened in silence.

Ché motioned to Alberto. "These are not good times for

journalism. Why don't you bring him over to the Ministry of Foreign Commerce?"

I was taken aback, but Alberto said he thought it a fine idea.

"What do I know about foreign commerce?" I objected.

"The same as I do about the industrial world, and here I am, Minister of Heavy Industry."

"But I don't know anything about protocol or international commercial trade," I insisted.

"You'll learn it all in three weeks," said Alberto. Just then an aide entered and placed a lunchbox on Ché's desk.

"It's my supper. No one can persuade my wife not to send it over to the ministry; that's the way it is."

Alberto rose from his chair, but Ché motioned him to sit back down. He said it would be better for me to leave journalism behind for the moment and Foreign Commerce would be an excellent apprenticeship. "Don't worry about a thing. What is needed in these situations is a satisfactory level of communication skill, and that you have. The rest will be done by a bunch of able nobodies; they will tell you what to do, just as a theater director does with his actors."

And that is how I became director general of CUBARTIM-PEX, a subdivision of the Ministry of Foreign Commerce concerned with the exporting and importing of all items related to art and culture. In my new position, I also became a member of the advisory committee of the ministry. I should say at the outset that my work brought me face-to-face with the basic economic problems of Cuba at that time. Every meeting at the ministry demonstrated the lack of control and the contradictions within the three elements of this branch of government: (a) The Central Planning Group (JUCEPLAN), responsible for the establishment of budgetary priorities for the internal economy. (b) Foreign Commerce, which analyzed the industrial requirements within the nation. These would then be converted into orders for machinery and equipment to be acquired abroad in accordance with the analysis established by JUCE-

PLAN. (c) The National Bank, which effected payment to the vendors abroad.

In practice, there was no coordination among the three economic directorates. Fidel Castro subverted their functioning by sending abroad his infamous "special missions" with orders to purchase anything that the dictator felt was urgently needed. These purchases were paid for in cash, and this in turn affected the grand designs established by JUCEPLAN. In reality, there were two Ministries of Foreign Commerce, the most powerful and arbitrary being that personally directed by Fidel. Finally the moment came when the National Bank no longer had any cash reserves left to cover the expenses incurred by the "special missions."

When the crisis erupted, Fidel found a quick solution. Alberto Mora was replaced by Marcelo Fernández, president of the National Bank; Regino Boti, formerly head of the Central Planning Committee, was replaced by the country's president, Osvaldo Dorticós. Once again, blame for the supreme leader's actions was foisted on others.

Alberto Mora was never to occupy another important post in the Cuban government. For a time, Ché took him on as an advisor in the Ministry of Heavy Industry, and later he worked in the Sugar Ministry. Feeling himself relegated to the sidelines, he requested a stipend to study political economy with Charles Bettelheim in Paris, and it was granted.

For my part, I requested permission to travel as a roving representative of the Ministry of Foreign Commerce, with the pompous title of Director of Overseas Activities. The title was an ad hoc creation within the bureaucracy so that I would be the equal of any minister of the same rank in whatever foreign country I was in. My areas of concern were the Eastern bloc and Scandinavia. The main office was in Prague.

A few days before Alberto and I were to leave Cuba, we went over to Ché's offices to say goodbye.

"We're turning into characters in a revolving door," he said. "But you people do want to see the world, don't you?"

Alberto was unable to hide his depression, and Ché noticed that something was wrong. "And what's the matter with you? Don't forget, I've still got something of the doctor left in me."

Alberto described his emotional difficulties, though as neutrally as possible.

Ché listened without interrupting, then asked, "When do you feel depressed?"

"In the morning, when I wake up."

"When you wake up, you feel depressed," Ché repeated.

"Yes, when I wake up."

Ché walked up to Alberto slowly, put his hands on his shoulders, and shook him, looking straight into his eyes. "I live like someone torn in two, twenty-four hours a day, completely torn in two, and I haven't got anybody to tell it to. Even if I did, they would never believe me."

That was the last time I saw Ché, but the scene is still vivid in my memory.

A few hours later I received a call from the Writers' Union with the message that someone was looking for me. That person, a woman, had left her name, but the switchboard operator had written it down illegibly, and the person calling me could not make it out. It was something like "Francis," or "Florth," or "Florence." "Florence," I said. "That must be it." "Yes, it's Florence." She had been looking for me for six months; every time she called, she was informed that I was abroad. She said she would call back, but did not leave an address.

I told the operator to give her my telephone number in Havana and my address in Prague if she called again, but I never had news of Florence at either of those places. I persuaded myself that I had forced the operator to read "Florence" on the piece of paper when in fact some other name had been written there. Besides, it made no sense for her to make a trip to such an alien country as Cuba. I was her only link to the place, and that link had been curtly broken when I was last in New York.

My stay in Prague turned out to be brief, the point of departure for visits to other nations, all on instructions from the ministry in Havana: Hungary, Yugoslavia, Bulgaria, Rumania, East Germany, Sweden, Norway, Finland, and Denmark. Insofar as the socialist countries were concerned, Cuba wanted to bring its commercial trade into better balance. Up to that time, trade had been systematically in their favor. The newly appointed vice minister in charge of these negotiations was a man who thought he had practical solutions for everything. He handed me a breakdown for each country, in three columns: "present trade," "desired trade," and "possible trade." If I could achieve at least a 30 percent increase over the present level, and in our favor, the negotiations would be deemed successful.

I returned to Europe believing that I could succeed in my new assignment, but in Prague I found the same bureaucratic authoritarianism, the same political espionage, the same censorship, the same fear, the same nihilistic resignation. Antonin Novotny continued in his presidency-for-life, domineering a country which was still living under the shadow of Stalin's purges of the Czech CP. The execution of the former party secretary, Rudolf Slansky, and the punishments meted out to those accused of being his collaborators continued to weigh on the country. Sex and alcohol were the only achievable paradises, bought with the special money called *tusex*, a scrip which circulated among high-level bureaucrats and foreigners; its convertibility to any world currency was guaranteed. With *tusex* you could purchase anything, from food to appliances and automobiles. All Prague revolved around *tusex*. It was even a determining factor in juvenile prostitution in Czechoslovakia. For the youth of that time, it was the key to a world of competitive options, a dazzling opening to things of the West. I thought they had false notions of a reality which I knew at first hand. The young people of Czechoslovakia couldn't wait to get rid of those badly dyed, ill-cut clothes produced by

Czech garment makers. They admired the elegant stylings in *Vogue* and other Western magazines.

I did have the opportunity to meet with writers, painters, and musicians. The composers were the ones who moved about with the greatest freedom, and their works seemed attractive and innovative to me. But the greatest poet of the country, Vladimir Holan, lived in voluntary confinement in his apartment, inaccessible to anyone who did not belong to the select group of his closest friends. Nonetheless, he was widely read and admired. His long poem "A Night with Hamlet" is considered a masterpiece of twentieth-century Czech poetry. And, too, Milan Kundera had just published *The Joke*, the novel which brought him to the attention of an international audience. The French Communist Party had endorsed the book through the intervention of Aragon, but the hierarchy of the Czech CP was already plotting to suppress it.

I kept myself informed of cultural developments in Czechoslovakia, read poems, short stories, and portions of novels in translation, thanks to the generosity of my friend Mariella Kutzerova, who spoke Spanish well. She was the wife of the Cuban painter Tony Evora and she guided us through the labyrinths of Prague, showed us the hidden city, and did so without bitterness. She wanted us to miss nothing of the country she loved, but what resulted from that contact with "reality" was collective frustration and anguish. It seemed as if Prague were still an occupied city. I returned to Cuba after a year, convinced that if the Soviet Union was emerging from the monstrous deformations of Stalinism, Czechoslovakia remained its hair-raising parody.

14

THE HAVANA I RETURNED TO was also oppressed by caution and fear. The government had canceled all scholarships (including that of my friend Alberto Mora) for study in capitalist countries. The official line was that Europe seduced Cubans into a *dolce vita* and made them susceptible to corruption. They cited the case of Rolando Cubela, who had been sent to Spain by the revolutionary government and, it was said, had been recruited by the CIA and had plotted to kill Fidel.

Cubela had been condemned to death by a revolutionary tribunal, but his sentence was commuted by Castro to twenty years. Since then, there had been heightened vigilance in all revolutionary organizations. An aura of suspicion was prevalent in the country.

In the Writers' Union, the presence of State Security seemed much more evident. In order to assure that its *dolce vita* was entirely eradicated, the government had come to the conclusion that it was necessary to cleanse the institution of homosexuals, who would be sent off to concentration camps in Camagüey. Under the rubric of Obligatory Military Service, these camps also became places of incarceration for people disaffected with the system because of their religious beliefs, such as Jehovah's Witnesses. The camps were the creation of Raúl Castro, who thought he had discovered in Bulgaria new and efficacious methods for "curing" homosexuals. In fact, the procedure was quite rudimentary. It was purest Pavlov—pleasure and revulsion being produced by particular erotic stimuli. For instance, they would show a film of two men having sex; when the patient's pulse was at its height and he was at the point of orgasm, an electric shock would be applied. The procedure would be repeated frequently, until a conditioned reflex of repellence had been achieved.

This treatment drove many people mad. Unquestionably, the system, called UMAP, was among the cruelest ever invented by the regime. But in spite of adverse criticism voiced by a few sensible people in power, State Security went on sending young people to the UMAP camps through 1967; often, they were students and artists who had done nothing wrong.

I remember encountering Juan Marinello as he was leaving the National Hospital. He greeted me effusively, but seemed very nervous. He asked me about my last trip abroad and praised Prague, "the lovely city of the poet Nezval." Marinello seemed old and decrepit. His comrades from the pre-revolutionary CP were under close surveillance, he told me. It was no secret that many of the old-time militants had criticized the political and economic leadership of Castro, and everyone knew that Fidel was fully cognizant of everything that was going on in the remnants of the old party.

In matters of culture, things were no less tense. Castro, as always unwilling to create a Ministry of Culture, used every imaginable pretext to keep culture on a short leash, maintaining a modest National Council of Culture, which he finally handed over to José Llanusa. Yet Castro did accept Carlos Franqui's proposal to bring to Havana from Paris the prestigious exhibition Salon de Mai. Franqui himself supervised the installation. These were crucial years—the Salón de Mayo exhibition, the Havana Cultural Congress, the scandal caused by the so-called microfraction of Aníbal Escalante and the old-line CP, whose repression by Castro eliminated the last shadow of dissent. A new era was inaugurated whose motto was: "Wherever you want us, whatever it might be, and for whatever purpose you desire, Commander in Chief, just give us the order!" If there was a difference between Cuban society and its "fraternal equivalents" in the Soviet Union or in Czechoslovakia, it was the cheap, crude tone which in Cuba dominated everything.

One evening, I received a phone call from the weekly review *El caimán barbudo* (*The Bearded Alligator*); they were putting together an issue dedicated to an insignificant novel written by Lisandro Otero, whom Llanusa had made an advisor at the National Council of Culture. They wanted to print my assessment of the book along with that of two other critics, all under the caption "Three Generations Give Their Opinion." And I did give my frank opinion of the book, in an article hardly worth reprinting now. I will only say that I criticized Otero's novel and defended *Tres triste tigres* (*Three Trapped Tigers*) by Guillermo Cabrera Infante, a novel which was being clandestinely read in Cuba at the time. Guillermo had already been removed from his post as cultural attaché in Brussels because of intrigues fostered by the political police. His independent opinion and his outgoing and acerbic character could no longer be tolerated.

After the article was published, Alberto Mora appeared at my house in a panic. It turned out that my article was just what State Security had been waiting for to finish me off. From that moment, I became a marginal person. I was thrown out of work. Llanusa had proposed me as international director of the Cultural Council, and Haydée Santamaría had offered me a post in the Literary Institute of her Casa de las Américas, but they both received a direct order from Raúl Castro to withdraw their offers.

But my ostracism needed a stronger raison d'être. At the time, I was putting the finishing touches on my book of poems *Fuera del juego*; a few had already been published in the literary magazine put out by Casa de las Américas. At twelve midnight, seconds before the deadline for submission for the National Literature Competition (sponsored by the Writers' Union) and just when State Security was sure it had vetted all the texts submitted for the competition, my wife, Belkis, handed over the manuscript personally to a friend of ours at the Writers' Union. He, in turn, slipped the entry into the pile of submissions. By the time they found out that I had gotten my text into the competition, it had already been sent out to the members of the jury, along with all the others.

The jury was heavily pressured by the Writers' Union and the police, but to no avail. Neither Lezama Lima nor J. M. Cohen nor José Z. Tallet nor Manuel Díaz Martínez gave in to the strenuous suggestions that my book be disqualified. It won the prize unanimously, but the award—consisting of a trip to the Soviet Union and one thousand pesos in cash—was never given to me.

Between my being "awarded" the prize and my incarceration for activities against State Security, three years of isolation intervened—their "sending me to Coventry." The presence in Cuba of the first Chilean diplomat accredited after the triumph of Salvador Allende made my situation even more precarious, because that diplomat was Jorge Edwards, a novelist whom I had known for years. A leftist from his youth, Edwards had supported the Cuban Revolution during its most critical moments. As a career diplomat in the Chilean corps, he had never wavered in his public support of and his expression of solidarity with the Cuban government, even when many Spanish American countries had broken diplomatic relations with Cuba. It was only logical that a man with such a background be chosen as the first Chilean representative to revolutionary Cuba. Everyone felt that Allende had done the correct thing—everyone, that is, but Fidel Castro. The story of his short-lived service in the Chilean mission, no more than three months, has been told by Edwards in his book *Persona non grata*. Whenever we see each other these days, whether in New York, Barcelona, or Madrid, we entertain ourselves recalling scenes from that time. When I want to learn something of the desperate and self-destructive being that I was then, I read a few chapters from *Persona non grata*, where I emerge as a stubborn Pulcinella from whom Edwards cannot separate himself.

In his own way, Jorge Edwards suffered my fate, as did my closest friends, also condemned to ostracism. They and others ended by benefiting from the incident. From 1969 to 1971, many politicians, professors, publishers, novelists, and poets passed through Havana. That is to say, they barely touched on our reality, and with only a few, like Mauricio Wácquez, Enrique Lihn, Mario Vargas Llosa, and Ángel Rama, was I able to speak about our problems in depth. The rest were too taken with the delirium of a revolution which had "blown the whistle" on American imperialism. For them, a Cuban like me was only an anecdote; besides, all Cubans were inferior to Comandante Castro, the only man able to converse face-to-face with history.

During this period I wanted to express in some way the context over which Cuban reality was being projected, and so I wrote my novel *Heroes Are Grazing in My Garden*. The book is not a denunciation or an allegation, not even testimony which might aspire to verisimilitude. Rather, it is a text through which certain conflicts and certain beings pass like shadows. Since I had no need to hide what I was writing, I placed my novel at the disposition of the rector of the University of

Havana, where I had been ordered to work. The rector refused to read it. He said to me that he would not exercise the functions of a censor. However, State Security convinced Fidel Castro that Jorge Edwards, who had not read one line of the novel, was the intermediary through whom I was going to get the book to the Spanish publishing house Seix Barral, thus provoking a future political scandal.

The evening before Jorge's return to Santiago as *persona non grata*, I knew he would be the pretext for my arrest. I remember asking Belkis to call the Hotel Havana Riviera, where Jorge was staying, so that he might know my whereabouts. I returned to my apartment at midnight, and at seven in the morning State Security broke open the front door and two policemen took us both away in a car to the old residency of the Marist Brothers, in the nearby suburbs of Havana. From outside, it is the most placid and agreeable building that one can imagine; within, the residency, like an imitation medieval prison, is a labyrinth of corridors and stairs, with cells lined up along dark hallways.

Once inside, one of the guards asked me to empty my pockets. He counted out the money, wrote down the amount on a piece of paper, and placed it in an envelope, which he sealed. Then I was taken to another room for mug shots (profile and full-face, showing a prisoner's number around my neck). In yet another brightly lit room with huge green overstuffed chairs, a desk, and two plain wooden chairs, I took off my clothes. They searched my underwear, shoes, and socks. When I was dressed again, another official, short, with a dark complexion, handed to me a document which accused me of "having plotted against the powers of the state." Below appeared the name of a Lieutenant Álvarez, who had signed the indictment. The official pointed out my name. I asked if he was Álvarez. He replied that the lieutenant would be in later. I told him I would wait.

"But it was thought that at this time you would deny the charges. Deny them and sign. That's all."

After a while I was taken along several corridors guarded by heavily armed police who let us through only after a password was given. In a small room, a prison uniform was chosen for me from a large pile of clothes. Then they took me to another office, furnished like the first, but containing technical equipment of the kind I used to see in a radio station. Seated at the desk and wearing an imposing military uniform as he toyed with the indictment was another policeman, of a lighter complexion, who tried to intimidate me by expressing great irritation:

"So, you never thought we would pick you up, eh?"

"True."

"You thought you were the untouchable one, the rebellious and untouchable artist who goes around accusing us of being fascists? And that we were going to forgive all your counter-revolutionary antics? So you could plot against the security of the state without being placed at the disposal of Military Tribunal Number One of La Cabaña prison? You can sign the document any way you want—it won't be the only document you are going to sign. With all the poison you've been spitting at us, *all* of us, you must have your own little story of infamy."

"It's all a mistake."

"Oh, so now you give yourself permission to pass judgment on the legal measures of the Revolution?"

"It's a mistake to accuse me of something that everyone knows is not true."

"So there might be a 'gigantic international reaction'?"

"I never plotted against the powers of the state."

"So write a denial and countersign it."

I signed.

"An international reaction."

"Those are your words, Lieutenant."

"That is what you expect. Intellectuals are untouchable. That is what you hope for. Your friends will begin to mobilize—if they did that kind of voluntary work for the state, we would have more consumer goods than anyone else in the world."

"My friends outside Cuba will be troubled, and they are our friends, they support us," I said.

"They support whom?"

"Us. They support Cuba."

"*Your* friends support Cuba . . . ?" he asked sardonically. Then added: "Those friends of yours support Cuba? These friends, for instance?"

The office was filled with sounds of a party in progress—voices in Spanish with different Latin American accents all mixed together. It was impossible to hear anything clearly. Bursts of laughter blotted out the words. I finally made out a voice telling a story in impeccable English; indeed, in the exaggerated accents of a British lord. It was a typically obscene tale of the kind often heard in Spanish America. Everyone became quiet when a woman's voice announced the arrival of Jorge Edwards. The host of the party had a Mexican accent, and his name was Carlos. All of a sudden, the sounds ceased.

"Do you recognize them?"

I said I thought I recognized some of the voices, but could not be sure exactly who they were, and even less what the purpose was of making me listen to it all.

"Because I want you to remember the voices of our friends, as you call them."

I didn't know what to say. The situation was straight out of the theater of the absurd. I could not understand why they were making me listen to that recorded fragment without telling me what it was.

"Your friends," said the lieutenant ironically. "The ones who support us."

The recording started again.

"Tell us, Jorge, tell us," said the Mexican voice.

"Listen to the friends Jorge Edwards and Carlos Fuentes. Listen to them well," shouted the lieutenant over the sounds on the tape.

The Mexican voice gravely insisted that the Chilean voice tell him more, much more. The Chilean voice—it sounded a bit drunk—said that he had come to Mexico in order to be able to send to Chile a report on the true nature of the Cuban situation, without danger of his diplomatic pouch being opened in Cuba. He was convinced that the real diplomatic relations between the two countries were being carried out by their respective intelligence services; that Fidel Castro had inundated Cuba with Chilean wine of the Baltazar brand, out of pure caprice, without giving other Chilean producers a chance; that Cuba was placing its own people everywhere in Chile; that the Cuban embassy in Santiago had an oversized staff; that the personal escort of Allende was completely Cuban; that when he left the house where he had dined with Allende, just as he crossed the street to get into his own car, voices with a marked Cuban accent had shouted out "Adiós, compañero" from their various guard posts. The Chilean voice continued, saying that one of the daughters of Allende had married an official of the Cuban intelligence service; that Fidel Castro knew more about Chile than did Allende himself. "The situation there is very serious, Carlos, I'm really worried. *El Mercurio* is the only newspaper with any sense; their editorials are splendid, right on the mark. It's just as well that Pablo wants nothing to do with Fidel Castro now that he has been attacked by all those Cuban writers, who are all 'his master's voice,' anyway." (At this point you could hear the other's laughter.) "I always said to Pablo that Eduardo Frei was the best president Chile ever had, and now, with this government of Allende, I realize more and more that this man is an idiot."

The Mexican voice reacted to all this with consternation, but the one who was terrified at what I was hearing was me. Someone had brought a tape recorder to that party. Not long ago, as I talked over the incident with Jorge in New York, he assured me that he knew who had brought the recorder in, but he would not tell me the person's name. Clearly, that was the voice of Jorge Edwards, and he did remember the conversation. Yes, of course, they had had a lot to drink, as always. Yes, he had run off at the mouth. In New York, he laughed as he recalled the final moments of the conversation with Fuentes, but hearing those same moments resounding in a Cuban jail was like hearing a bomb going off. The Mexican voice said, "I've lived in Chile off and on and I can't understand how Chileans can swallow the fact that Fidel might have an influence on their policies."

"Allende is a fool. No one can stand Castro in Chile."

"Really solid people like the Chileans," insisted the Mexican voice, "have let themselves be seduced by that bongo player of history."

The Chilean voice became hysterical with laughter. He repeated the expression time and again; everyone burst out laughing. "That bongo player of history." He couldn't get over the expression. The Chilean voice began to sing it: "Bongo player, bongo player of history, caballero. Doesn't that sound like Nicolás Guillén, doesn't it sound like the voice of that mulatto whom Pablo Neruda imitates?"*

At that point, the recording stopped. The lieutenant looked at me without speaking, openly contemptuous. After a pause he said, "We don't want to be defended by such comrades."

He glanced at his watch and stood up. "With all your critical remarks, you will have more pages in your complete works than those of Comrade Pablo Neruda. Now, off to your cell." He called the guard.

"We have a lot of time to continue our conversations."

* I should note that although neither Carlos Fuentes nor Jorge Edwards recalls the phrase "that bongo player of history" as my memory brings it back to me, Carlos Fuentes did indeed use similar language in my defense in an article written around that time, where he noted that, because of the Padilla affair, ". . . Cuba has once again been turned into a country of (monolithic) bongo players and (inquisitorial) rumba dancers. There is no reason for Cuba to adopt the methods used by Stalin." Carlos Fuentes, "La véritable solidarité avec Cuba," *Les temps modernes*, Paris, June 1971, p. 2320.

15

ON MY FOURTH DAY in detention, I lay stretched out in my
narrow cell on a pallet of thick wooden planks suspended from
the wall by two chains, like something in a medieval dungeon.
I heard the big steel door crank open. A guard ordered me
to stand up. It must have been very early in the morning, since
there were no sounds of life from the neighborhood outside
the walls. Once again I was surprised to see that the guard
was heavily armed, since at every door in that fortress, with
its labyrinth of hallways, there was a guard who challenged
you and gave you permission to pass on. Again I walked down

the long stretch that separated me from the small, overlit office of Lieutenant Álvarez. I was his "case."

In Cuba, prisoners are interrogated by the same officer. The socialist world's outstanding contribution to jurisprudence is the fact that policeman, detective, and examining judge are one and the same person. Perhaps it's done that way to speed up the trials, whose only function anyway is to hear the prosecutor's charges and hand down the sentence, without anyone's examining whether or not the investigation was a fair one or its conclusions justified. The lawyer for the defense merely pleads for clemency in the name of the generosity of the Revolution.

Before entering Álvarez's office, I once again went through the ceremony of abasement, simple and quick, which all political prisoners must submit to. The guard grabs you by the bare shoulders (since the prison uniform is a kind of sleeveless gown, the color of baby shit, distributed randomly, so that one week it may swallow you up and the next clamp around you like a straitjacket), shoves your nose against the wall, and stands at attention before the closed door. Then, adjusting his voice to make it sound more martial, even though a speech defect makes what he says incomprehensible, he shouts out: "Tinint, prizner yasíntf'rzere be-éyendmi!"

The memorized phrase is too pompous for most Cubans, and the guard pauses for a split second and, almost choking, finishes: "Mishin-talettimintr."

Of course, if one is a Cuban and has heard it often, he or she may manage to decode the phrases as follows: "Lieutenant, the prisoner you sent for is here behind me. Permission to let him enter." From inside the office I heard a voice imitating Fidel Castro's, since every Cuban police official's aesthetic or emotional goal is at least to try to *sound* like Fidel: "Permission granted, comrade. Have him come in."

The first time I was taken to his office, Álvarez was wearing a dress uniform and he behaved with the ceremonial air appropriate to receiving a captured general on the field of battle; this time, he wore U.S. Army fatigues. His jacket was held in at the waist by an imposing green belt, from which hung a no less imposing pistol. I was afraid that something was going on outside, because he seemed ready for combat. His silence and aggressive body language added to my unease. This time he didn't order me to sit down. He was standing before the desk flanked by the two plain chairs we had sat in before. The door behind him, which had intrigued me the first time, was open and our conversation took place to the background of the incessant clatter of many typewriters, where secretaries were making transcriptions of recorded interrogations that would later be submitted for expert analysis.

"We've had Misié Pier Golendorff, a notorious enemy agent, here with us for a month. We know what you said about our detaining him—'To convince me Pier is guilty, you have to show me proof of his guilt.' And who are you that we have to show you proof of anything? We have in our possession all the notebooks in which you keep your 'literary observations.' They are nothing but reports to the enemy. Am I wrong?"

I stated that Golendorff was a member of the French Communist Party and a friend of Cuba.

"Like you, right?"

By then he was shouting, and abruptly took the manuscript of my novel *Heroes Are Grazing in My Garden* out of a desk drawer. I recognized it immediately by the two thick hard plastic covers that Soviet export agencies use for their catalogues, which I had used as binders. There could be no mistake.

"We've got all the copies. You turned out more than the entire print run of *Granma*, except that *Granma* spreads the ideas of the Revolution, while you spread poison from the CIA."

He stroked the shining covers and smiled as he looked toward the door. "And your wife should be here with you. Both of you are cut from the same cloth. She says she suffers from claustrophobia, but the doctor has already diagnosed her—she's a hysteric."

I said that she had nothing to do with what I had said, done, or written, that she should not have to suffer my fate, much less be detained for no reason at all.

"Is that a provocation?"

I said no, but I knew I was wasting my time. A cold chill ran through my body when I heard her tense, anguished voice coming out of the tape recorder, refuting the accusations this same officer was leveling against her. What did she have to do with my poems, my novel, my opinions? Why had she been locked up in one of those cells? I could never have imagined that they would resort to these tactics, dictated by blind hatred. If my imprisonment for "conspiring against the state" was a setup, her imprisonment—when they knew she suffered from a nervous condition—could only have been the result of "policy," the term used for high-level decisions which, though unjust, are considered necessary. What they were doing, of course, was taking their revenge, some years after the fact, for not having been able to stop the Writers' Union from awarding me the poetry prize. Now, they said, my recently completed novel was another attempt to create an international scandal. Even the title, *Heroes Are Grazing in My Garden*, infuriated them; only *animals* graze—horses, for instance. Fidel Castro's nickname in those days was "Horse."

To understand the level of paranoia with which State Security read the work of Cuban writers, consider the case of Virgilio Piñera. He had published his collected poems under the title *A Whole Life*, and included the poem "The Horse's Path," originally published in the magazine *Espuela de plata* (*Silver Spur*) in 1941; thus, "horse" there could in no way have been an allusion to Fidel. But though Virgilio had shown the authorities the tattered 1941 issue, the police eliminated the poem from the volume at the last moment. Ironically, "The Horse's Path" did appear, buried in the prose of the "Introductory Note." The vigilance of the censors did not extend, it seemed, to the prologue.

I took the title of my novel from a short poem by Roque Dalton, which begins and ends with the line "Heroes are grazing in my garden." Roque had been a friend for many years. He was a member of the Central Committee of the Communist Party of El Salvador and was later assassinated by his comrades of the radical left who had for some reason condemned him. Roque had a great sense of humor, of the irreverent, and he was highly amused to think one of his lines might be used as a book title. But whenever the novel was mentioned at high-level police meetings, the line was read as a direct and insulting reference to Fidel.

So there could be no doubt that vengeance would inform the "policy" toward me, but what need was there to extend it to my family? I felt a knot at my throat and tears came to my eyes. Álvarez looked at me as if from on high. "Cry if you want; men cry. But before you declare war on us, you'd better ask yourself if you're ready for a shoot-out. You are a clever man, and we have no problem admitting that. But the thing is, we have to put an end to the problem of intellectuals in Cuba. Otherwise, we'll wind up just like Czechoslovakia, where the intellectuals are standard-bearers for Fascism, like that little Russian friend of yours, that Yevtushenko—he's anti-Communist and anti-Soviet."

Though I knew it wouldn't do me any good, I answered Álvarez by stating that I was ready to assume my historical responsibility. He shouted back, "Counterrevolutionaries have no history!" I kept insisting that no one could ever prove that my wife and I were anybody's agents; I had sent the novel that was so exasperating to everyone to the rector of the University of Havana so that he might read it and give his opinion. I had no intention in writing it other than to mirror some characters and conflicts which emerge only in a revolutionary process. The very fact that we were under arrest for a novel that had not yet been published illustrated my point better than anything else. "You know that I've been to almost all the socialist countries," I said, "and worked as a representative of the Revolution in two of them. And in every country, I saw very clearly that the political apparatus in the end became a force of unquestioning authority. The political leadership inevitably became alienated from its base in the people. Instead of being shut up in a cell like criminals, my wife and I should be discussing my book at the Union with my fellow artists and with the political leaders of the cultural sector, not with the police."

"Yes, of course, over a cup of coffee and a good Uppmann cigar, so you could become president of the Union yourself."

"You have a very poor opinion of writers, Lieutenant."

"Because they're all the same."

"All of them?"

"All," he shouted, "without exception. Did Ché make exceptions when he said that all writers are in a state of Original Sin?"

Certainly, Raúl Castro made no such exceptions. Years before, in Prague, addressing the Cuban diplomatic and commercial mission I was attached to at that time, Raúl had alluded to the controversy then raging in the U.S.S.R. around Solzhenitsyn. "In Cuba, fortunately," he had said, "there are very few intellectuals, and those there are do nothing but get bogged down reinventing the wheel." This was the tenor of the editorials that had been appearing in *Verde Olivo*, the official organ of the Cuban armed forces. *Verde Olivo* had also run an article called "The Provocations of Heberto Padilla." Seemingly, Raúl Castro was at last realizing his long-standing ambition to purge the cultural sector, applying the same methods he had used before to elevate the morals of the country by creating the infamous UMAP camps. I will never forget the impression of Raúl that Waldo Frank left me with in Havana in 1960: "There is some deep abnormality in Raúl. He's cold and cruel and is capable of any crime." César Leante, a Cuban writer who was with me at the time, gave me a terrified look. We were upset by Frank's summary judgment, which we believed to be somewhat subjective. In retrospect, of course, we know Frank was right.

"The moment will come," Álvarez continued, "when every citizen will be a member of the Interior Ministry, just as Fidel wants. Then no one will have to be detained. But these days the party has assigned State Security to this task, and we are carrying it out."

He grabbed the manuscript of the novel and began to pound with it on the desk. "Do you know what the title of your novel ought to be? Can't you guess?" He came within a few steps of me. "*The Novel without an End*, baby, where nothing happens and where nothing *can* happen—just a few pages read by a tight little group, pages which will be tossed into the garbage, because that is what they're worth. And anyway, what's it all about, stuff that's fragmentary, unfinished, incomplete? Fidel doesn't like this poisonous shit, the leadership doesn't like it, the party, nobody." He held the manuscript with a degree of rage I hadn't thought him capable of, and that was the last thing I saw or heard.

When I came to, I don't know how much later, I was no longer in Álvarez's office. A huge weight seemed to press down on my head. I was stretched out on a pallet, and a doctor was taking my pulse and listening to my lungs and heart. When he was through examining me, he left without a word. For a few moments, I tried to reconstruct the scene, but my head felt three times its normal size, all the blood having rushed to it. My ears rang. It was a struggle just to breathe. I managed to get up and went to the faucet in the corner of the minuscule latrine—a hole in the floor. I splashed cold water over my face and head. I pissed blood. My nose was bleeding, too.

It was cold in the cell, strange weather for March in Cuba. I could feel the draft from the three slits high up on one of the walls. The cell was in a kind of mist, through which I could make out letters scratched on the walls probably with the end of a spoon—poignant scrawls, farewells to the world, bits from old prayers, which I quickly forced myself to stop reading. There was a light bulb above the doorway, enclosed in steel mesh. I heard voices coming from the hall used by political prisoners to go to and come from interrogations. The prisoners never saw one another; to avoid that possibility, the guards would whistle out when they were bringing along a detainee. Once, when I was outside my cell and about to cross paths with another prisoner, two whistles sounded at the same time. They shoved my face against the wall until they removed the other man; I could then proceed down the hallway.

I felt terribly weak, terribly tired, and went back to the wooden pallet, but when I raised my leg to get up on it, my strength failed me and I fell to the cell floor. My feet must have knocked against the door as I fell, and the noise must have been heard. A flashlight shone in through the peephole; the door opened quickly.

I woke up in the Military Hospital at Marianao. The place was roomy and bright; you could see trees through a high window. The nurse had finished making an electrocardiogram, and a man's booming voice filled the room. "I'm a friend of Ramirito Valdés and Sergio del Valle." He went on dropping names of political leaders, but no one was paying attention. The guards, doctors, and nurses carried on with their duties. After a bit the iron grating which served as the door to my room opened and a fairly young nurse came in—ugly, but cheerful—and placed a thermometer in one of my armpits, in the Cuban manner. I took advantage of her nearness to ask about the man with the loud voice. She would tell me only that he was under psychiatric observation.

"But if he's crazy, what's he doing here?"

"He is undergoing treatment, but of course his case is different from yours. I've read your books, we talked a lot about them when we were young—you have had a baleful influence on us. But now we have instructions to give you the best treatment possible. I have orders to take down your choice for lunch and supper." She removed the thermometer and examined it with a frown. I snatched it away from her.

Now the man with the voice was jumbling together all sorts of political figures—those in government and those in exile. He was a friend of Raúl Castro and Raul Chibás, of Ramiro Valdés and Huber Matos. It was maddening.

"He's crazy," I said to the nurse. Just before leaving, she turned to me: "But he was caught making bombs."

She soon came back with two aspirins, and in a half hour my fever began to subside. As it did, in my growing lethargy I conjured up images of my wife locked up in a cell at State Security; of my children, who probably had not gone to school, to avoid questions and taunts from their teachers and their schoolmates; images, too, of the friends who might feel the repercussions of my arrest. I had no doubt that this was the beginning of the iron-fisted policy Raúl Castro had been urging on the government for so long and had so keenly desired to direct personally.

Vitali Boroski, the first *Pravda* correspondent sent to Cuba, a man who used to visit Raúl often, said to me one day as we were walking along the Avenida del Puerto: "Be very careful of what you say—very careful." He said it warily. Vitali had an intense nature, a keen intelligence. He was a well-read man who had fought in World War II and was a member of the Soviet Communist Party. Knowing what I now know of such things, I have no doubt that he was a Soviet intelligence agent.

"Listen and listen carefully. Enemy number one of all of you is Raúl Castro. One of his biggest phobias is culture. They say the only thing cultural whose existence he recognizes is the waltz."

This iron-fisted policy knew no scruples. When we had a first glimpse of the libels and insults published in *Verde Olivo*, we wondered how Fidel Castro could tolerate it and whether he supported it. We Cuban writers were not unconscious of the hostility with which foreign intellectuals, who almost unanimously defended the Cuban Revolution, had reacted to the government's approval of the Soviet invasion of Czechoslovakia. It is true that, after this first voicing of support for the invasion, the Cuban press did publish an unprejudiced and objective account, which in turn led readers to assume with some certainty that Cuba really condemned the invasion. Fidel Castro himself, in a speech in which he noted the "bitter necessity" of approving the action, acknowledged that his words of approval had let a lot of people down. If he accepted this and admitted it, why his fury at the international condemnation of his behavior? And, we wondered, why make scapegoats of Cuban writers and artists? We were not even permitted the out offered Yevtushenko, who, though he had condemned the invasion while he was abroad on one of his many poetry tours, was greeted on his return to Moscow with not even a slap on the wrists. Was all this a symbolic act—knocking me around a bit, throwing my wife and me in prison—as if somehow it was Jean-Paul Sartre and Simone de Beauvoir being subjected to a harsh punishment, and not Belkis and me?

To stand up to such a perfectly timed and wholly unscrupulous maneuver would have been utterly futile. There is no courage more inconsequential and doomed to anonymity than that of a Cuban who struggles to shout out his truths as he faces a police unit armed to the teeth. Your friends will tell you not to get riled up; they know how much power a petty official has, and how much his victim has to lose. The only weapons against such a bully are guile and cunning. It's not a question of whether you have balls. Those of the Chief of State are well protected by his repressive apparatus, whereas a jailed writer's balls are highly vulnerable to a well-aimed kick.

While I was in the Military Hospital, Fidel Castro came to see me. I remember the clanging of the iron doors and the panache of the escort making way for him in a place where even inanimate objects would have dropped to their knees to let him pass. I remember him shouting at the guards: "Out, all of you, wait in the hall." The bodyguards slithered away as he waved a dossier, pacing back and forth with giant steps, but never looking me in the eye. "We two are the only ones who have to be here. Today I have the time to talk to you, and I think you have the time, too; and we have a lot to talk about."

Yes, we had time to talk—time for him to talk his head off, to heap scorn on the literature of the world, because "getting revolutionaries to fight isn't the same as getting literary men to fight. In this country they've never done anything for the people, neither in the last century nor in this one. They are always latecomers jumping on the bandwagon of history . . ." He must have seen himself as an impressive leader standing majestically before a no less impressive adversary dressed in a faded uniform, a scar still fresh on his forehead, his body still aching from the kicks of history.

16

~~~~~~

I SPENT A FEW MORE DAYS in the Military Hospital. As I recuperated physically and emotionally, I began to take a certain liking to the place. They had cared for me attentively and served me the food I had requested. But then I was returned to the Marist Brothers Residency, and the interrogations, always starting early in the morning, began again. Álvarez tried to keep me off guard, with surprising revelations or with veiled threats. Names and events (no matter how insignificant, episodes I myself had forgotten) were trotted out during these conversations. The clear intention was to frighten me, to convince me that I was a plaything of the police, that, in fact, they could go much further than they had up to that point. I remained convinced that their list of accusations consisted of nothing more than the criticism of the system voiced among friends or gleaned from things I had written, and that nothing could connect me to international espionage, nor was there anything related to the CIA, an organization which, judging by the opinion of the Cuban police, was omnipresent within Cuba.

Perhaps because they were about to close the case, or because they wanted to weaken my faculties even more, I was left isolated in my darkened cell for five days, with no guard coming to take me to interrogation. After the sixth day of not speaking to anyone, I became a little mad. Since there was no one to listen to me, I began improvising conversations aloud. I would speak with my friend Günter Maschke, a young German revolutionary of the New Left, who had deserted from the West German Army and gone into exile in Vienna. There he had sought the help of the Cuban embassy; he was given refuge, sent to Cuba, and put up at the Hotel Nacional. In Havana, Günter would come to see me every day around noon, bringing the latest works by Marcuse, Adorno, Ernst Bloch, and other writers of the Frankfurt School. As a leftist sociologist, Günter had expected to find in Cuba a practical confirmation of his own Marxist aspirations. However, Cuban reality dashed his hopes and he began cautiously to express criticism of the Revolution, odd comments which were picked up by a microphone somewhere.

One day he called me from his room in the hotel. In a shaky voice, he told me: "State Security is in my room. They've given me a few seconds to say goodbye; I'm being thrown out of the country."

In my cell, I found myself saying to Günter, "They threw *you* out, but look where they put me!"

The cell door opened abruptly.

"Where you should be, baby," screamed Álvarez. "And that little Kraut with his philosophical airs should be right here with you, too. Half-baked intellectuals were born to be counterrevolutionaries. Get up. And what the fuck are you doing, talking to yourself? Do you always talk in your dreams? All along the hallway here, your comrades tell me that you snore and talk all night."

When I tried to go out into the hall, I found I could barely stand. Six days of darkness, of lying on my pallet, had drained my strength. I felt dizzy, as if I were floating, but I made every effort to stay upright. A guard caught me by the arm.

"Better take him to the infirmary," ordered Álvarez.

I do not know how I got there. The infirmary was just another office. It had the same vinyl couches that could be found everywhere in the Marist Residency. I sat down; after a while a fat, rosy-cheeked doctor approached me, smiling.

"What's the matter with you?" He asked the question while taking my pulse.

"Nothing."

"What do you mean, 'nothing'? What are you here for?"

I told him everything that I did not know, and he watched me closely, showing some interest. "Listen, are you Fischer's case?"

"Who?"

"Fischer's case, old boy, Fischer. Aren't you the Padilla everyone is talking about on the overseas radio?"*

"I am Padilla, but I don't know who Fischer is."

"The officer, the one who's been interrogating you. How many days since you were last in his office?"

"Six, more or less."

He nodded. "Ah, it always happens."

He asked me to follow him. From that moment on, everything changed. He led me into what turned out to be a small emergency clinic. There was no one in the room he brought me to.

* I later found out that my interrogator, Lieutenant Álvarez, was an avid chess player, and since the American Bobby Fischer was the chess rage at the time, Álvarez's nickname in the prison was perhaps inevitable.

Asking me to lie down on the table, he listened to my heart. "The problem is that you are in a state of nerves and drained of energy. I'm going to give you a booster shot and you'll feel better soon."

As he prepared the injection, he kept on talking of my "case" in a modulated, cordial tone. "In matters of ideology, decisions are made rapidly. Feel fortunate that you are here. This is only preventive detention—a halfway house between prison and freedom. From what they tell me, your case is related to ideological deviationism."

He gave me the shot and smiled. I went on squinting in the bright light.

"That's because you have spent too much time in the dark." He smiled again and turned off the lamp closest to me. "You'll feel better this way."

But I did not feel any better. The growing effect of the shot turned into an inchoate mixture of languor and drunkenness. The light that was still on seemed to spin in circles, and I did not know where I was. I imagined being in different places. I was in my own home and in a foreign country, and in places I could not name. Suddenly I thought I was in the Havana Riviera Hotel, where Belkis and I had been staying for a few weeks. I could see the wide lobby of the hotel, and I heard someone calling to me. I recognized Davidson, my first professor of German, who had always kept his eyes nearly closed— a symptom of the disease which finally left him blind. Davidson had on the same bellboy's uniform worn by the staff at the Waldorf in London, where in 1960 Enrique Labrador Ruiz and I had a picture taken standing at the entrance. He had on the same round cap, the same cream-colored tight-fitting uniform with large brass buttons. Davidson called to me in a thin voice and asked me to sit down.

"Everyone here is saying that you are in prison. Tell me, is it because of your novel? Your friend Günter got away with some copies, didn't he?"

The child's cap that Davidson was wearing seemed vaguely

ridiculous all of a sudden. But that parody of an English lobby attendant was speaking to me about very serious matters.

"And you sent another copy off with the Chilean Jorge Edwards, and you surely must have other copies hidden, no? Don't forget that I am your German professor, and I am also your friend. We have known each other since we met at the Cuban embassy in Cologne. Or have you forgotten?"

This skeletal, half-blind, well-turned-out parody of a bellboy kept up his inexplicable ceremony of seduction.

"The truth is that neither one of us believes in Communism. We should do things together. I can arrange things so that Rika, my wife, gets you a scholarship to study in Germany. Tell me, where are the other copies hidden? Tell me, where? I can keep a secret, you can count on me. Now listen, I am the only one around who can personally carry your last report on the internal struggles within the Cuban CP to Jorge Edwards. Where have you hidden it?"

Dizzy, and completely unsettled by this crazed interrogation, I was finally able to shout, "I don't know what the fuck you are talking about, Davidson, I just don't know."

People were hitting me hard with their fists, cold water then thrown on my face and on my chest.

"How long do you intend to keep up this crazy monologue?" I heard someone shout at me. But the voice was not that of my German professor in bellboy uniform with brass buttons but that of Álvarez, standing beside the attentive doctor. The room was getting colder by the minute, and everything seemed to have acquired an extra dimension. I was revolving in an interminable downward spiral consisting of the London bellboy, the German professor, Álvarez, and the fat, rosy-cheeked doctor. The separate parts kept multiplying, becoming a twisted mirage.

I do not remember how I got back to my cell, but after a while, squinting into the darkness, I was able to make out the opaque light bulb enclosed in mesh over the steel door. It must have been seven in the evening, the hour in which power was cut as an energy-saving measure and all the homes in a great number of barrios of Havana were plunged into darkness. In the prison, of course, there were emergency generators.

That April was even more inexplicably cold than March had been. But in spite of the chill I took a shower to try to recover my wits. I dried myself and put my prisoner's uniform back on. It seemed extraordinarily cozy to me. I threw myself down on the pallet and attempted to reconstruct the past few hours. But my efforts were full of blurred outlines, confused images, and worst of all, nothing seemed to relate to anything else. It was a jigsaw puzzle whose parts could not be made to fit together.

A bit later, the door opened. It was a guard with some crackers in his hand. "Take these," he said. "You were asleep at suppertime."

He gave me a handful of crackers and I quickly put them under my pillow, to save them for when I was really hungry. Two hours later, another guard came to say that Álvarez wanted to see me.

I had barely sat down in his office when he said, "Head-quarters has given me instructions for you to write a letter which will acknowledge the errors you have committed, errors which you yourself know better than anyone else. Our comrade here will accompany you to another office. Write it all out there, and have it sent to me."

In the other office, I saw my own typewriter—I recognized it immediately; alongside, a pile of blank sheets numbered in strict numerical order, each one to be accounted for. There was also a basketful of crackers. Later, a guard brought in a large glass of soda water.

I figured that it would be enough to write a declaration in which I would admit that, after my conversations with members of State Security, I had come to the conclusion that my friends and I had acted in an irresponsible manner in our dealings with foreigners. I also added a touch that the police would want to have—that our literary ambitions were, unfortunately, out of sync with our political responsibilities, and this indicated the need for periodic meetings between members of the party and the Writers' and Artists' Union, so that norms of conduct might be established. There should, I said, be regularly scheduled exchanges of ideas which would help us avoid future errors.

After swallowing the last cracker, I took a sip of soda. I was convinced that I would be free within twenty-four hours. After all, at no time during my many interrogations had there been any substantiation of the charges against me. What was important in this document was to prevent them from reading into it a guilty verdict. I wanted the accusations to be reduced to the level of "deviations" from correct opinion. After a moment, I asked that what I had written be sent along to Lieutenant Álvarez.

The next day, I was called in once again. It was late in the afternoon, and I could see the pages written by me spread over Álvarez's desk.

He picked them up slowly and said, in a cold tone, "This is unacceptable. Do you know what headquarters thinks? They think you are a wise guy who wants to pull our leg right down to the last."

"How is that?"

He crumpled up the pages and stood. "So, in your conversations with us, you finally came to the conclusion that you and your friends have acted irresponsibly." He was shouting. "And you did not know any of this before talking to us; we revealed the truth to you. You've got balls. These pages are no good. Look." He ripped up the crumpled papers and threw them in the wastebasket.

Then he sat down and spoke to me very slowly. "No, what you are going to give us is a multi-page confession in which you go on record, describing step by step all your activities with the enemy. This has to be done on your typewriter, your own typewriter, the same machine used to turn out all those defamations of Fidel and the Revolution. We have plenty of time. So I want you to think about all the poison that you have spread about us, telling everybody that the only thing missing here is the Kaiser's spiked helmet."

He called the guard and ordered me back to the same office as before. And, as before, crackers and soda water.

"When you finish, give me a call. Take your time."

What had unsettled me were his instructions relating to my "activities with the enemy." This could mean inventing crimes which had never taken place. All the other accusations were based on opinions of mine critical of Castro's revolutionary government. But in suggesting "activities with the enemy," they were putting me on notice that they would destroy me if they felt it necessary to do so.

"If you keep on dreaming about the effects that an inter-national scandal might have on your person, I warn you that the Revolution has many ways to put a damper on such a scandal. Go along now, think about what you are doing, and write."

I went along, and of course thought for a long time, and I began to write. I persisted in my initial idea of staying close to the phrase "deviation from correct opinion" so dear to the Communist world, while dramatizing in vehement fashion my ungrateful attitude toward Fidel and the Revolution. I would emphasize my repentance—this would make them happy, I thought. My imprisonment would be seen as a just sanction, and my friends would not suffer the consequences of errors brought on by my actions. In less than three hours, the "confession" was written. It came to more than thirty pages.

Álvarez was impassive as he read it. He was not at all reluctant to praise the alacrity with which I reacted to his counsel, and he noted admiringly the fact that I had not needed to change the pre-numbered order of the blank pages. I was sent back to my cell.

Just as the door was being opened, the cart carrying supper came along. That night the food on the aluminum plate was white rice, white beans, and a hard-boiled egg. The door closed behind me; I took the spoon and marked off another day on the wall. The meal tasted fine.

I could tell that it was dawn by the light filtering in through the slits high up on the wall. The door creaked open and I was ordered to stand up and follow the guard. The guard knew the way. By this time, I was familiar with the office with the glass walls where you could see an old guard in a uniform and two or three plainclothes agents with cameras who always whispered as I passed by. But after this area I went up and down many sets of stairs till we arrived at a double door. Through the door you could hear the grunts and heavy breathing of people who seemed to be practicing boxing or karate.

The guard announced our arrival as usual.

I could hear Álvarez above the din. "Let him in."

I was in the midst of a group of athletes. Two men were wrestling with considerable agility. One of them leaped away from his opponent and landed on his back on the gym floor. In a corner, a uniformed guard was slowly sweeping the floor.

Mopping off the sweat, Álvarez laughed at the guard with the broom. "Alejandro!" he shouted. "Why did headquarters punish you with this job for today?"

The guard stopped, and with the grand gestures of an actor he emoted a sentence which made everyone laugh: "Because, to sweep, 'there is nothing better than a pair of good hands.' "

Still puffing, Álvarez exclaimed: "You see, even the guards know your verses by heart. I have to leave for a moment. Wait for me here."

As he walked away, he shouted to the group: "Listen, do you know who this guy is? It's the poet Padilla."

Everyone glared at me. The first to speak was the guard with the broom. "Padilla? And with those specs?"

He came close; the others followed. "A prick with glasses on."

He raised his hand and ripped my glasses off, screaming,

"Because in trying times there is nothing better than a pair of eyes."

Roars of laughter. Then they began a kind of macabre ritual, repeating lines from my poems as they picked me up and bounced me back and forth. I hit the wooden floor again and again. My head, forehead, legs, my entire body became a punching bag. The last thing I remember through the pain was a fist across my nose and temple. Later I tried to open my eyes in a tub of freezing water.

The chubby, rosy-cheeked doctor was pushing my head under the tap until I thought I would drown. "It's therapy for horses, baby, but you'll see, in twenty minutes you'll be quite presentable."

I was brought over to a table in the emergency room. I realized that I had gotten another shot, because, along with the accustomed exhaustion, I felt the same drunkenness as before, but now it was as if I were floating above the pain. The lamp was going around in circles, and the scenes I saw were from my childhood, the New York streets covered with snow, the many airports I had passed through. But I heard no voice, nor did I see my German professor dressed up as a London bellboy trying to get me to confess to being a spy. I was sinking into a placid space which gradually dissipated the blows. When I woke up in my cell, I felt alive as never before, and I understood that I had been the victim of that ancient cruel ritual which all police states put their subjects through.

I cried from shame. With the passing of the years, I realize all too well that I was a privileged witness to horror as well as its accomplice until that moment. Whether or not I was conscious of what was going on in Cuba at that time, I had never taken the trouble of finding out for myself that in Cuba people were being tortured on the most preposterous pretexts. Later I thought of Huber Matos, Gutiérrez Menoyo, Sorí Marín, Pedro Luis Boitel, all those who were with Fidel from the first days of the insurrection, and who were later beaten, tortured, even executed with a degree of sadism more refined and monstrous than in the worst tyrannies.

"Oh God, compared with the others, not much has happened to me. Those who really suffered are those who fought for freedom and were then betrayed." Through the peephole, a beam from a flashlight poked into the cell. "Go to sleep, and stop talking out loud—anyone would think you were in church."

I kept quiet until the guard with the flashlight went away. I wanted rest, but that was impossible. I did drift off into a half-sleep; I saw myself in my twenties, walking along a Havana street with a young girl from Santiago. She was being awarded a literary prize by the Casa de las Américas. She was nineteen, slender—you would think she was from the Mediterranean, with her huge dark eyes. I never thought that poetry could be so exactly linked to personal attractiveness, but that certainly was the case with Belkis Cuza Malé. She embodied in an amazing way the alliance between two things I did not think could be joined. With her, the decisive chapter of my youth had begun.

Around five in the morning, the door opened. Álvarez and someone I had never met before stood in the brightly lit hallway.

"We are going to get your clothes; the doctor is waiting at the hospital." I was taken to the same room where I had been issued a prison uniform; a guard brought me my clothes. He then gave me a sealed envelope and asked me to open it. There were the keys to my house, along with some money. Nothing was missing. He asked me to sign a receipt attesting to the return of my valuables; I went out into the street with the two officials. We got into the same car which had taken me to the hospital before. We were headed there again. In those first moments after sunrise, everything around me seemed so strange that I was convinced that we were driving around the streets of a city I had never visited. The people I observed waiting on the sidewalk for the light to change or chasing a last bus seemed so relaxed. Stopped at a red light, I heard the voices of mothers wafting out of house windows, trying to get their kids out of bed and ready for school. It was just a Cuban morning, like all the mornings of my past. I never felt more depressed than when I heard those mothers' voices.

We went through the main door of the Military Hospital and were directed down a long corridor on the ground floor to a place reserved for prisoners. We went into a kitchen where a young soldier was cooking up something for himself on the stove; Álvarez ordered coffee for us. We went out to a patio; there were shade trees and stone benches scattered around a garden.

"Headquarters has decided that the treatment you require is not available in this hospital. Your attending physicians think you are suffering from long-standing emotional problems and that you are prone to hallucinations—well, you know more about that than anyone."

Álvarez stood up and strolled among the empty stone benches. "Look, we've come to the conclusion that you are a guy who eats a lot of shit but at the same time is driven by wildly grandiose ambitions. All your verbal fluency comes out of your being, essentially, a sloppy and lazy person. You declare war on us, but then you avoid the shoot-out."

The soldier called from the kitchen that the coffee was ready. Álvarez ordered him to bring it out to us; he poured me a demitasse. The bitter taste upset my stomach.

"A team of specialists will examine you. Speak to them frankly. And, by the way, tomorrow some other friends will be passing by to pay you a visit. They will also be able to speak to you without restriction."

I was taken off to the same room as before. Now it had a few more chairs and desks. The doctors looked me over and made a cardiogram.

"I'm pretty sure that your case does not fall within our field of competence," one said to me. "At any rate, we will wait for the results of the tests." The man speaking to me was dressed in the kind of white smock often seen in laboratories or in sanatoriums. He seemed too young for his salt-and-pepper beard. His companions remained silent.

The next day the officials Álvarez had mentioned came to my room. There were four of them. They sat in the stuffed chairs, I in the desk chair. One member of the group placed an enormous manila folder on the table and began to sort through a stack of photographs. Though I saw the photos upside down, I could tell that they were shots of my face, my apartment, many of my friends. He continued sorting.

"We will speak of this later," he said, without telling me what the postponed subject was. He then showed me an impressive number of restaurant and bar bills charged at the Hotel Havana Riviera to the account of the Chilean diplomatic mission. I recognized the inimitable signature of Jorge Edwards.

The man glared at me. "Don't get the idea that the Revolution has stolen these chits from the Chilean mission. Not at all; every one of them has been paid by the Revolution. Señor Edwards contributed nothing, nor did his bosses at the CIA, but we can show them to you now. We have figured out that the consumption of Scotch accounts for just about half of the total restaurant and bar bills signed by Edwards. The little boozer drinks up Scotch that the Chilean people would have had to pay for."

I could see that the bills for Scotch consumed rivaled in their enormity the equally sizable bills for beef, not to mention the astronomical number of kilos of coffee purchased. I said nothing.

"Why don't you say something?" asked one of the officials. "Do you suppose that Edwards, coming as he does from one of the most reactionary families in Chile, came to Cuba to express his solidarity with the workers? Of course not; he came to recruit all of you spiteful intellectuals as spies. And you were the first.

"Here, look at these photos taken during some of those big suppers Edwards threw for you people, there, you can see all of you kissing his ass. Look at the little group of whores fawning over the foreigners, but it's okay, we have them on a short leash. You know that a new society is not built in a day. For the time being, even these antisocial elements are of use to us. That's what whores are for, right now—they tell us everything."

There was a long silence. Then the member of the group who had seemed the most insignificant of them all, a blond and painfully thin young man, spoke up. "We don't think that you are a Marxist–Leninist, Padilla, but your deeply seated social resentment might be useful to us on some matters we are interested in. For instance, what is your opinion of all these splurges of Señor Edwards?"

I said that I had not expected to be asked to judge the expense account of any consulate or mission but that I was convinced that those enormous tallies were the direct result of Jorge's generosity. The supposed excesses were actually an indication of the miserable economic situation of Jorge's friends, who, thanks to him, were able to eat and drink during the three months of his stay in Cuba. These things did not typify and were not characteristic of any particular embassy. I knew that when Jorge had insisted on paying the bills, he had been told not to worry about them, that they were included in the courtesies offered by the state to the Chilean consul.

Another official broke in. "You know very well that Edwards is an agent of the enemy, the boss of all of you. By this time, Comrade Allende has in his hands the file on his representative in Cuba, and it is devastating. This time he will not be able to be protected by his buddy Pablo Neruda. Edwards will be tossed out of the Chilean diplomatic corps in disgrace; then Fidel will decide what is to be done with him, his friends, and his accomplices. I am now going to read you what Fidel said at the university, a statement which is being distributed abroad by Prensa Latina."

He read the text of a cable, attempting to imitate Fidel's tone of voice: ". . . In a few days we will publish some revelations which will outrage the public at large. It is not only the so-called Padilla affair; many more are implicated along with him."

I realized then that Castro was looking for the opportunity to liquidate the first wave of intellectual dissidence in his regime, just as he had done three years earlier with those old Communist militants like Escalante whom he had put out to pasture for having constituted a microfaction. This kind of purge is frequently instituted when criticism or discontent appears within a Communist state. But I had only known of purges as an intellectual possibility. I never imagined that I would be given the opportunity to observe the careful organization of such a farce, aimed at destroying a group of people. Moreover, it was inconceivable that I would head the list.

Everyone was awaiting the reaction of the Allende government. If Jorge Edwards was expelled from the Chilean diplomatic corps on the basis of the Cuban dossier, then it would be a clear indication that Castro was capable of dominating things in Chile and imposing upon Salvador Allende his own criminal methods.

Edwards recalls in his book *Persona non grata* that two high officials of the Allende government resolutely opposed Castro's libel. One was Clodomiro Almeida, Allende's Foreign Minister; the other was Orlando Letelier, later killed by a bomb blast in the streets of Washington, D.C.

The sessions of the recently convened Congress of Education and Culture were being broadcast on television in the hospital. The guards and nurses were all attentively following the proceedings. When an old veteran of the Chilean Communist Party for whom Castro had great respect—Volodia Teitelboim, friend and later biographer of Pablo Neruda and an important figure in the Chilean Popular Unity Party—appeared at the rostrum to give a speech to the Congress, you could feel the tension. The officials at my side must have been thinking the same thing I was—that the Chilean politician would take advantage of this occasion to speak to the Congress about his government's position on the scandal that had been unleashed, with me at the center of it. But when his calm speech included only passing references to the usual boilerplate, the fraternal relationships newly established between Cuba and Chile, I understood that his appearance before the Congress had only one objective—to let Fidel Castro know that the Popular Unity government of Chile refused to accept his recommendation, that Jorge Edwards would not be expelled from the diplomatic corps as a CIA agent, as there was no proof for such an allegation. The maneuver by the Cuban government had been adroitly blocked; Castro had no choice but to act within Cuba itself.

Over the applause coming from the TV following the Teitelboim speech, I heard the phone ring. A nurse answered and motioned to one of the officials. He took the message and returned to his seat. "Álvarez and Gutiérrez are coming over. We'll be back later."

As I sat alone, thinking about what Teitelboim had said and had not said, I was greatly relieved, but then I began to seethe with resentment toward Fidel Castro, a man without scruples who had tried to display before the world the Robespierre-like image of the incorruptible leader.

Once again, my complicity with an authoritarian regime became evident to me. Arthur Koestler, in a warning of 1943 heeded by no one, had told us: "There is no excuse for you— for it is your duty to know and to be haunted by your knowledge. As long as you don't feel, against reason and independently of reason, ashamed to be alive while others are put to death, not guilty, sick, humiliated because you were spared, you will remain what you are, an accomplice by omission."*

At noon, Álvarez and Gutiérrez appeared. They ordered

* Arthur Koestler, *The Invisible Writing* (New York: Macmillan, 1954), p. 429.

the nurse to bring in the clothes I'd been arrested in, and told me to get dressed. "Let's go to the beach—you need a little air."

We left the building and got into a car whose only peculiarity was the remote-control device on the dashboard which signaled to headquarters the precise location of the vehicle. We went from one end of the city to the other, from Marianao (where the Military Hospital is located) to the bay tunnel; then we went down the Vía Monumental, which runs along the lovely beaches of the eastern end of Havana. At Guanabo we stopped, got out of the car, and made our way through heavy underbrush to the isolated beach.

"Feel better?" Gutiérrez inquired. Álvarez sat down on a big rock. He invited me to sit down as well, but I said I would rather stand.

"Well, if you want to stay on your feet, you should think very seriously about what you are doing. We can destroy you even though you know we have no legal justification for doing so. You haven't done anything; you haven't planted any bombs or carried out any sabotage; no black market dealings in currency. All these things will be acknowledged by the Revolution at the opportune moment and we will not be reluctant at all to rehabilitate you. But right now you represent a very dangerous tendency in the nation and we have to eradicate it. So you have only one alternative—come to an agreement with us." We returned to the hospital in silence. I remember getting out of the car without saying a word.

The thirty-seven days I had spent in the Marist Residency and in the Military Hospital were punctuated by daily routine interrogations. It soon became clear that Jorge Edwards hadn't even read my novel. The suppositions made by State Security or some ill-intentioned informer were without any basis in fact. It was also obvious that the government was trying to find a way out now that my situation had turned into an international scandal.

At last, they came up with a formula to cool things down. I

would memorize the "self-criticism" I had written in the State Security office, recognizing my errors and those committed by my friends. From this document the authorities would extract a text indicating "repentance," which in turn would justify official clemency. And the entire text would be recited aloud by me in a closed meeting of the most important members of the Writers' and Artists' Union. The audience would be limited to a few of the select. José Lezama Lima and Virgilio Piñera would not be invited. But they would be informed of the event before it took place.

I was freed at midnight; the next morning I boarded a bus to Lezama Lima's house. He was terrified when he opened the door and saw me, but he asked me in. Just a little later his wife, María Luisa, appeared, also frightened and confused. I explained the situation to Lezama and told him that a man from State Security would come to see him that same day.

"Those people don't have to ask permission to come into our houses," he observed. "They are always inside, and you know it as well as I."

17

~~~~~~

IT IS UNFORTUNATE that there is little allusion, in Lezama Lima's correspondence, to the events we all lived through after 1971. Doubtless, those experiences touched him deeply and he could not write about them even in his letters.

The meeting with my friends, Lezama, and the agent from State Security took place the same day I was released. The purpose was to organize a session of the Writers' Union at which I would recite my "self-criticism." A half hour into the gathering at Lezama's house, it became clear that things were not proceeding in a satisfactory manner. The agent kept fidgeting in his seat, his patience wearing thin. Lezama had assured him that he accepted, as we all did, the scenario for the "self-criticism." However, he avoided answering the agent's questions directly, taking refuge in complex metaphors, with allusions ranging from the black angels of William Blake to the "house of philosophy," an expression borrowed from Georg Simmel. Lezama had been able to convert an interview into an event that self-destructed. Still, the agent was speaking from a position of power and sought out ways to frighten everyone and to encourage cowardice among the defenseless.

Perhaps because of Lezama's asthma, or his three-hundred-pound weight, or because of the particularity of his poetic world, which was so distant from actual history, or because of all these things, he was the most vulnerable in the eyes of State Security. The poet got under their skins as no one else had done. Perhaps their irritation was due to the influence he exercised on a new generation of younger writers. Twelve years of revolutionary history had only intensified his influence. For my part, in spite of my headlong opposition to Lezama's poetry and that of almost all the poets from his *Orígenes* group, I always tried to keep separate the man Lezama from his aesthetic positions.

In contrast, Spanish and Spanish American poets admired him and his work. Vicente Aleixandre had described his poetry as ". . . visceral and probing, plunging into the soul—exquisite and transcendent poetry." Luis Cernuda had written to him: "I spoke to Octavio Paz about your poetry, and we are both intrigued by your work." Even Wallace Stevens had informed Lezama that, although he had not enough Spanish to fully comprehend him, his books were of the kind that made Stevens regret his poor command of the language—". . . all your pages tantalize me."

To me it was clear that his work embraced the worst vices of literature in the Spanish language, although his baroque style is not simply that "which borders on its own caricature," to use the words of Jorge Luis Borges. Lezama transcends such classifications with his impressive extravagance. To use his own language, he was a tenacious proclaimer of things at once astounding and dazzling. Every time I approached his poetics, his "doctrines of the windflower," I found myself violently dispatched to a realm of pure language, his one and only kingdom. Lezama admired Valéry, and it is not difficult to find traces of the French poet in his theoretical statements. As with Valéry, Lezama esteemed books with *obstacles* in them—clarity meant glibness, only the difficult was stimulating. More than once he cited enthusiastically that paragraph of Huizinga about the secret power of hermetic expression:

> The close connections between poetry and riddle are never entirely lost. In the Icelandic skalds too much clarity is considered a technical fault. The Greeks also required the poet's word to be dark. Among the troubadours, in whose art the play-function is more in evidence than in any other, special merit was attributed to the *trobarclus*—the making of recondite poetry.*

But far from considering the troubadour as having a "play-function within a society," Lezama insists upon "the presence of that hermetic minstrel who follows the methods used at Delphi—nothing is openly stated nor are things hidden; there is only the making of signs." All of Lezama's work is a universe of signs similar to that of Góngora. "The roots of the jongleur's art come from a vast underground tradition, except that the beam of light thrown out like a comet by the jongleur disappears into its own parable . . . The Delphic signs are traced out on a slate of night which the oracle himself assiduously erases."

When he gave his famous lecture on Mallarmé in the fifties, the leftist critics and others made fun of him with a play on words: "I heard Lezama speaking on Mal-larmé and I was a-larmèd." Nicolás Guillén enjoyed repeating the joke, because his own poetry constituted the poetic system Lezama had condemned most strenuously. In his *Colloquy with Juan Ramón*

* J. Huizinga, *Homo Ludens* (Boston: Beacon Press, 1955), p. 135.

169

Jiménez, you can see his rejection of the kind of poetry which takes "race" and "blood" as its point of departure. For Lezama, what was Cuban was a category of the spirit. Although Lezama considered himself a Roman Catholic, more orthodox believers, including members of the *Orígenes* group, severely criticized his novel *Paradiso* (many would not permit their wives to read it) because some of the episodes depicted a homosexual world which Lezama never stood in fear of. In his last years, Lezama was troubled by the political situation in Cuba. He used to say to me that the ordinary Cuban was a man of the sun who did not know how to live in the subterranean world imposed on him by political repression.

He was tolerated by the regime because of its respect for his literary prestige. At the same time, he was closely watched because of fears concerning the influence he was having on younger writers. When *Paradiso* was published, veiled attacks began to appear, some from his old cohorts. His opinions were always galling to the regime, particularly since they were almost invariably expressed in an ironic, even sarcastic tone. The people who visited him at his home began to inform on him as well. These were people who wanted to remove him from the posts he held in the Writers' Union and, for that matter, from the literary scene. As I was, he was a member of the Literature Section of the Union and also participated in the activities of the editorial board of the *Revista*. His dutiful attendance at the meetings and his willingness to read materials for possible publication were astonishing. Obviously, his opinions weighed heavily in the final decisions of the board. A good number of Social Realist texts and others of an opportunistic nature fell by the wayside under his searing critiques. A born polemicist, he defended his opinions with assurance, but he was a man of breadth in aesthetic matters. When *Fuera del juego* won the Poetry Prize of the Writers' Union, Lezama was one of my most energetic defenders. He never caved in to the many suggestions that he change his opinion of the book. When I had learned that he was to be a member of the jury, I had been afraid that his opinion of my poetry would be hostile; I certainly never dreamed that my poems would interest him, since they were written with a conscious economy of verbal means that only incidentally allowed for images or metaphors. But not only did my book win his approval; as vice president of the Union, he opposed the decision of the higher authorities to condemn the book. He took a hand in drafting, along with the other members of the jury, the defense of their opinion. This is the text which appeared as the prologue to the Cuban edition. That was the nature of the man Lezama.

The practitioners of Social Realism never forgave him. It was not a matter of aesthetic disagreement, since that was of little import to them, but rather that his reputation made their task more difficult. Writers from abroad would visit him, treating him with reverence and sympathy. No one sought out the Social Realists.

During Hans Magnus Enzensberger's long stay in Cuba, we would often meet with Lezama. On one occasion Hans Magnus invited us to lunch at the Hotel Nacional. Lezama had read my translations of Hans Magnus's poems, and he was especially pleased by my version of his "Lachesis Laponica." It was a splendid meal. Lezama punctuated his conversation with long puffs on his cigar. Hans Magnus followed him intently, hanging on every word. When Lezama talked about classic German literature, he mentioned names and dates as if he were discoursing on his contemporaries. This was December 1968, the time of the Havana Cultural Congress. Writers and artists from all over the world had gathered. The visitors from the United States included Robert Silvers, editor of *The New York Review of Books*; the economist and writer Emma Rothschild; and Susan Sontag, who had brought along her son, David Rieff, then just over sixteen years old. Hans Magnus and I met with them in one of the conference rooms set up for visitors. We were later joined by Julio Cortázar and a few other writers. Lezama's name had begun to circulate in the publishing houses of New York; Silvers said he wanted to meet him. Two days later we all went to his house. Bob was impressed with Lezama's personality. Once again Lezama displayed his passion for literature and his knowledge of American writing. Bob asked him about the relationship between poetry and science, whether they coincided or diverged. Lezama answered by discoursing on the energy at the center of all creative acts. Both, he said, coincided in the world of hypothesis and conjecture. The aim of science was poetry, he stated; both poetry and scientific proof were versions of man's delirium.

As Silvers continued the interview, Lezama himself seemed to undergo a transfiguration in that small living room with its suffocating heat. Although he breathed in asthmatic gasps, a hidden energy seemed to be released in him. It is a pity that only State Security has in its possession this wondrous display of Lezama's conversation, braided through with its most arcane allusions. He spoke with high praise of Emerson's poetry, and recited aloud the Spanish versions done by Juan Clemente Zenea. When Bob asked his opinion of Martí, Lezama looked at him with friendly enthusiasm, as if the question had been posed by a member of his circle. "We can say of Martí what Martí said of Quevedo," he replied. "Those of us who come after him speak the language he spoke."

When Bob asked him point-blank: "And do you think that Martí would have been happy with the political changes which have taken place in Cuba, with the way things are today?" Lezama pressed his cigar with his fingers, brought it to his mouth and puffed on it three or four times in his accustomed way, then inhaled for a few seconds without taking his eyes off Bob. "Ah well, ah well," he said, answering not at all, as if he were signaling his hidden intention behind the afternoon's only moment of reticence. After all, this was shortly after the invasion of Czechoslovakia, the polemic surrounding *Fuera del juego*—months in which mediocrity triumphed in Cuban cultural life, the time of abject submission to Soviet policy. Long after the conversation, Bob Silvers would repeat fragments of Lezama's surprising declarations. Twenty years later, he can recall them still. Late in the afternoon, the sky aflame with the setting sun, Julio Cortázar appeared with the photographer Chino Lope. Cortázar had brought Lezama a box of cigars.

"My friend," he said to Cortázar, "you are contributing to the fact that tonight my dreams will be different. Cigar smoke is an ally of my happiness and an ally of my death." He added ironically, "The people from the Casa de las Américas bestow upon me one box every two or three months, as if that sufficed, and I smoke five of them in less than a day."

It was true. Lezama's anxious desire for cigars was increasing as he waited for his visa to leave Cuba to accept literary awards in Spain and in Italy. The visa never came. As he noted sadly in his letters to his sister, the denial was bringing him nearer to death.

It was interesting, after Lezama did die, to see how the police managed to turn his funeral into a reception for courtesans. The bureaucrats called everyone on the telephone to make sure we would all attend. Bringing together all the writers in the great salon of the funeral home was one of the infamous "oblique images" of which Lezama used to speak.

But that afternoon, as Bob and I were taking our leave, Lezama displayed his customary high spirits. Taking advantage of the presence of a photographer, he asked that a picture be taken of the group. I still have it. It must have been a delayed-action shot; from right to left, you can see Cortázar, the photographer Chino Lope, Lezama, Bob Silvers, and me. By mysterious design, someone (perhaps to eliminate Lezama from the print) had folded the photograph at the point where Lezama appeared. "Odd that they decided to fold it just there," Bob noted not long ago.

But in the months before his death, Lezama still seemed to have the strength to keep up his resistance to the regime. I would frequently meet with Lezama during Jorge Edwards's three-month stay in Cuba. At times the three of us would be joined by Mario Vargas Llosa and Julio Cortázar, they as so often in those days *de passage* in Havana. One evening Edwards and César López organized a supper to celebrate Lezama's sixtieth birthday. César and his wife, Micheline, cooked a magnificent meal. Since Jorge enjoyed diplomatic privileges, he was able to purchase everything, not only meat, but simple things like olive oil, salt, and vinegar. At midnight, as we were eating and smoking through the good graces of Edwards, we heard someone knocking at the door. We looked at each other. We knew that at any moment our shared fraternity might be stolen from us by our enemies. So we were not that surprised to see at the door a human being who was malignity incarnate—a languid spy with long black hair and soft dark skin and huge eyes (evil *can* be beautiful, after all); he had come to ask us please for a little olive oil to cook with. The clumsy pretext didn't deceive us for an instant. After he left, Lezama noted in his slow, grave voice: "There you have a case of someone living by the phallic sword, but it can also be a sword over our heads." We all laughed, but we knew his words were a forewarning.

After I was arrested by State Security, many of the visitors to his house told him that what had happened was not a result of general policy but exclusively the "Padilla affair." Lezama, who was trained as a lawyer, answered such assurances by shaking his head and saying, "No, it's against all of us." He said the same thing when he refused Cortázar permission to supervise the French translation of *Paradiso* that was to be published by Editions du Seuil, where Severo Sarduy had long been employed as an editor. "No, that would be an attack against Severo."

Lezama was not surprised when he was invited to discuss the details of the "self-criticism" which I was to perform at the Writers' Union a little later. After the political peroration of the agent from State Security, Lezama took a long puff on the cigar that had been offered to him a few minutes before. If the planned event at the Literature Section of the Union would be useful to ease the international scandal caused by my arrest, he thought it should take place. The man from Security told him that he did not have to attend, that even Nicolás Guillén, the president of the Union, had refused. José Antonio Portuondo would be in charge. Lezama listened attentively and, after a pause, asked, "What I do not understand is this—what value can such a meeting among ourselves have to put an end to the scandal?" The policeman replied, "This was a decision made at the highest level."

"But you could put a stop to it all in two minutes if you sent Padilla off as cultural attaché to Bulgaria or wherever," said Lezama, "and then Pablo Armando Fernández to London, and reappointed César López to the Foreign Ministry, to the job he lost because of intrigues."

The agent became enraged. "Do you mean to imply that the comrade lost his job because of intrigues? Intrigues on whose part?"

"My friend, intrigues are like calumnies in opera plots—they grow and grow, one on top of another."

The agent leapt to his feet. "I really don't understand you."

"Nor do I understand you, sir. I don't think you are more than thirty years old, but you enjoy enough power to pillory us all. Sir, you are the power of the state."

The agent burst out nervously: "We have proof and we can go much further than we have, sir."

"My friend, I do not know how far your reach is, but I do not fear anyone."

"Lezama, I am here to ask for your cooperation."

"You will have it."

"But you began by attacking decisions of the revolutionary government."

"That is your way of seeing things, sir. I am not of the same opinion."

"I'm not stupid."

Lezama didn't contradict him; he let him continue: "You have defamed the Revolution on more than one occasion. You ought not to make me prove it to you."

Then Lezama, making an almost superhuman effort, got on

his feet as he crushed the half-smoked cigar in the ashtray. "Lieutenant," he said excitedly.

"Second Lieutenant," shouted the official.

"Second Lieutenant, all our lives are being threatened by gossip and malicious innuendo. I cannot be an exception, but you cannot prove anything that I do not already know, unless my dreams or my nightmares have given me away, a possibility which I do not at all discount. Man is an unforeseeable being."

The Security man looked at Lezama without saying a word. He went toward his briefcase, opened it, took out a small Sony tape recorder, and turned it on. A voice of mixed inflection came out of the machine; it was easy to recognize. It was the voice of this man expressing himself with extraordinary eloquence.

"It is painful that all the governments in the history of this country have concluded that writers are their enemies. They remind me of all the filthy trials from colonial times onward. They are always screaming at a poet, whoever the poet of the time is: 'So, you're Cuban, you're sensitive and we are crude; therefore, we will give you the iron fist. If you are a traitor, we will surround you with cackles and derision. If you are pure of heart, if you are open to pristine exhalations from the earth, we will crush you with belly laughs and derision.' The way things are going around here, one of these days there will be no one left on the island, only me left to hand over the key of the city to a counterrevolutionary like Señor Rolando Masferrer."

He stopped the tape and looked steadily at Lezama. "What do you think?"

Lezama didn't look at him. He said only: "One day all after-dinner conversation and even the orgasm of lovers will turn into material for political crimes. You, Señor Lieutenant . . ."

"Second Lieutenant," he corrected irritably.

". . . You, after all, have me in your hands."

The man reacted nervously to this. "I am authorized to tell you that there is no official intention to destroy anyone. I am sorry to have upset you with this demonstration."

Lezama burst in: "Not at all, Lieutenant—that is me talking, and those were my words on one particular day. I don't believe that this is the first or the last time that a man has confronted his own discourse."

We were all deeply moved.

"I will leave now," the official declared.

Lezama said only, "May God protect you!"

The official stared at him as if he had heard an obscenity.

The night of my "performance" ended as had been sketched out in the scenario we had agreed to a few hours before. Afterwards, many people went on to Lezama's house. Luna was the first to arrive. He feverishly recounted what had happened, unaware that Lezama was already fully informed.

"But you, my friend, a devotee of Derrida, are you surprised that a man destroys himself as he confronts his own discourse?"

After Lezama was buried, there were many promotions in the subsection of the political police responsible for watching over writers. They thought that after his death discord would grow and that the intrigues meant to divide the writers and artists who still remained in Cuba would flourish. At the cemetery, we could not fail to notice the brigades of State Security men milling around, as if on maneuvers.

However, the clever strategists in the regime could not have foreseen the historical challenge which culminated in the Mariel exodus. Although they attempted to repair the damage by pretending Mariel was made up of the dregs of Cuban society, those strategists knew the truth. In the end, even they had to depend on writers whom they themselves had cast into obscurity and whom they despised. The triumph, therefore, belonged to poetry. This is the special lesson of José Lezama Lima. He knew that the world of poetry was obliged to reject the temptations of political conformity posed by those who hate poetry, those who hate us. For that reason, he decreed Zenea—the poet executed by the Spaniards in the nineteenth century—the prince of Cuban poetry; we should now name Lezama the prince of resistance and honor.

18

BEFORE THE MEETING at the Writers' Union was to begin, I met
with José Antonio Portuondo, who was to preside, Nicolás
Guillén having roundly refused to participate in what he called
"this farce." And it *was* a farce. The meeting, however, did
stray from the program previously outlined by the officials
with whom we had met at Lezama's. Fidel Castro was enraged
because the protests on my behalf by American and European
writers had not let up. As a last resort, he ordered that the
meeting be recorded and the transcription of the proceedings
distributed by Prensa Latina. This would prove how generously
the revolutionary government had treated a group of self-

confessed counterrevolutionaries. However, the tactic was too clumsy and there were too many precedents in Communist countries in cases where a reputation had to be destroyed. Indeed, far from convincing Castro's critics, the farce made his real purpose all the more clear; this legalism could not conceal the abuse of power.

In any case, Prensa Latina did not publish an exact transcription of what I said. There were sections that the authorities felt should be censored. Neither did they publish the speech by the Haitian poet René Depestre. Since he was under the impression that the meeting was entirely spontaneous, he read out a letter to Fidel concerning the situation of Cuban writers, drawing some parallels. He described as exemplary the approach which the North Vietnamese had used to resolve problems in the cultural area. The letter recommended Cuba emulate their example. After reading his letter, Depestre commented on the meeting, saying that for the first time he found himself attending an encounter of criticism and self-criticism among writers where State Security had conducted itself in an exemplary way; for my part, I had recognized my errors with the same frankness as had my other comrades, who had not hesitated to criticize themselves and vow to correct their ways.

Depestre is alive, but he lives in France. Two days after his speech he was removed from his post at Radio Havana and was never again given the opportunity to read his commentaries in Creole which were broadcast to Haiti. He had no recourse but to ask for an exit visa for his wife and children, which he finally obtained, though with difficulty.

Should anyone want to verify the more concrete aspects of the farce, the letter which I am supposed to have written to the revolutionary government from my cell on May 5 is available. Though shorter, it is basically the same text which I memorized and recited almost down to the last word, as the police had instructed.

The farce seemed to give Fidel Castro pleasure, above all

because of the skill with which I repeated in front of my friends the paragraphs in which the elaboration of my ingratitude toward the leader acquired the requisite degree of vehemence. After I had finished, I was seconded by several friends, who repeated, with the same degree of conviction, the same complete set of errors attributed to us by State Security. After it was all over, we hugged each other. Not even Norberto Fuentes, who brilliantly acted out the role of dissident that had been assigned to him, was able to escape from the histrionic emotion shown by all those present. It was an orgy of revolutionary embracing, aided, no doubt, by the fact that my confession ended with "Fatherland or Death, we shall triumph," the liturgical formulation of revolutionary emotion.

After the hall had emptied, only the actors in the melodrama remained. The last embraces came from the police, who were celebrating along with all of us a meeting where repression had triumphed, where effusive submission to orders had transformed us into docile marionettes for the satisfaction of the Comandante.

The Security man in charge heaped praises on us. Before leaving our group, he said gravely, "Be sure to denounce to Dr. Portuondo any fool who cuts you dead in the street tomorrow. It is very important that we know who goes on being our friend and who does not." My friends were optimistic. "With that kind of support, we have nothing to fear." But I could not hide my own premonition. "After tomorrow," I said, "we will have to tell Portuondo that everyone has greeted us in the street, even our worst enemies."

That night, neither Belkis nor I could sleep. With some Vivaldi playing in the background, we continued our silent conversations. We had already decided to say nothing aloud to each other, because of the hidden microphones. Everything we wanted to say we wrote out on pieces of paper which we piled up before eventually putting a match to them. Belkis told me things that I was unaware of. The more she wrote, the more evident it was that the meeting at the Writers' Union was not going to stifle the international uproar. Far from it. My case had opened up a breach, if not an irreparable rupture, between the repressive policies of the Cuban government and the thinking of writers and artists around the world, who until that moment could not imagine that Fidel Castro would reproduce the methods of Stalin in such a distant and different country.

Clearly, if their objective was to convert Jorge Edwards into a heavy-handed recruiter for the CIA among Cuban writers, the campaign had been a disaster. The equally torpid masquerade that was our "self-criticism" was no less so. No one was taken in. But the morbid fascination felt by a tyrant as he succeeds in humiliating an adversary has other objectives. Even if everyone knew that my debasement was achieved by terror and torture, Castro wanted to make known to the world that Padilla and his friends had acquiesced in the ceremony of self-degradation as the cowards that they were, just as Aníbal Escalante and the rest of the old CP had done. Escalante's own "self-criticism," written in the now classic terminology of the old purge trials, had also been published in *Granma* and other journals as binding evidence of his cowardice.

Just after the publication of the text of my declaration, Octavio Paz analyzed it in an article written for the Mexican journal *Siempre*: ". . . Let us suppose that Padilla is telling the truth, and that he did defame the Cuban regime in his conversations with writers and journalists from abroad. But since when is the destiny of the Cuban Revolution to be played out in the cafés of Saint-Germain-des-Prés or in editorial offices of literary reviews in London or Milan? . . . In order to cleanse the reputation of its directorate, supposedly stained by a few books and articles which cast doubt upon their competence, the Cubans oblige one of their critics to declare himself an accomplice of abject and ultimately insignificant politico-literary intrigues.

"All this would be grotesque," Paz continued, "were it not yet another symptom of the fact that the fatal process is already on the way in Cuba, a process which turns the revolutionary party into a bureaucratic caste and its leader into a Caesar."

My former wife, Berta, and my children, Gisele and María and Carlos, had already heard reactions to the event from foreign broadcasts on the short wave. The general view was summed up in a statement attributed to Gabriel García Márquez: "I do not know if Padilla has done damage to the Revolution as has been alleged, but I do know that his 'self-criticism' is doing damage, a lot of damage."

The government's first mistake was to distribute, through Prensa Latina, a "letter" purportedly by me, asking for clemency. The obvious falsity of the document doubtlessly generated widespread lack of confidence in the other assertions made by the regime. Yet, according to State Security, Fidel had seen a film of the ceremony made exclusively for him; he was satisfied.

A few nights later, Alberto Mora appeared at my apartment in a highly nervous state, and told me that the international campaign against Fidel had intensified; he made a sign to Belkis and grabbed me by the arm. As we went down the hall he told me in a low voice, "I assume that you don't say anything in that apartment."

I told him that we were writing out anything that might be dangerous. As we headed toward his car, he said that we should talk in generalities as we were going along. I thought we were driving to his apartment, but after a while we stopped in front of his mother's house. We entered through a side door into a room separate from the rest of the house. He told me that the situation was getting more complicated and more dangerous. He recounted what Belkis had already described to me—that a few days after my arrest he had written a letter to Fidel expressing his concern about the matter and had handed the letter to Carlos Rafael Rodríguez for him personally to deliver to Fidel. No sooner had Fidel read the letter than he ordered Mora's arrest. Alberto spent only forty-eight hours in State Security, thanks to the intervention of Fidel's close collaborator Celia Sánchez, who had promised Alberto's mother as she was dying that Celia would protect her son from the dangers the old woman saw looming over him. Alberto showed me a copy of the letter. It was long, but I do remember the beginning almost verbatim. Using the intimate *tú* form, the first sentence read, "Fidel, you know that I did not become a revolutionary because of you."

Castro had long before stopped using the *tú* form of address with almost all his old comrades-in-arms. That Alberto had taken up my cause was enough for Castro not only to order Alberto's arrest but to come later to Alberto's cell, where he loudly berated him for giving support to an enemy and casting doubt on revolutionary justice. When Fidel finished, he told Alberto to go see the chief of State Security. This man, named Abrahantes, greeted Alberto effusively, and told him that Fidel had ordered him to send Alberto off on a special mission to check up on some agricultural projects. Fidel wanted Alberto to see how they were going and write up a detailed report. And Abrahantes handed Alberto the keys to a Chevrolet Bel Air.

Alberto told me all this and said, "Monday I'm off to Las Villas Province. I'll be back on Thursday; try to be prudent, because things can really get bad for everybody."

After forty-eight hours the first international reactions to the meeting at the Writers' Union started coming in—round condemnations of Castro's repressive methods. I even received a few cables. One was from Cortázar: "I feel that more than ever I am your brother." Another from Yevtushenko: "Your Russian brother supports you and embraces you—Eugenio." All were supportive, but there was one communication I never expected. When I heard the voice on the telephone—the unmistakable voice of Blas de Otero—I was stupefied. His tone was determined and lively, but there was still his laconic intonation: "Heberto, I'm calling from Madrid. I want you to know that I am on your side and I embrace you. I will sign nothing against you. Don't let anyone have you think otherwise.

Now listen to me, I will *never* sign anything against you. Give a hug to Belkis and everybody else. I know we will see each other soon."

He didn't let me get a word in. He only wanted to convey his message of solidarity. All I was able to say was "Thanks, I love you, Blas." And just then his image took on sharper relief; it was as if he were near, and I continued to think of Blas de Otero as if he were at my side, as he had been during his stay in Havana.

We had met in Paris—1952. His entire life had been dedicated to politics, but his poetry—some of the most original in Spanish in the fifties—was read and esteemed throughout the Hispanic world. Blas de Otero was the poet the Communist Party had been waiting for; invitations from the Soviet Union, China, and the Eastern bloc countries were abundant. He was particularly thrilled by the idea of going to Cuba. Indeed, he spoke of writing an entire book on the subject. More than anything, he wanted to get to know a Spanish-speaking country in the throes of a revolution.

Walking along the streets of the Latin Quarter in Paris, stopping at bookstores, drinking espresso, or smoking one cigar after another, Blas was the image of enthusiasm and vitality, or at least he was to me. Others assured me that he was self-absorbed and churlish, almost inaccessible. I never saw him that way. We visited the places he loved and talked about the poets we were interested in and the poetry that needed to be written. He was a convivial type, and it was only later that I finally realized how disturbed he was. Nonetheless, the telephone call from him in those circumstances was the most moving show of loyalty I could imagine.

It is true that I had received calls from Juan Goytisolo and Julio Cortázar after *Verde Olivo* began its attacks on me and everyone they considered a liberal writer; but then neither Juan nor Julio was a militant Communist of the stripe of Blas de Otero. When he sent me his book *Mientras* in 1970 in the midst of the growing campaign, Blas was breaking with the rigid discipline which Spanish Communists had adopted during the Franco years. But in May of 1971 I was someone just out of prison, surrounded by the confusion that the Cuban government was fomenting through distorted reports sent abroad by Prensa Latina. All of a sudden I had been condemned as an enemy of the Revolution. That was the official posture, and it is well known that no party militant can deviate from it.

I remember our conversations in Paris in the early sixties when Blas spoke to me worriedly but forthrightly about the expulsions of Jorge Semprún and Fernando Claudín from the Spanish Communist Party. He did not hide his sympathy for both men, but he was utterly convinced that the party's decision was not capricious; a true militant was obliged to submit to such a decision. With me, he was acting on his own and at considerable risk. Only then was I able to understand that what was important in life was shared experience that transcended ideology. A revolutionary process can be judged authentically only by those who live through it. Blas had devoted three years of his life to Cuba; from the night when I introduced him at the poetry reading which was to begin his stay in Cuba, we gradually discovered the surprising artistic and literary affinities between us. Blas threw everything he had into the Revolution. Together we traveled to cities and towns, inspected agricultural projects. We took note of idiocies and injustices. What irritated him the most was the self-satisfaction of the bureaucrats, people who had turned Marxism into its own caricature. What he thought of as a caricature I knew by that time to be the real face of things.

Had he discovered upon his return to Spain identical evils in his own party, or, on the contrary, had the party arrived at the same conclusions as he? I do not know. But his spontaneous message of support coming at just that moment went straight from my telephone to a State Security tape recorder, and Blas must have been aware of the fact when he made the call. He had decided that the Cuban Communist Party should know of his support for me, and that its "highest levels," so sensitive to messages in my favor, should know as well. "Nobody can make me sign anything against you," he had said, and he signed nothing. His name never appeared among the small group of professional Communists who had scurried over to the Cuban embassy in Madrid to receive orders from Havana on the Padilla affair. Blas never asked what those orders were, and no one dared suggest that he do so. He was the only Spanish poet who had lived for years in Cuba, written poems in praise of revolutionary labor, performed voluntary work in the fields side by side with the peasants, and published in Cuba the first uncensored edition of his fine book *Que trata de España*. He, Blas de Otero, had refused to accept the rebuke, "Down with intelligence," which the infamous Franco general had delivered to Unamuno. Indeed, Blas and Unamuno were parallel lines in history, and like Unamuno, he never renounced his principles.

Blas had first been invited to visit Cuba in 1964. At that time I was the director of CUBARTIMPEX. Blas brought the complete, uncensored version of *Que trata de España*. I read it immediately and suggested to Alejo Carpentier, who at that time was director of the Editorial Nacional, that we do a generous printing of the book. My organization would pay Blas only $1,500, a ridiculously small sum, but it would nonetheless help the author. Alejo agreed and I sent the stipulated amount as an advance to Blas's bank account in Spain. The book was printed right away. However, according to the Editorial Nacional, Blas was only supposed to receive $750, not $1,500. The grand campaign against making the agreed-upon payment was instigated by Alejo's secretary, whose hatred of the old-line Communists was limitless. For her, the party began and ended with Fidel. Blas never found out the true cause of the conflict, and I am not at all sure it was ever straightened out.

The years 1964 and 1965 were happy ones for Blas. We were both invited to become members of the poetry jury for the Casa de las Américas Prize, along with the Argentine Juan Gelman and the American poet Marc Schleiffer. This gave us the opportunity to read and discuss the many books under consideration. As we did so, our affinity began to grow into a real friendship.

Blas made many friends in Cuba—above all, among younger writers. He was very much taken with the colloquial poetry being written in Cuba at the time. He, too, wanted to free himself from the closed forms so typical of traditional poetic practice in Spain, and he succeeded particularly in the poems written in Spain after his return from Cuba. In all of them there is a sense of ease and unpredictable rhythmic movement, driven constantly by the will to displace the old forms which he had mastered in his earlier work. There were no technical devices in the Spanish language that he could not make use of. His favorite poet was Juan Ramón Jiménez, whom he read assiduously over the years. The writer he was least interested in was Miguel de Unamuno. He loved the work of Camus. He told me that there were two books of Camus that "drove ecclesiastical fear from me—*Noces* and *L'Eté*." Although he had obviously read Camus intensely when he was a young man, his partisan militancy prevented him from identifying with the Algerian's broader and more humane vision. Blas used to complain that the feelings of solidarity evident in *La Peste* never led Camus to discover the true solidarity which for him was to be found only in the ideology of the "working class."

I remember an occasion when Blas called me to say that he wanted to see me and "tell me something." I went to see him, this time at the Hotel Riviera. He seemed happy. He had on sandals, gray pants, and a white shirt with the sleeves rolled up. That was when he told me that he had fallen in love and that he was getting married, and he wanted me to be at the wedding and act as witness. We had a few drinks to celebrate the occasion.

Blas decided to bring Yolanda, his Cuban wife, back to

Bilbao to visit his family. In a letter he wrote me from Spain, nothing seems to cast a shadow over his matrimonial or familial relations.

Dear Heberto:

After our long trips and visits, rested now, we write these lines to you to see how you are and to send you above all our warmest embrace. We stopped for a while in Prague and then in Paris, where I had a few publishing matters to take care of. We have been in Madrid too, and have asked about you when we saw some of your friends. We have delayed writing you, because we hoped to see you here. We are staying in Bilbao for a while, catching up with paperwork; you know that when you are on a trip you can't even think about such matters, because there are other things that are so much more interesting. We've decided that Andresito should return home, where he can get a better education. And we regret it very much, as you can imagine. We want to go back to Cuba as soon as everything is settled here. Soon we will go to Madrid to see if I can get things moving and make a little money . . .

. . . It turns out that on one of our rainy afternoons I came across a book of poems quite by chance. I read it and I have to tell you that I thought they were very good (and I hardly ever get to the word "good" when judging poetry). It was your *El justo tiempo humano*. There's a diffuse climate there, a bright poetic mystery which you've joined with what is real and what is experienced, with a kind of verse and rhythm really free, but closely adapted to the meaning. Tell me if you've been writing more, if you've been publishing . . .

I'd love to hear news from you. Has it been HOT HOT? Don't let your pen fall asleep. A big hug for you from

Blas

Bilbao 5-XI-64

In 1965, when I was in Europe as a representative of the Foreign Ministry, we saw each other again in Prague. He called me from the hotel where he was staying with Yolanda. He was going to return to Cuba for a while, he said. The Spanish Communist Party had organized the trip and his house in the

Santos Suárez barrio was waiting for him. I found out then that he had finished his book *Poesía e historia*, which he dedicated to me. Perhaps it is his worst book, the most repetitive, the one with the most superficial and mechanical kind of political enthusiasm, but even there you can find some observations made in his usual subtle manner. He said that China was wonderful but "one must leave it for the moment." He felt a genuine sympathy with Cuba, but revolutionary chauvinism drove him crazy. As always, his poems were aimed at the "immense majority," that generic entity which, like Spain, formed part of a prior fervor.

19

ONE SUMMER AFTERNOON in 1968, Blas called me on the telephone, as he did so many times, to ask me to come over to the Havana Libre, because "I have to tell you something important." I could hear in his voice the first signs of one of his nervous collapses; in a few minutes I knew he would be overcome by asphyxia and bouts of weeping. For many months before, I had been witness to many of these crises; and I had been his only confidant. Before going to the hotel, I called Enrique Oltuski to tell him my fears. Although Oltuski was no longer a minister, he still had some influence in the government and was the only person I could enlist when Blas had the initial attack in Havana.

On that first occasion, I was unable to find a single vehicle in the vicinity, and the nearest physician was at the Military Hospital. Because I thought that it might be the beginning of a heart attack, I had asked Oltuski to come over quickly. He was there in fifteen minutes, and during that time the pills that Blas took to weather the crisis began to have their effect. With tears in his eyes and barely breathing, he apologized, and then went on to describe this illness that no doctor anywhere (and he mentioned consultations in France, the Soviet Union, and China) had been able to cure. It always started with a sudden attack of depression, followed by bursts of tears and hallucinations in which he saw himself wandering the streets of Bilbao, with his family glaring at him as if he were a condemned man. In the dream, he would then board a ship, and the dream would end abruptly with a vision of hordes of worms coming out of an immense nose.

Whatever it was, he never found a cure. Just after that first attack, Oltuski had suggested that we take him to the Naval Hospital, whose chief administrator happened to be his brother-in-law. The psychiatry section was headed by a Dr. Fleitas, a young man trained in the United States and in the Soviet Union. He diligently assembled a team of specialists, some of whom knew Blas's poetry. They treated him with an empathy which relaxed him, and Blas raised no objection to staying on at the hospital. That evening he would be given a tranquilizer. The next day Dr. Fleitas and his associates would study the case. Blas kissed his wife goodbye, asked her "to forgive him once again," and went into his room.

As we left the hospital, I asked his wife, Yolanda, what his words to her meant. She burst into tears. Though she said nothing at the time, she did reveal on the way home that her husband's crises were becoming more frequent. She described to me the same dream that Blas had told me. "He feels ashamed every time he recovers, and asks forgiveness. Didn't he do that with all of you?" In effect, he had. I asked if the party was aware of the situation.

"Well, he tells everyone that it is a case of mental fatigue, and the only person who knows the truth is General Modesto. He is like a father to Blas."

Blas's new request that I come by the hotel was alarming, so I again called Oltuski. Blas was waiting in front of the hotel. He was wearing the same clothes that he had on when he entered the hospital. It was clear that he hadn't shaved, but his smile as he greeted me reassured me a bit.

"Where did you leave the car?" he asked me calmly.

"Right there, on the corner."

"Good, why don't we take a drive around old Havana."

As we were going down 23rd Street toward the Malecón, he craned his neck every which way and, as he spoke, never stopped looking around.

"Do you trust Oltuski?"

"Absolutely," I said vehemently.

"Calm down. I trust him, too. I even think his brother-in-law might be innocent."

"What's going on, Blas?"

He laughed. "It's no big deal. I was finally able to escape."

I am trying to remember his words just as he said them. At that moment I felt as close to insanity as he did.

According to Blas, he was about to become a victim of the best-organized kidnapping that the party was able to pull off. He added that certain breaches in party discipline on his part had made a drastic corrective necessary; during the Cultural Congress in Havana it had been suggested ("to avoid using another word") that his colleagues in the Spanish CP felt that a Spanish militant should not ever marry a foreigner, even a Cuban.

"But Yolanda is a foreigner only in a relative sense," I argued. "Besides, she speaks Spanish and comes from a socialist country."

He smiled wryly. "That is what I thought."

I went on, saying what he already knew, that Yolanda was the chief librarian at the Writers' and Artists' Union, and, on top of that, was a writer from a humble family. What better qualifications?

Nonetheless, the "suggestion" had been made, and Blas was convinced that Dr. Fleitas was in charge of carrying out the kidnapping. The pills given to him at the hospital were made in Russia and the doctor insisted that he take them every hour or so, something which of course Blas was very careful not to do.

"The Chinese would have been more subtle," he said. Surely, Fleitas had not noticed his absence. He would go back that night.

"You must speak to Oltuski. You must warn him. This plan could only have been cooked up by the party. You must warn all Cubans. I must see someone important. Do you understand?"

I brought him over to my house and asked him to wait for me in the library, which had the advantage of being separate from the rest of the house and having its own entrance. When I turned on the air conditioner and the cool air began to have its effect, he slumped into a chair and asked, "Do you think they would dare come and get me here?"

"We would put up a fight," I told him. "Take it easy; I'll talk to Oltuski."

I asked if he wanted water or something to drink.

"If you have a beer and some soda water, that would be nice. I'm exhausted."

It took a long time to convince Blas that he should go back to his home in the Santos Suárez barrio. I tried to reassure him; I promised him that everything would be all right. When Oltuski arrived at my place, Blas gave him a hug and suggested that we both take him home, feeling safe in our hands. Someone must have forewarned Yolanda. When we came in, she showed no sign of surprise that her husband was out of the hospital. Blas seemed calm. He kissed her and then went to bed.

We left Blas's house and again went to see Dr. Fleitas and the general administrator at the Naval Hospital. They were worried. Fleitas in particular believed that Blas's behavior was more significant than he had thought at first. He said he had spoken to Blas, trying to find topics of mutual interest. He had mentioned the Soviet Union, but that seemed to upset the poet. It was clear that Blas was terrified of the country he thought Fleitas was working for. These associations were typical of specific pathologies, but who would have imagined that a militant Communist of the stature of Blas de Otero had gotten himself into such a state? The psychiatrist was unable at that time to make a definitive diagnosis, but everything pointed toward schizophrenia and the crises would become more frequent during periods of tension. Did we know if anything more deep-seated was troubling him? I kept silent about what I knew.

The psychiatrist emphasized that this was a situational crisis from which Blas could recuperate only if the underlying difficulty was resolved. Fleitas was intrigued by what he saw as an ideological involution of the poet's primal beliefs. According to him, the basic religious foundation of Blas's upbringing was in conflict with his more recent political militancy. That was the most likely cause of the crisis, barring other, unknown psychosomatic causes. Dr. Fleitas could not hide his frustration in dealing with his patient. "I would have liked to help him, but he had made a transference in which I occupy the place of the enemy." He asked that we keep informed; perhaps Yolanda would be of assistance. Yes, she would be the one to talk to.

As Dr. Fleitas spoke, his face showed real concern. Oltuski's brother-in-law repeatedly emphasized that they had tried to set things up so that Blas would feel as if he were in his own home. The doors of the hospital would always be open to Blas; even more important, those were direct orders from the party.

That evening we found out that the party was indeed concerned over the problem, but their solicitude did not turn out well. We went back to visit Blas at home to see how he was. Through a grilled window we saw him covered with sweat, wearing the same rumpled white shirt; he looked out at us with bloodshot eyes and the expression of a madman. He laughed at us, but didn't open the door.

"A Russian came by," he shouted. "Somebody named Vladímir. He even showed me his identity card. Vladímir Rodríguez. The Chinese would have been more subtle."

He kept on laughing and repeating the same line. ". . . more subtle, much more subtle. Vladímir Rodríguez. The first and last names don't match. Only a nut would think up such a ruse."

Just then Yolanda appeared at Blas's shoulder. She seemed more defenseless and harried than ever. She said to him, "Open the door for them, Blas," and he obeyed. His crazed face changed immediately. Once again he became the helpless infant—he had placed himself in our hands. He described in a detailed and eloquent manner the unexpected visit of the so-called Vladímir Rodríguez, "who was trying to trick me by pretending that he was a Cuban functionary, a member of State Security. Of course I didn't open the door. I did the right thing, no?"

Both of us told him no, he had done the wrong thing.

His eyes filled with tears He spoke in a kind of strangled voice, sobbing. "So, both of you, too? You, Heberto, and you, Enrique, you too are against Yolanda?"

"We're against the idea that somebody wants to harm you," I told him. "You know very well that I would never want anyone to do anything to either of you."

He sat there looking at me for a long time.

"I'm not a member of the party, Blas. I owe nothing to its discipline. Neither does Enrique. You know very well that no one wants to harm you. You must believe us and speak openly to us."

He fell back in his chair, weeping.

Yolanda whispered to us, "He hasn't eaten a thing." I asked

her why. "There's nothing to eat in the house, we've used up the ration card for the month."

"Come on," I said. "Let's go out to eat. It's on me." Yolanda wanted to change her dress. Blas would go as he was. When Yolanda went off to change, Blas fell silent. Enrique and I said nothing for a few minutes, not knowing what to do. From his chair, you could hear him muttering without looking at us: "They are there and say nothing. They don't speak to me, they say nothing to me."

He got to his feet and walked around the room. He was speaking about us as if we didn't exist. Mercifully, Yolanda returned. "Let's go, Blas, we're all hungry."

Still disoriented, he was brought back to normal, more or less, by his wife's words. We finally left the house. My breezy invitation turned into a meager meal at the Havana bus station restaurant, where my friend Moisés Sierra was a waiter. I had known him since childhood, and he converted our late appearance into a sort of family gathering, joined by the other employees. Blas seemed to cheer up in their company. He loved to be with ordinary people and learn local turns of phrase.

The isolated location of Blas's house in the Santos Suárez barrio couldn't have been more inappropriate for someone like him. Rationing in Cuba was insufficient for any normal person, let alone for him, since the doctors had recommended a diet rich in proteins and vegetables, which were completely unobtainable.

I don't remember the name of the functionary in charge of his case at the Central Committee of the party, but I do remember down to the last detail the man's unusually pale skin, his nonexistent eyebrows and balding head of hair. He told us soberly that he was fully aware of the Blas de Otero case, and he seemed to be as worried as the rest of us. A decision had been made to invite Blas to take up residence in the Hotel Havana Libre.

"That way, there will no problem with food, and he will be attended to by efficient revolutionary employees."

His later stay at the hotel was the happiest part of Blas's three-year residence in Cuba. He was able to communicate more openly with Yolanda and spoke very frankly to her about his situation. Convinced that divorce or separation would endanger her situation in Cuba, Blas decided that Yolanda and her child, Andrés, should take Spanish citizenship, and he promised that he would make no mention of a possible separation until they were in Spain, safely removed from any threat of repressive measures. The decision was made for all three to leave.

As I said goodbye to Blas for the last time, I felt that I was embracing a very ill man. I never saw him more defenseless or so melancholic. As I was leaving the airport terminal, I ran into the party functionary in charge of his case. This time, he had thick eyebrows and I barely recognized him.

"Well, we can relax now that the poet has left us," he said, smiling. There was another man standing next to him, about the same height, with flushed skin and thick gray hair. It was Vladímir Rodríguez. When the functionary introduced him, Rodríguez described what happened the day he went to visit Blas at his home. "When I showed him my State Security identity card, it was if I were from the CIA. The only thing he said to me was 'Let's see now, say it again'; I told him I had been sent by the Central Committee to help him in any way possible, and he said I would have to knock the door down if I wanted to come in. They say he is deranged. Of course, with the struggles he must have undergone in his own country, one can understand . . ."

For me, Blas de Otero's departure was the end of an era. A few weeks later I received a postcard from Bilbao which ended with the same formula as always—"A hug from Blas." I am not sure how Blas found out about some of the more flagrant injustices in Cuba which took place after he left. Perhaps tales of some of these things filtered out through members of the Spanish Communist Party. I received a note from him at the height of the scandal caused by my being awarded the Poetry Prize from the Writers' Union: "Prudence and calm," he wrote. Then five years passed and I did not hear from him. Someone had told me that he was ill, and I found out later that he had been operated on for cancer. But in 1978, when Fidel Castro sought to inaugurate a policy of greater communication with the Cuban exile community through a so-called Dialogue (this was around the time of the visit of the Spanish Prime Minister Adolfo Suárez to Cuba), a Spanish journalist brought me two books of Blas's, *Todos mis sonetos* and *Poesía con nombres*. Slipped into the pages of the books were two poems in typed script, apparently unpublished, with Cuban themes: "Imberbe Imago" and "Me complace más que el mar," a title taken from a verse by Martí. The first poem was set in the Santos Suárez barrio and simply describes one of Blas's recurrent dreams during his illness; in the poem, Paris is now the city in which things appear "with a hat of Spring / and great straw wings / and ashen eyes and pimply mouth and a nose bursting forth with tiny worms." The second poem is a kind of self-portrait in which he sees himself as "simply in the midst of a Revolution, opening my eyes wide to learn all that is good and all that is perhaps avoidable."

To learn, then, not only all that is good but also all that is perhaps avoidable. Around that time I got news that I would be given permission to leave Cuba. Since the most energetic pressures to obtain an exit visa for me were coming from Spain, my first thought was to go there and see Blas again. But a few days before I was to leave I was officially informed that I could travel neither to Miami nor to Madrid; I had to go to New York via Montreal. It was then that I received news of his death.

So we were never able to speak, as we had so many other times since we had first met in Paris in 1962, talking perhaps of all that is perhaps inevitable. Those were years when we discussed anxiously whether Stalin's concentration camps were inevitable, whether the lack of political debate within any Communist Party was inevitable, whether the lack of freedom and the accompanying predominance of State Security were inevitable elements of that "classless society" which he so ingenuously believed to be possible. Blas always said, "Perhaps, perhaps it can be avoided." Our talks often lasted till dawn, as we walked around the torrid streets of Havana after all the cafés had shut for the night. Blas used to say to me, "I say *perhaps* because there are always semibarbarous procedures in any attempt to transform a society. What is so terrible is that the Communist tribunals so closely resemble the Spanish Inquisition."

Blas strode from crisis to crisis, trying to put together the hidden, broken world of his religious faith. "Oh complexion of the world, oh beautiful God, / oh flesh of my flesh and of my soul / flesh which without You drifts away like the fog."

In his last poems, the thirst for God becomes more explicit than ever. His return to Spain and his long residence in Madrid were an odd fluke which only his death put an end to. I do not know where he is buried, but his work does belong integrally to the Spanish language, a classic of our century without folklorism or regionalism.

20

BETWEEN 1971 and 1978 I was under constant surveillance and under a kind of de facto house arrest, only permitted to stay in my apartment or to visit my old house, which was still occupied by my former wife, Berta, and my two oldest children. I was fortunate to have that house, which had never been closed to me either before or after my troubles. Most of my friends lay low and took refuge in their homes, because State Security continued to persecute everyone they classified as "disaffected." One group of young people, who had been in the habit of meeting in front of the Rivero funeral home to talk about literature and politics, found they had been infiltrated by agents pretending to be writers and artists—the most active and vociferous dissidents in the group found themselves denounced to the police.

The party was ready to impose drastic measures on all the artists and writers who remained active in the Union. They distributed new identity cards that would be necessary for continuing membership; whoever did not receive a new card was automatically excluded from the Union. Thus the membership was reduced to a fraction of what it had been. State Security organized the literary competitions, and the works awarded prizes were typical imitations of the worst of Soviet literature and Central European writing. The number of participants from the Soviet bloc increased, but writers such as Yevtushenko, Ilya Ehrenburg, and Voznesensky became forbidden names. Literature was now at the service of the party, and its themes had to be carefully chosen by appointed study circles—a direct importing of the Soviet line from Stalin's time. My friends were reduced to the group which had participated in my "self-criticism" at the Writers' Union. Often I was visited by Alberto Martínez Herrera, who sweated through many weekends in my apartment, and of course Alberto Mora, who, though he tried to remain optimistic about his future, was never able to recover his position within the government.

I remember that on the 13th of September of 1972 at three in the afternoon Mora dropped by the apartment to leave a copy of Hemingway's recent novel, *Islands in the Stream*. The work had greatly impressed him and he had read it more than once, but since it was the property of the Writers' Union library and there was a list of people waiting to read it, he thought he would save a few steps by giving it to Belkis in our apartment. Belkis worked at the Union. But she was in fact at work, and he stayed only a few minutes. That night, just before supper, Mora went into his bedroom and shot himself in the head. I was aware that, in addition to his general state of depression, he was going through a personal crisis. He had put too much hope in his recent marriage, but it was not going well, just one more in a long line of failures.

Carlos Verdecia and I had worked with Mora in the Ministry of Foreign Commerce, and Carlos greeted me with consternation at the funeral home. He, too, knew everything that Mora had gone through and this only intensified his grief.

During that time I saw Verdecia often. He was out of work and was being closely watched by State Security because he had resigned his post as vice minister, with the intention of leaving the country. For years he helped me with my clandestine work. He would type out Spanish versions of Russian books that had been bought by the State Publishing House. I earned some money by polishing up those texts before their publication. We were paid three dollars per page, split three ways between the original translator, who did the rough version, and Carlos and me. We had to take precautions so as not to arouse the neighbors' suspicions, since the typewriter could be heard day and night. Occasionally, Alberto Martínez Herrera would stop by and tell us about his latest run-in with the State Security people who were following him. He was expert at identifying them and usually had no trouble losing them in a crowd.

For State Security, the truly dangerous people were the foreigners who tried to see me. The neighborhood block committee was in charge of keeping track of all visitors and passing along the details to the higher authorities. The foreigners would always call first on the telephone; I was told to ask them to call back the next day. No sooner would I hang up than the telephone would ring again. A voice from State Security would order me to "squash him"—that is, reject any invitation by that person—or would say that someone from the Cultural Council would call and tell me what to do.

In the end, the government decided that the most efficacious way for me to avoid journalists from abroad was for us to move to the country, to one of Fidel's famous model farms.

They sent us to a plantation in the Escambray area. There a house was set up especially for us, freshly painted, with an electric stove and a refrigerator. For the peasants working on the farm, these amenities made us seem like higher-ups who were studying the project to which Fidel would give the go-ahead in due course. Fidel was determined to change the character of the region, which had been sympathetic to counterrevolutionary activities. He decided that all families known to be anti-government should be transferred to distant towns, so there would be no trace of them left. Some were sent to La Yaya, an urbanized development typical of Fidel's stubborn drive to make organized collective farmers out of simple peasants.

Belkis and I were invited to this new town, which Fidel himself was to inaugurate two months later. The houses had that hard, sterile look of prefabricated Soviet structures. La Yaya had been built atop a hill from which we could contemplate the thick vegetation that had served for years as a base of insurgency.

Our guide was the head of the party for the region, whom everyone called Chao—an easygoing, cordial man who was attentive to our every need. After he showed us around the town, he stopped at the last house at the edge of town, and as he stomped his boots on the ground, he said, "You can't imagine the tons of rock we had to bring up here to build this town."

I asked him why.

"Crazy Fidel decided to build La Yaya in the only place the engineers said it couldn't be done. There's no bedrock here at all—we had it all brought up from below to make the foundations for the houses." And he burst out laughing.

He would laugh for no reason at all as he pointed out the rows of orange and banana trees or as he passed around cigars of the highest quality; he would laugh when he gave the order to have the best cheese and milk brought to our house, or when he would shout out, "Bring them a couple of cartons of

Milián's meat," a canned minced meat which the head of the party in the province (a man named Milián) kept on hand in case of a sudden appearance by Fidel.

In our kitchen, the cartons of canned *picadillo* piled up; some of the officials from the town would even stop by to ask us to share these with them. They simply could not figure out what our function was supposed to be, or the reason why Chao would visit us so often, always laughing. Belkis and I began to worry about how such excesses would be justified.

We were in a jeep on the way to a town called Trinidad when I brought the matter to Chao's attention. He said nothing. He stopped on the bridge over the Guaurabo River, where Hernán Cortés had anchored to clean and caulk his ships. A flock of ducks was gliding serenely through the water. He took out his pistol, aimed, and hit the nearest duck, which disappeared underwater only to reappear a few feet away a moment later.

Chao was really laughing now. "Padilla, you've got to learn a lesson from that duck. See, even though you shoot him, he's unsinkable."

So we went on living in the house in this anomalous situation. The whole town benefited from the food that was given to us. And Chao went on doling out those high-quality cigars, the kind cigarmakers keep for themselves rather than sell.

I learned through Alberto Mora that Fidel wanted me to become acquainted with the Revolution's plans for the development of the countryside. The model farm was only one example. Fidel had the erroneous idea that my discontent was caused by ignorance of the government's achievements. Every morning a horse would be saddled up for me and Chao and I would trot off for a morning ride, occasionally accompanied by his assistant, an old man who carried his own stock of cigars. The ones he smoked kept going out, while the ones I was smoking glowed down to the last puff. One day I asked him why he smoked such bad cigars in a province that produced the best tobacco on the island.

He answered laconically: "Comrade, these are the only ones I can get. You're lucky, getting them direct from the party as you do."

Chao had assured me that everyone in Cumanayagua smoked the same high-quality cigars, and I told this to the old man.

He smiled. "It's that we buy them in different state stores, comrade. Ask Chao where he gets his, and you'll find out."

I soon discovered that all of Chao's statements and reassurances to me were alike. The local cheeses, the milk, the meat, the butter—all of it came from a mysterious reserve set up for us alone. If that was the reality that they wanted me to get to know, it was a privileged reality which only exacerbated my depression and discontent.

One morning when Chao came to visit us, I said to him, "We're leaving, we are not staying one more day. We're leaving, we're leaving right now."

This time he didn't laugh. "I have no orders to stop you," he said. "If you want, I'll have a party car pick you up to take you back to Havana. I did everything I could, but in your case, frankly, no one is going to change you."

Those were the same words Alberto Mora repeated to me when I came back to Havana. "They say that you keep having the same critical and arrogant ideas as before. That's what Fidel thinks. You're going to have to eat that cheese if they give it to you, smoke those cigars if they give them to you, eat the *picadillo* if they give it to you."

That morning Alberto was going off to Pinar del Río, where he would supervise one of the "planifications" that Fidel had assigned him after his return from Las Villas. He had asked me to join him so that we would be able to talk along the way. When we got back, around dusk, I asked him to drive by the "Puerta de golpe," where my grandparents' farm was located. I particularly wanted to see "El colmenar," the place where I had spent my childhood and where my uncle and aunt still lived. I wanted to see it at sunset, in the same fading light which had exalted my imagination when I was young. There stood the house of my maternal grandfather, who had been born in the Canary Islands. When I was a child, I would pester him with questions about the landscape and the climate of his native land. "It's hardly any different from here," he would insist.

I should say here that I was brought up with a love of Spain, something that doesn't happen even to many Spaniards. I never experienced any kind of regionalism, nor did I have to express myself in a language other than the one I learned as a child. Cuban provincial towns, and for that matter Havana itself, are full of centers where Galicians, Basques, Asturians, and other groups from the Spanish provinces gather on social occasions. For me, it was that diversity of peoples on the peninsula which made up the essence of Spain. I was convinced that even the climate of the different regions of Spain was reproduced in Cuba, a geographical extension of those Canary Islands which my grandfather assured me he never missed for a moment.

Many years later, in 1981, I would visit the Canary Islands, "hardly any different from here," my own island. I was on a plane from Barcelona to Las Palmas, the capital of the island group, accompanied by Rafael Soriano and J. J. Armas Marcelo, executives from the publishing firm Arcos Vergara, which had just brought out my novel *Heroes Are Grazing in My Garden*. Just before landing, I looked out the window, peering anxiously down toward the earth. Armas Marcelo said, "There they are, look at them . . . crouching like animals about to pounce."

The islands are enormous promontories of rock and ash, with the towns and cities perched on the gray-black lava. From above, the houses are inviting and attractive, painted in a myriad pastel colors. We stayed at the Hotel Iberia, facing the ocean. I hardly slept that night; I opened the window and looked out onto the water. On the horizon I could see a single boat; closer, some docks with blinking lights as in any port town. It was Cuba again, but without the abundant vegetation of the tropics. When I walked through Las Palmas with my new friends, as effusive and carefree as my own countrymen, I discovered a city like Havana, with the same climate and the same colonial barrios. I then understood why my grandfather never returned to the Canaries, which had been for him, and for so many others like him, the portal to the New World. On the other side of the ocean he had found a verdant, prodigious, outsized replica of the islands. He must have thought that his opportunity, after much sacrifice, to buy two tobacco farms was a gift from God. He lived on one of them for the rest of his life, and that is where I was born.

That time which I spent with my grandfather was the only part of my childhood that I remember with a real sense of joy. They were solid days, with everything in its place. The familial order was maintained in an unchanging fashion: grandfathers, parents, uncles and aunts, sisters and cousins. Until I was ten years old, I lived in harmonious surroundings centering on the two growing seasons of the island. In the summer, the peasants would rake the fields clean until they appeared burnt and desolate. We loved to walk behind the machine which piled up withered tobacco stalks and the dry hay, which were later stacked at the four corners of the property. My grandparents were both producers and sellers of tobacco. My trips from Pinar del Río to Havana were always associated with crates of the leaf. On either side of Monte Street stood the wholesalers' stores. My grandfather's store was there too, spacious and spotless, with a bitter, acrid smell.

When I started grade school, the family began to have financial problems. Although my father was a full-time lawyer, I heard him make a few remarks late at night about the fate of the family properties, which had been mortgaged heavily in a vain attempt to keep the rapidly declining tobacco business going. My paternal grandfather tried to commit suicide at the age of ninety. The maternal branch of the family was more prudent and better organized. It was able to hold on to its properties. But after I was twelve my visits to the country grew less frequent and the family never again spent school vacations there. The financial help that came from the wholesale tobacco store in Havana also disappeared, and my parents' situation became precarious just as my sister Marta and I started secondary school.

Alberto Mora and I did drive to the property, but though we stopped for a moment, I refused to get out of the car. There stood the old house of my childhood, now surrounded by pine seedlings. The house itself lay empty and abandoned. As I looked at it, I felt a strange horror, and I asked Alberto to drive on. I know that we should never return to the places where we were happy, because such places belong to memory and cannot stand up under the weight of nostalgia, veneration, or homage. Now I did not have a home anymore, not even in my memory.

When I got back to the apartment, I found Belkis asleep and I tried not to wake her. Far more than the nostalgia that linked me to a lost childhood, Belkis was what was keeping me alive.

In December of 1972 our son Ernesto was born. We had wanted to have a child before it was too late for both of us. Of course, the baby's arrival changed our life, but the years dragged on, identical and monotonous. Our son grew and our close friends died. First it was Alberto Mora, then José Lezama Lima. In 1975, St.-John Perse died in the France that he never thought he would return to when we met in Washington so many years before.

Our reduced circle was joined by a painter from Murcia, Spain, named José Cid, who lived close by. Belkis had begun to write her novel *Juan y Juana*, and every Saturday, Cid and Alberto Martínez would stop by to listen to her read the pages she had just written. Belkis was painting with enormous enthusiasm and energy, but we were both convinced that our working lives in Cuba were over. None of our work was being published. Once Nicolás Guillén, who was editing the magazine

Unión, tried to publish my translations of five poems by William Blake. State Security forbade it.

We were closely guarded. And we were working in lower categories than before: Belkis was assigned as proofreader to the *Nueva Gaceta de Cuba* at the Writers' Union, and I went from published writer to translator in the Editorial Arte y Literatura. After our return to Havana from the countryside, the regime became even more openly hostile.

In 1978 the monotony of those years was suddenly broken when Fidel Castro decided to usher in a more liberal policy toward the exile community abroad. Many thousands of Cubans returned for short visits to the island, and former political prisoners and members of separated families were given permission to leave the country. These new conditions allowed my former wife, Berta, and the children to leave for Spain, where they took up my cause with the then Prime Minister Adolfo Suárez. I, too, lost no opportunity to approach anyone I thought might help me to leave—that is, to choose life once again. With that objective in mind, I decided to contact Gabriel García Márquez during one of his visits to Havana.

I knew that the Hotel Riviera, where he was staying, was full of State Security people; so, around nine in the evening, I entered the hotel through the side entrance facing the sea, which led to the basement, where the cafeteria was located. Next to the men's room there was a bank of telephones. Since I knew the house phones were tapped, I used one of the public telephones and dialed the number of the Riviera and asked for his room.

A man's voice answered in a Cuban accent. I told him my name and I heard him repeat it aloud. García Márquez came to the phone. He greeted me cordially; I said that I wanted to see him as soon as possible. He told me that he could not just then—he was with friends. But "tomorrow at nine in the morning I'll be waiting for you here in the hotel."

I was afraid that in the intervening hours State Security would try to prevent me from seeing him. I told him that I wanted to talk to him about my desire to leave the country; that was the only reason for my call.

"Do you think I can help you?"

I said that I thought he could, because he was at the head of a human-rights group called Habeas Corpus.

"Come tomorrow at nine and I will be waiting for you."

"If I don't come, it is because I have been prevented from coming."

I got up early and told Belkis that if I had not called by noon, she should call me at García Márquez's room. At that early hour in the morning it was almost impossible to find a taxi. I stood by a clump of trees near the closest traffic light. I could see any car coming, but they could not see me. At seven-thirty a shabby taxi slowed down for the red light. It was empty; I opened the door and got in, somewhat startling the old, thin driver. I told him that it was an emergency and that I would pay him well if he took me where I wanted to go—first I would have to pick up my wages at a certain spot at eight o'clock, and then to the Hotel Riviera, where I had an appointment at nine. He said it would cost twenty pesos; I gave him twenty-five. Everything went as planned. At nine sharp I entered the hotel the same way as before and called García Márquez. He said he would be right down to ask permission to bring me up to his room for our talk—visitors were not permitted in the guests' rooms in Cuban hotels. I calculated how much time it would take him to get to the lobby. After a while I saw him come out of an elevator, looking to the left and the right. I walked toward him and he shook my hand warmly. Suddenly we were approached by two agents from State Security. I could see another man, Gustavo Casta-ñeda, the agent in charge of my case, coming toward us breathlessly. I told him to come closer; I shook his hand. García Márquez did not seem to understand the situation.

"Gabriel, this is an official from State Security and these two other men are agents who want to prevent our conversation from taking place."

Gustavo answered calmly, saying that I was exaggerating, that García Márquez should not pay any attention to me. The three men then left.

As we went up in the elevator, García Márquez said, "Your friend was not happy with your introduction."

"That's his job."

We sat down on the big sofa in his suite. He began to talk. "Rolando Rodríguez, the director of the Book Institute, assured me that you were working for him without any problem, and that you avoid the foreigners who want to take up your cause, but I can see that things are not going well."

I told him of my desire to go to Spain, where my older children were living. So as not to alarm him, I insisted that my reasons for leaving were not political but "humanitarian."

"You have chosen a bad moment. Your case is still being talked about, and if you go off to Spain now, there are plenty of Cuban counterrevolutionaries waiting to turn you into a symbol."

I tried to make clear that I had no political connections with any group of exiles, but he insisted worriedly that there would be journalists waiting for me at the Madrid airport, and plenty of them. The Padilla affair would be revived at the most inopportune time. "I urge you to think about that," he told me. He then went on to say that the Padilla affair had caused a breach between himself and his best friends. All the Latin American intellectual community had been affected by this business.

"I've wanted to erase your case from my mind." He made a gesture with the palm of his hand to emphasize what he was saying. Now he was finding out that the man in charge of the Book Institute had not told him the truth, and that the problem had not been resolved. I said that my children and other relatives in Spain had used the occasion of Suárez's trip to Cuba to plead my case through diplomatic channels. But the Cuban government denied that the Spanish delegation had brought up the matter officially. García Márquez asked me who had told me those things.

"The official who tried to stop me from seeing you downstairs."

"And why do you think that what he was telling you was a lie?"

"Because I have many letters from my family in Spain telling me that I would be able to leave after a group of Spaniards in Cuba who wanted to return home had boarded the planes sent to Havana by the Spanish government. I would follow them. José Luis Cueto of the Spanish Secret Service and Señor Aza, Suárez's administrative assistant, explained the procedure to my family."

My friend Pablo Armando Fernández had told me that Cueto had stopped by his apartment in Havana one morning to show him a photograph of himself with my family in Spain, and that I should know that the Cuban government had decided to allow me to leave. García Márquez asked me for details concerning the efforts made on my behalf by members of the Suárez delegation, but I said I did not want to go on with that petition. Instead, I preferred that he, García Márquez, take up my case.

"I repeat that I want to take advantage of the opportunity being offered former political prisoners, and persons who feel out of place in Cuba. It has been officially stated that all such persons may leave the country. I say it to you here in this room because I know that what we are saying is being recorded on tape."

García Márquez burst out laughing. "You have too much faith in State Security."

"Why do you say that? It seems obvious that the government would want to know what you talk about with visitors. Everyone knows who you are. If I were Chief of State I would hang an invisible microphone inside your shirt."

"I should tell you that I am the first to criticize this revolution."

"But you haven't been invited here because of your criticism. We would all like to say what we feel, but you have been invited because you grew closer to the Revolution just as the majority of writers abroad stopped supporting it."

He kept moving his leg up and down. I saw he had on maroon boots of tanned leather. They were very popular in Spain at that time.

"You are right in thinking that I can help you," he said slowly, "but I won't. I think you should think it over. Your leaving Cuba at this moment would harm the Revolution."

The suite occupied by García Márquez was identical to the one used by Jorge Edwards. The same furniture was set up throughout the room and in the same way. The only thing different was a new refrigerator and a bar with bottles of mineral water and Johnnie Walker Black Label. García Márquez drew back the curtains; through the picture window the tropical sun flooded the room with light.

"Would you like a drink?"

I said that a character in Graham Greene had said that at certain moments a drink was inevitable.

"They owe the old man a Nobel. I tell him every time I see him. You also worked in Prensa Latina, didn't you?"

"At the same time as you did."

"I don't remember you. What section were you in?"

"With Rodolfo Walsh in Special Services. We saw each other once or twice at parties given by him and his wife, Poupé, in their apartment in the Foxá building."

"I saw her in Buenos Aires. She was sure that someone had seen Rodolfo in a provincial jail in Argentina, I think it was in Santa Fe; it's more likely that he is one of the disappeared."

"I can't imagine him as an urban guerrilla," I said.

"Well, can you imagine Masetti leading a guerrilla group in the north of Argentina? Our generation is filling up with corpses."

At eleven-thirty I got up to leave, and I thanked him for having listened to me. He shook my hand warmly. "I've given you what I think is my best advice. If you think about it, you'll see that I am right."

Of course, I paid no attention to his counsels, nor do I think the government cared much either.

García Márquez was not alone, however. Alejo Carpentier took the same view—that in spite of the errors committed by the Revolution, one had to remain faithful to the cause and avoid making enemies of the international left.

I ran into Carpentier during one of his last visits to Havana. By then, he was mortally ill. We met in a bookstore near the old Hilton. I would have avoided him, because the scandal had made his life more difficult as Cuban representative to UNESCO in Paris, and I was aware of that. But he spied me at the end of an aisle and strode toward me with a tired smile. All of him was exhausted; he was sweating profusely now, whereas before he never had a drop on his forehead even on the most torrid day. He asked me to join him, and we went out to the street and into one of the Hilton bars. He sat down and said, "What I want is a beer; I'm suffocating. What about you?" We ordered two.

"What has happened to you could have been worse," he said. "At least you are alive and at liberty. What are you thinking?"

What difference would my "thinking" make? In the end, his affable treatment of me only made things worse. But I thought it best to say nothing.

"Are you staying long in Havana?"

"Look, my boy, I don't even know how I was able to make the trip here. One can know nothing about the future. I am being treated in Paris by the best specialists, and that alone gives me a vague hope. I have to go back, there's no choice for me." He spoke slowly, in a long lamentation. "I've got no choice but to stick with the left. I have to admit that revolutionary literature in Cuba still remains to be written. I have to go back. You are to blame for everything that has happened to you. I told you all this more than once in the past, but of course you young people can't wait to shit on any advice handed down by older people. Look, we just can't get into a fight with the left, and that's all there is to it."

I said nothing, and he kept on. "We can't get into a fight with the left even though it is lame, one-eyed, and ugly. What is the right? What can it offer us? The right never gave me a thing. Those are the people who tell us that the poor are poor because that is God's will. What have they ever given you? Tell me, Padilla, just exactly what have they given you?"

He asked the question with such vehemence that I decided to answer. I told him that the right had never given me a thing and I expected nothing from it.

He seemed infused by a burst of energy. "Ha! They've bestowed on you the worst reputation that any writer can have these days—a prestige given you by the same people who spend their lives shitting all over us."

"But I haven't got any prestige, Alejo!" I shouted.

He laughed at that, and leaned over to murmur, "You are the darling of the Opus Dei in Spain, and of all the rock-ribbed European right."

"Why?" I asked, shouting again.

"Come on, why don't you think about it? Perhaps you know already."

"What kind of shit is this?"

At my wits' end, I was ready to hit him over the head with the beer bottle. I couldn't take any more criticism or scolding from people who would have preferred to see me in jail than enjoying even the little freedom I had. Then suddenly I realized that Alejo's tone was now that of a co-conspirator. "Don't you understand why they were not able to lock you up and throw away the key, as they did with so many others? Can't you figure it out? Look, they don't give alternatives to people they don't respect. They are not afraid of people they don't respect. That's it."

I had to laugh. For me, a political prisoner was an adversary of the government who had proved it in action.

"No, you've got it wrong," he said. "In matters of policy,

adversaries are chosen. A CIA agent is not an adversary, nor is a terrorist—one of those trigger-happy nuts from Miami. You grab such people and throw them in jail. They have been condemned by history. But a young man who comes out of the revolutionary process, who has shown himself to be a supporter of its objectives as you have been, and has been present in critical situations? That man is not an adversary. They let you out because it was not necessary to imprison you. You have to retain a deferential attitude toward the Revolution, and study the reasons why they didn't treat you like the others."

For a moment, as he nervously talked and sipped his beer, I thought about deference, but I was in no mood to give it much attention. I thought that I had been forced to degrade myself, in a manner typical of the Communist world. Alejo should have known all this much better than I. Why was he speaking this way to me? He obviously was aware that our meeting might be spied on, that the fact that we had seen each other and were having a beer would be immediately known to State Security. In retrospect, I think it was one of his last independent acts.

Well before our meeting, he had been named to the National Assembly by the simple expedient of having his name appear unopposed on the ballot. He had behaved with the iron discipline of a member of the party when it was necessary to make a break with the old hard-line leftists, and when letters protesting my arrest began coming in, he behaved the same way. Above all, he was ill now, which in the Communist world is probably the only safe-conduct of any value.

In the end, my wife, Belkis, was permitted to leave Cuba in 1979 with Ernesto. She traveled on a three-month visa to visit her sick mother, whom she had not seen for fourteen years. The authorities knew, of course, that she was not going to return. During the year or so that we were separated, she did everything in her power to obtain permission for me to leave Cuba.

During that year when Belkis and Ernesto were alone in the

United States, I lived in a state of permanent tension. Letters from them and from other friends aroused in me an anguished expectation rather than keeping my spirits up. In the mornings I used to work on translations for the Editorial Arte y Literatura; every afternoon, when my nerves became intolerable, I went to the beach at Miramar and swam until I was exhausted. One afternoon the poet Manuel Díaz Martínez called to say that Virgilio Piñera had died of a massive heart attack. Although he was one of our most distinguished dramatists, his passing went unnoticed in the world of official culture. He had been a friend of long standing and my colleague in so many things that his death at that moment of great uncertainty only accentuated my solitude.

21

~~~~~~

THE ACCEPTED IMAGE of Virgilio Piñera is of the pederast incessantly pursued by the Revolution, as if the Revolution were a cop in a silent movie. That image, created with such energy by Guillermo Cabrera Infante, who knew him well, is difficult to elaborate on. And yet I will try to provide a portrait of the man *I* knew—a tenacious writer, fully conscious of what he was doing, witty and generous. The Virgilio Piñera whom I met in 1954 just after he returned from Argentina cannot be easily reduced to the set of festive peripatetics of the ordinary homosexual.

He was twenty years older than the rest of us and had

already lived a full life and written a great deal. I know now, from experience, that the only things a mature writer can hand down to a younger generation are his multiple and ever-changing masks. He was allergic to professorial posing and had been a literary loner, but in the fifties Virgilio found himself lionized by a group of younger writers. Yet he was separated from them by the arid years of his youth, in which, in Cuba, culture was nothingness.

Where Guillermo Cabrera hit the mark in his portrait of Virgilio was in tracing out the impression Virgilio gave of always being on the lam, his sudden disappearances. Which Virgilio did Guillermo Cabrera Infante know? Unquestionably, the one he describes. My version is the man I first got to know as we sat at adjoining desks every Sunday morning in the editorial offices of *Revolución*. He would write his column, which he signed with the pen name *El escriba*, at the same time that I was putting together a roundup of international events for the previous week. We would arrive punctually at nine o'clock and leave around one in the afternoon. Since I had a car, I would drive him back to his apartment in El Vedado, next door to José (Pepe) Rodríguez Feo, one of the founders of and a contributor to the review *Orígenes* (who had an extensive correspondence with Wallace Stevens). We would sometimes go up to Rodríguez Feo's apartment and talk with him while he finished lunch; on a few occasions, we shared a meal with him. Virgilio, too, had been in the *Orígenes* group, but he and Justo Rodríguez Santos were associated with the magazine more because of their friendship with Lezama Lima and, of course, with Rodríguez Feo than because of any stylistic adherence.

Virgilio was a marginal figure in the *Orígenes* group, whereas Cintio Vitier and Eliseo Diego, who seemed parodies of Lezama, were central to its existence. Virgilio was a gloss on no one. His membership in the group was based on his being included in the poetry anthology selected and introduced by Vitier in 1948. The anthology was an exquisitely produced book; every poet treasures it. I still have my copy, and when I look at it, it is both appealing and heartrending. But I was and am unable to identify with its hermetic character, the cryptic and overblown structures of the poems. There is no life to them. The circumlocution for a woman's place was the "zone of the wife"; for a man, the "place of the husband." The homosexuality of a few members of the group, including Lezama, was reduced to one very beautiful poem, "Desirable is he who flees from his mother." I do not know why the anthology began with an epigraph from Paul Valéry, since the only thematic interest shared with the French poet was a will toward the rationalization of poetry and a concern with Narcissus.

Virgilio's poem in the anthology, "Life of Flora," is like an explosion in an ensemble of metaphysical and mystical adventures. The verses accentuate Virgilio's unmistakable voice. "You had big feet and a clubfoot, Flora," he wrote. In his acrid and incisive compassion toward a being of flesh and blood, a poor lame Havana woman (in such marked contrast to the mysteries of the Eucharist and the unseen gardens of an imagined aristocracy), Virgilio Piñera is at his essential best.

He was the epitome of the artist who has been called an "oppressed man"; that is, someone who cannot take part fully in the work of his own generation because his oeuvre contains elements that will burst forth only with the next generation. He really did feel relaxed working with us younger writers. As editor of the official newspaper of the July 26th Movement, *Revolución*, Franqui had given us enormous freedom. The cultural supplement, *Lunes de Revolución*, championed a literature in which many alternatives were possible. Perhaps Virgilio saw in *Lunes* the fulfillment of the objectives of the magazine *Ciclón*, which Rodríguez Feo had founded in the forties, after his break with *Orígenes*. Virgilio was the guiding spirit of *Ciclón*, whose logo was a stern-faced cherub with cheeks puffed up, blowing furiously. *Lunes* itself was more like a hurricane at times, because we were not able to put forward our program in a sustained and ongoing way, as we would have liked. Many issues of *Lunes* reflected the fact that we had to make compromises with official policy—compromises made with those ingenuous high hopes that so often leave people in a bind. For instance, in the number devoted to modern Soviet culture, we behaved with "discipline": the issue had to be recast to adapt it to the pressing need of that moment; that is, the need to lie. The same thing happened in the issues devoted to North Korea and China, which were put together to the background of Ithiel León's bitter laughter. Ithiel was the man who collected the material we were publishing, on his trips through those countries—the classic horrified tourist.

Virgilio often wrote for *Lunes*; and appreciative essays on him as well as his own work were frequently published in its pages. The offices were always open, an enormous room just behind the teletype machines. These machines separated us from the reporters and editors of the daily, who treated us like peculiar animals. The clatter from the machines did serve as a sound curtain that muffled our literary discussions. Seated at his tiny desk, Guillermo Cabrera Infante presided over the sessions, always in a coat and tie. His appearance and his desk matched his white Nash convertible, which bore him around Havana. Guillermo played the role of provocateur in the group, which, more or less, was made up of Virgilio, Pablo Armando Fernández, Antón Arrufat, Fausto Canel, Humberto Arenal, Luis Agüero, Álvarez Baragaño, Severo Sarduy, Jaime Saruski, Ambrosio Fornet, and Edmundo Desnoes.

Often, after midnight, Guillermo would conduct a cruel interrogatory, asking who among us would earn a name in Cuban literature. Virgilio would serve as presiding judge, and he handed down the sentences in silence, with only a grimace or a gesture.

Guillermo would ask: "Master, will El Pocho [Ambrosio Fornet] win a place in posterity?"

A doubtful shrug of the shoulders. Everyone would laugh, and Fornet paled.

"And the Cow [that is, Saruski]?"

Raised eyebrows, the beginnings of a smile. Saruski would break out in a sweat.

"And Desnoes?"

A slight twist of the mouth.

"And Pablo Armando?"

Eyes raised to the ceiling.

"And Padilla, Baragaño, Arrufat?"

An impassive expression, which then brightened somewhat.

"And Lisandro Otero?"

Guffaw.

A born actor. It is too bad that Cuba never had a major theater in which dramatists could rewrite their plays right onstage, correcting them from the wings—and not as theater has always been written, with indications to the actors set down dryly on the page. Both Virgilio's theater pieces and his vocation as an actor would have come into their own. Our dramatists were always obliged to annotate everything, down to the backdrops. When *The Night of the Assassins* by José Triana was awarded a Casa prize despite the opposition of two members of the jury, it was the mise en scène that was awarded the prize, and malicious observers were heard to remark that the value of the work was in its staging and the "extraordinary" direction by Vicente Revuelta. The play as published was a dry script; the variations that had been introduced during the performances were altogether absent.

When Virgilio would read us his plays, he would act out all the parts like a quick-change artist. Fortunately, we also had the opportunity of seeing him perform in public when the Teatro Estudio permitted him to give a poetry reading. It was unforgettable. The floor of the stage was covered with a woolly rug. There was a small lectern. A single spotlight from above shone down on Virgilio, following his thin body dressed in fatigue pants and a bright blue shirt; he was shoeless. He began by reciting some of his best poems from memory, as if they were monologues. The applause went on and on. Virgilio left the stage and returned, took a bow. His movements seemed to reflect his own hallucinatory pattern of appearances and disappearances. How was it that Virgilio, that invisible man, could fill a stage? The light on his face brought out his gray eyes, sockets set off by the mauve light; a glimmer of tears. Although he would never confess it to anyone, his hyper-aesthetic sensibility was born of years of suffering—of being a homosexual in a macho country, a writer in a cultural ambiance whose only literary magazine was *Orígenes*. I saw him cry twice, once when Baragaño, whom he had admired as a poet and *enfant terrible*, suddenly died; the other time, at Lezama's death. He embraced me then, sobbing as he spoke in my ear: "The fat man has left us."

I remember him reading poems from his younger years, full of an infinite melancholy. He could recite whole passages in French from the *Phèdre* of Racine. Cabrera Infante reports that Virgilio liked me, but the reasons given are not quite clear. Virgilio and I did share a phobia of the baroque. We used to spend hours trying to figure out why the literature of Spain, written in times that were so fecund for science, was so chaotic and overblown. Our mutual irritation at the theories of Alejo Carpentier about the innately baroque nature of culture in Latin America was boundless. Virgilio was entranced by an anecdote of José Bianco's, the Argentine novelist, told when he visited Cuba. Borges, blind, happened to meet Bianco and recognized him instantly by his voice. "Pepe," he exclaimed, "what are you doing here?" Bianco responded with a verse of Borges's: "Being in the vain night / the man who counts the syllables." Borges, pleased perhaps, couldn't help adding, "Don't you think that's too baroque?"

From the work of Borges, Virgilio had learned to mistrust any writer who "used Spanish" for camouflage or with empty pomp. The defenders of such deceitful language, such as Alfonso Reyes and Pedro Henríquez Ureña (even though they themselves did not use it), reproached Borges for preferring second-rate English writers to certain eminent Spanish writers.

Of course, they were being unfair, since few people have written anything better or more exact about Quevedo or Cervantes than Borges. But Virgilio recognized that Borges, with his farfetched opinions and his critical excesses, was destroying the lair of those "advocates of the baroque" which Antonio Machado had spoken of.

Virgilio and Borges do not share a "will toward style," but they do employ similar methods of plunging into the imagination. "El baile" ("The Dance") of Virgilio could have been written by Borges, but this short story was published well before the Argentinian's major work appeared.

It is odd that at the time Severo Sarduy, a close student of Borges, thought that Virgilio and I were correct. Only years later would he determine that "to be baroque today means threatening, judging, and parodying a bourgeois economy based on the miserly distribution of goods at its center and at its very axis, against the space of signs, language, symbolic support of society, against a guarantee of its smooth functioning and clear communication." Of course, Sarduy is not speaking of the Spanish baroque but of the Spanish American neo-baroque, of the imbalance which is the "structural reflection of a desire that cannot attain its object."

For Virgilio, that "structural reflection" was not expressed at the level of old and new languages working at the same time, but rather in the articulation of imaginative planes which should nonetheless be transparent in order to be intelligible. He was never interested in play on words or parodic discourse. He strove for an oblique or allusive representation of thought, which he would vividly accentuate by the use of words which expressed that thought so perfectly that they seemed in the end to disappear from the page. It is too early to tell if he achieved his ideal. He sublimated nothing. His metaphors were his reality, his flesh. The title of one of his stories and one of his novels, "Simple Flesh," seems to describe his very being, the form of his desire.

In the political realm, we were also close. The contemporary world nauseated him, but he never lost a sense of lucidity and humor as he subjected the world to his scrutiny. During my absences from Cuba we wrote to each other often, above all when I was posted to Moscow. A letter written a few months after I left Havana manages to conceal his worst fears within a catalogue of frivolous detail.

Havana, November 30, 1962

My dear Padilla:
    You come to mind through a trivial association of ideas—the "chill" given me by the air conditioning in my office and the "chill" of Moscow. I cannot avoid this question—also trivial: What could Padilla be up to right now? We immediately make some calculations concerning time zones. Let us suppose, for instance, that it is three in the morning, Moscow time. It is more than probable that Padilla is asleep. On the other hand, maybe not—he is staying up late. If he is not staying up late, he is the victim of a toothache which is the cause of his being awake; the toothache has forced him to find solace reading *Four Quartets* again. Setting aside this little mental game, what is convincing in this matter is the depth of affection which accompanies my little game. To be concerned is to be touched by someone; to put someone else out of one's mind is to despise human beings. All this to tell you that I am preoccupied and concerned by your stay in Moscow, and not because I imagine that you are about to be given a crushing hug by a gray bear on a Moscow street, but rather because of what life might bring. To want to know what Padilla is doing in Moscow is an ennobled curiosity based on affection. Here and there I have found out things about you, from your translation of a poem by Yevtushenko published here, because Arcocha informed us that said poet had introduced you at a Moscow poetry reading, because Martínez gave me a few vague tidbits. Now I want you to write me so that the bits and pieces turn into copious data. I will tell you about my case. Those people from the eighteenth century, ever more eighteenth-century every day, have gone to incredible Versaillesque extremes. For example, Fornet has shaved off his beard, fearing that he might be confused with a figure from the Renaissance, the era they hate most avidly. Lisandro is all puffed up because Goytisolo told him that all Paris was talking about him (sic). And on the basis of what, I asked

him. Here everyone is taking a pinch of snuff. As they say, they are on the way out. Finally, *La Guerra y los Basiliscos* by Llópiz came out. Its author was kind enough to dedicate it to me. I was not at all surprised by the bit about "Master of this generation," but I don't know what to think about the second part—"To Virgilio Piñera, Bulwark of Symbolism." I was aware that I owed much to many movements, but as for Symbolism . . . For the little I have read of *La G. y los B.*, I suspect that Llópiz is an indefatigable cultivator of Borges. We all hope that this start in his career with Borges ends in a blazing finale named Llópiz.

Continuing on in the "informative mode" (in a city such as ours, so alien to thought, there is no choice but to fill up letters in this mode), I'll tell you that Óscar Hurtado gave a reading (for specialists) of his recent poem, "La ciudad muerta de Korad." It consists of fifty-eight manuscript pages, numerous epigraphs in Latin and Spanish, references to and citations of other poets (including you and me, but not Arrufat). It is a poem subdivided into four parts: "The Princess of Mars" (alluding to the work of Burroughs); "The Phantom of the Opera" (transposition of the Leroux novel); "The Story of His Father"; and "The Abduction of the Princess." It is an excellent poem and, even more, a great achievement. It has passages which are true discoveries, and it is above all a *fiery* poem, romantic, reminding me generally of the incomparable poem of Hugo, "Noces et Festin." It will be issued by Ediciones R by February. I presume that you are aware of the imminent and threatening trip of Pablo Armando Fernández to London, where his stammering English will be the torture of the lords of both chambers. We have just about come to an agreement with Her Gracious Majesty as to protocol. Pablo will present himself before Her Majesty and, without opening his mouth, will make the expected reverential moves. Then his voice, recorded as corrected by T. S. Eliot, will be heard, pronouncing his discourse of greeting. On the eighth of December I will publish *Aire frío*. People are getting keyed up. We shall see. Here people want "entertainment" (is that the way you spell it?), but I am going to give them searing whines and lots of black smoke . . . Pepe Triana is writing a long essay (Is such a thing possible? Can he put enough thoughts together to make thirty pages?) about your book, Pablo's, and Arrufat's.

It will come out in *Unión*. The Parajón group is busy getting ready for the centenary of the poet Julián del Casal. A whole team is snooping around Havana seeking out traces of his life, clues, typography, sighs left on a corner, details of his clothes, perfumes, etc.—in a word, an entire thickly populated forest of that poet who after one hundred years seems so similar to our poets with "their long locks soaked up in melancholy." Now the Puente group (they have an office at the Writers' Union) will put out a magazine entitled *Catapulta*, and it is well titled, as the first number contains a hatchet job on Nicolás Guillén and praise for Lezama. The fat man has been touching up details on his family shield. Now the motto of it reads: "Tardy, but Inevitable"—a bridge, a great bridge now visible . . .

That's all, my dear Heberto. How are you? The family? Tell me if you and they have adjusted to Moscow. One more thing—don't forget the prologue to the anthology. Arrufat and I can follow your instructions for the selection. Tell me what to do. Tell me if you are doing any writing these days, how's the work, etc.

A big hug from
Virgilio

"The people from the eighteenth century" was how we alluded to Ambrosio Fornet and Edmundo Desnoes. The anthology was the first collective project of Ediciones R, directed by Virgilio. This anthology, along with my novel *Busca vidas*, was destroyed when Ediciones R was liquidated and Virgilio removed. I could tell that Virgilio wanted me to tell him what I was seeing, and I did tell him in my reply. Although thirty years ago we were not as cautious as every Cuban is nowadays, I tried to ensure that the letter would be seen only by Virgilio and my writer friend Calvert Casey. I later found out that the letter had disappeared; it would turn up in the State Security file as proof of my being an enemy of socialism. They had taken everything from Virgilio, my letter included. Our ingenuousness, or sloppiness, then was without limit. After I replied to Virgilio, Casey couldn't stand it any longer and he wrote a letter which I have among so many from both of them:

Havana, February 5

Beloved Muscovite:

From all indications and from what Arcocha tells me, my letter to you never arrived, because you have given no signs of life, though I did read your especially interesting letter to Virgilio.

I wrote you *motu proprio*, knowing full well how melancholic the first days in an unknown place can be. You can see how my best intentions were lost in the mails. So many other things get lost that way; I sent you a chapter of a novel of mine which came out in *Unión* and which you probably have received by now, clippings, etc. I've been put on the jury of the Casa de las Américas, and it is driving me crazy; they are engaging people, though—Cortázar from Paris, Emmanuel Carballo of Mexico, González Tuñón of Argentina, and others. They all love your poetry. Your book and Arrufat's seem to be the best. They saw *Aire frío*, which is very good—I'll send reviews.

I enclose some poems by Miguel Barnet, whom I had to endure one night when he read his poems in public. I couldn't take it; I threw a glass on the floor and went home. How the young poets admire you.

I miss your corrosive wit, your constant irritation, your intolerable voice, your insults.

There you have Pablo in London and Guillermo in Brussels—do you write to them?

So, no more time for anything; bother me all you want; I have had the *Revista* of the Casa sent to you, have you been getting the *Gaceta*?

A big hug
Calvert

P.S. Send me details of your successes, acclaims, etc.

Virgilio used to get up at six in the morning. He translated, read, and was immensely productive. People have wanted to build a monument to his anus, neglecting the fact that his homosexuality not only satisfied his eros but sustained his intelligence. Virgilio knew how to bind eros with the imagination in Cuban letters with unequaled force. He abhorred drugs, never touched alcohol. Indeed, he was the most circumspect, sober, and generous man I have ever met. Reading his

Aire frío, one can see what his life was like. In more than one sense, that work is the crude summing-up of the typical Cuban family. Virgilio was always on the verge of going hungry, but hunger never appeared in his works except as a metaphor, as in "La carne." In the State Publishing House, where he worked as a translator, they loved him. But though he was the first to do extra "voluntary labor," he was hated and condemned by the regime and its servants.

His masters were Gombrowicz and Central European literature: Kafka, Karel Čapek, Bruno Schulz. Probably because of his youthful friendship with Gombrowicz in Buenos Aires, Virgilio supervised the translation into Spanish of Gombrowicz's novel *Ferdydurke*. It is also impossible to overlook the influence on Virgilio of the tales comprising the *Anthology of Fantastic Literature*, edited by Borges, Silvina Ocampo, and Adolfo Bioy Cásares, published in Buenos Aires in 1940, when Virgilio was barely twenty-five. It was in Argentina, in Borges, Silvina Ocampo, José Bianco, and Witold Gombrowicz, that Virgilio found his literary mentors.

Besides Guillermo Cabrera Infante, other friends have doubtless written about Virgilio, but no Cuban of his generation wrote anything about him when he died suddenly on the night of October 18, 1979, during one of his proverbial games of canasta. The few photographs extant scarcely give an accurate impression; he always put on a grave face for the camera, that of a pompous and circumspect actor. But I remember him as I saw him on so many occasions over the course of two decades—a being whom the years were not able to change physically. He never gained weight or altered his way of combing his hair or his style of dress.

Virgilio died in absolute silence, reduced to the category of mere translator. In general, when a member of the Writers' Union dies, a notice is posted at the entrance of the Union, announcing the place and time of his funeral, just as soon as the arrangements have been set. The announcement of Virgilio's death, almost illegible, appeared a few hours before we were to accompany the casket to the Colón Cemetery. The only thing which seemed to worry the directorate at the Union was that the family should try not to select a "controversial type" to speak at the gravesite. As always, they suggested that stuttering phantom Ángel Augier, but since the burial service for Lezama we had learned to counter such initiatives. They had, after all, suggested Augier for Lezama's service, but his widow vehemently opposed the choice and asked Cintio Vitier to speak. After Virgilio's death, his closest friends met with his sister Luisa, and Pablo Armando Fernández was chosen.

Virgilio died late in the afternoon; his death was known by us the next morning. I was informed by the poet Manuel Díaz Martínez, who phoned and told me. I only managed to say, "And Pepe?"—referring to Virgilio's neighbor Rodríguez Feo. "I think he already knows." I then received the three calls which, after eight years of isolation, I had reason to expect— from César López, Pablo Armando Fernández, and José Rodríguez Feo, the little group which had shared Virgilio's last years. We had met often to eat and to comment on the news of the day, which we magnified just as bombastically as such things are being magnified today.

Pablo Armando and I went to César's house, just one block from the funeral home where Virgilio lay. It was a very windy morning, the first cold blast of the supposed Cuban winter. César's house was enormous. It faced the sea and was close enough to seem battered by the waves at high tide. What an unforgettable house that was, where pain and fleeting joy brought us together so many times, when so many people now dead were still alive.

We went in and went straight to the kitchen like conspirators. After a few sips of strong coffee, we went to César's library and sat down, saying nothing. César's wife, Micheline, had died recently; Lezama had gone. Now it was the turn of the man we had all thought would never die—Virgilio.

At the funeral home we met Antón Arrufat and Luis Agüero. We were worried about Virgilio's papers. One of us got a key and went to Virgilio's apartment to get his manuscripts, which had recently been typed clean. Virgilio boasted of always having things in order, as when he chose as literary executors his nephew Juan and Antón Arrufat. But whoever got to the apartment first found the door locked, with an official seal prohibiting anyone from entering. We understood then that Virgilio's manuscripts were already in the hands of the police.

We were all aware of what had happened a few months before between Virgilio and State Security. Agents had smashed down the door to his apartment, early in the morning, when Virgilio was in the habit of working on his translations. They screamed at him, calling him an old counterrevolutionary and a fag, and confiscated copies of his works. Virgilio had also told us that they came back later and threatened him, warning that it "would cost him a lot" if he met with foreigners or continued to attend certain literary meetings. He only told this to a few people, but soon everyone in the Havana cultural scene knew about the incidents. After that, Virgilio became even more of a recluse, but he did set up a code system for us to use if we wanted to visit him. One ring on the telephone would mean that we were waiting at the corner. On one of my last visits to him I was accompanied by my friend Carlos Verdecia, formerly Vice Minister of Foreign Commerce, who wanted to ask Virgilio some questions about literature on behalf of Verdecia's son, who was studying at an American university and was writing a thesis on Virgilio's work. Virgilio was not at all happy to hear about Verdecia's son and his thesis; indeed, he was quite upset. A few French writers and theater people had paid him a visit not long before with the same thing in mind, but he had refused to say a word. "In any case," he said in a low voice, "my work is done. Look at it, nice and tidy, cleanly typed so I can hand it over to my nephew and to Arrufat. I'm now seventy-eight years old and you never know when you are going to kick the bucket."

On the bed of the denuded room, so well described by Cabrera Infante, were the manuscripts, lots of them. Fear had not overcome Virgilio's will to survive. He rarely went out into the street. At nine in the morning he would hand in his translations to the appropriate department, where many "dissidents" in disgrace earned a living, a place separate from the editorial offices of the State Publishing House and located in the most unappealing spot imaginable. I, too, had to hand in, every day, the same number of pages of bad novels that I had been told to translate, and we often met there. We would leave the office together, walking back to our respective homes. Walking was the surest and also the most relaxed way to talk about what was going on in the country. At times, it was impossible for me to show up at nine o'clock, and when I would appear the next day I could usually tell that he had been disturbed by my absence. One week before he died, I did not go to the office for three consecutive days—a friend brought in my pages for me. On the fourth day, unable to restrain himself any longer, Virgilio wrote me a note: "Padilla, I make use of P. to come see you and hand you this little paper. I don't know, I got up in a bad mood and remembered the sentence of Rimbaud—'Par delicatesse, j'ai perdu ma vie . . .' Well, I'm almost in tears. Yours, Virgilio." I did not see him again. The heart attack occurred four days later.

In a Cuban funeral home, the body lies in a coffin half-covered by glass. One sees only the face and the upper torso. There is a long-standing tradition, a kind of art, I suppose, of cosmetically improving the faces of suicides, victims of accidents, and those who have died after a long illness. Funeral-home artists make use of all kinds of powders and creams, following a photograph of the person as model. And, in death, Virgilio preserved the serenity of expression that he had the last time I saw him; his face was illuminated by the theatrically unreal light given off by the candles. There lay, resolute and visible, the invisible man whom so many tried to decipher. He looked like a physical rendering of his soul.

Less pompously, his other friends shared my impression of the dead man. Finally, Pablo, César, and I went back to the mansion by the sea, where Pablo was going to write the eulogy on César's typewriter. He couldn't find the words. We agreed that the writer's block came from the fact that, though Virgilio was dead, he was still putting up obstacles to our treating his death with proper solemnity. So in the end we decided to treat him in death as we had treated him in life, and that ours would be a panegyric authored by three hands—Pablo Armando at the typewriter, César next to him to help him sustain the discourse, and I looking on expectantly. We would eliminate the funereal gravity which Virgilio had despised, that verbal pomp which used to sicken him so. We even eschewed those old-fashioned clichés which he might in fact have favored. But we only got halfway. The text was going nowhere. Then Pablo, like a Raymond Lully, that expert in dialogues of the heavens and the earth, leapt from the typewriter, saying that he was incapable of writing any more, that I should do it; he then went back to the typewriter, waiting for my words. The words of the eulogy for Virgilio may have come out of my mouth, but it was as if Virgilio were dictating them to me. Pablo Armando didn't leave the typewriter till I threw myself exhausted on the library sofa. We promised each other that someday one of us would describe what had happened during that ritual, that spectacle of anguish, love, and efficacy of three friends linked to Virgilio's memory. The political differences which separate us now are of no importance. What counts is that crucial moment that brought us together by the grave of our friend. If the experts in State Security submit the eulogy to one of their close readings, they will be forced to admit that it is a text that Virgilio obliged me to dictate and that he obliged all three of us to recite.

22

ONE NIGHT at the beginning of March 1980, the telephone rang in my apartment and my stepdaughter María Josefina answered. I was sitting in the farthest room, which Belkis had turned into a study. The person calling was Chomi Millar, chief administrator at the office of Fidel Castro. But María Josefina thought that the caller was Ramoncito Ante, a young man from the neighborhood who loved to play tricks on her over the telephone. When she realized who was really calling, she came running: "It's Fidel's office."

Chomi asked me when I could come to the office of the Comandante in the Palace of the Revolution. I told him that

I could be there in less than an hour. He made an appointment for ten the next morning. I was convinced by then that the efforts of Belkis, my sister, and my children, along with the support given me by my North American friends, headed by the dynamic Bob Silvers, not to mention the efforts of the PEN Club in New York, then presided over by Bernard Malamud, were finally having results. I also knew that Gabriel García Márquez was trying to sway the hard-liners in State Security. Although I never heard from him directly, he had sent messages on various occasions through Pablo Armando Fernández, whom he would run into in the hallways and dining rooms of Havana hotels.

I got up early and arrived at the Palace right on time. I went to the main entrance and identified myself; a soldier escorted me to the office of a functionary, who had instructions to bring me to Fidel's office. The place had a North American air to it, but there were paintings by Mariano and Portocarrero on the walls. Chomi was dressed in an olive-green shirt and pants; he had olive skin himself and an unctuous manner. He had been my superior when he was rector of the University of Havana, but now he was receiving me in the capacity of replacement for Fidel's confidante, Celia Sánchez, who had died of cancer.

Just then Fidel appeared, half real and half fiction. He told Chomi that he had left a few reports on his desk from members of the party in Camagüey; Fidel and I were then left alone.

"How long has it been since we last spoke?"

"Not long," I said.

"No, I mean really had a conversation."

"Almost twenty years," I said.

"But I've been seeing your face almost constantly."

"But we haven't spoken," I said.

"True, it was in groups, but we have spoken." He looked at me for a few moments and then said, "You are fatter, but I am older. There have been many years of struggle." And he got up and started to walk around the room.

"Your request to leave the country has been granted, just as it was granted for your wife, Belkis, last year. I don't deny that I would have liked for you to have direct personal experience of the work that is being done throughout the country, because—don't take me wrong—intellectuals are generally not interested in the social aspect of a revolution; they are interested only in their freedoms. I don't know what you all talk about, but you always wind up in a confrontation with the Revolution. You spend your time voicing opinions about our problems as if you were experts."

He stopped, and then added vehemently, "I have already told everyone that I think you should leave, and I am not doing this under pressure from outside, although it is true that your wife even wrote to the Pope. You can go to any country you want."

It wasn't so. The Cuban mission in Washington had told Belkis to move to New York. They refused to allow me to take a direct flight to Miami, and flying to Spain had been ruled out.

"No one will touch your things or your books, and everything will stay as it is now. How much time did you ask for, two or three years?"

"Three years."

"Stay as long as you want, and when you want to come back, give me a call. If you are a true revolutionary, you will want to return . . . Don't get the idea that happiness is waiting for you on the other side; your exile will be nothing like you think it is going to be. Remember what happened to Nicholas Berdyaev when he left the Soviet Union."

"There are differences," I said softly.

"I am not talking about intellectual categories. I am talking about attitudes. Lenin knew his adversary better than those Russian exiles who were waiting for him when the Soviet government asked him to go to Paris. His was a temperament which could not comprehend history, just as yours is."

I was silent.

Then he said, "What is most obvious in your conduct over

the past years is your blind hatred for State Security. Would you mind telling me what government on this earth is able to do without it? It is inevitable in a revolution. People who criticize a revolution may be mistaken, they may be sincere, but they are dangerous nonetheless. To create a new society, we have to demand national unity. Marx and Lenin are the prototypes of a revolutionary and they were both implacable with their enemies."

For Fidel, an enemy was anyone who displayed the merest disagreement with his ideas. Captain Borrego, who had run the Sugar Ministry, warned him at the beginning of 1970 that ten million tons of sugar simply could not be harvested that year. Fidel went into a fury. "Ten million tons there will be," he shouted. "There have to be." The harvest that year was well over eight million, but Fidel had "given his word" that ten million tons of sugar would be produced, and so the extraordinary collective effort seemed a failure. I had decided that those imprudent acts of Fidel's were an exacerbated manifestation of his optimism, but experience showed us that in fact they were a reflection of his contempt for others and his egotism.

Luckily, two years before, I had been able to read the *Diary of the Cuban Revolution* by Carlos Franqui. It was being passed from hand to hand throughout the country, a clandestine book. I had read the first section of the book when Franqui and Valerio Riva, the director of Feltrinelli, were putting together materials for a book to be signed by Fidel himself. In his essay "Concerning Cultural Dissension in Cuba," Valerio recounted in detail the work sessions that had taken place in the Feltrinelli castle in the Piedmont region of Italy. Valerio emphasized in his memoir the effort that had to be made to bring order to Fidel's speeches and writings so that a democratic orientation would prevail over his authoritarian tendencies. They were trying to show Fidel's better side. But when I was finally able to read all of Franqui's *Diary* and I read the letters Fidel had written to his wife and to his friend Naty Revuelta from Batista's jail cell, I finally understood that his Marxism was probably inevitable, since Marxism was the most suitable vehicle for him to create an authoritarian regime in which he would be recognized as Supreme Chief.

Napoleon was one of his idols. "The speeches of Napoleon are true works of art," he would write. "How well he understood the French! In each sentence he is able to play on each one of their emotional strings; he is playing with them . . . and how great he was with his enemies. I have already read much about him and yet I never tire of reading about him. There is no doubt that he was an Alexander without his disorder, Caesar without the personal vices, Charlemagne without massacring whole towns, and Frederick II with lots of guts and a soul open to friendship. I always considered him peerless. It should be remembered that Alexander received from his father, Philip, the powerful throne of Macedonia, and Hannibal received from his father, Hamilcar Barca, his army. Caesar owed much to his patrician blood. Napoleon, on the other hand, owed everything to himself, to his genius and to his will."

In another letter Fidel would say: "Robespierre was an idealist and honorable until his death. With the Revolution endangered, the frontiers of the nation surrounded by enemies, vacillators obstructing the way, it was necessary to be hard, inflexible and severe. It is better to sin through excess than through default, which can only lead to failure. A few months of terror were necessary to do away with a terror which had lasted centuries. We need many Robespierres in Cuba."

For more than twenty years, that was Castro's policy. The man who had spent his youth in a quest for power had little to say to me. He was in the place he had sought. From the wars he had read about when young, he took that impeccably pressed uniform, the big belt, the large pistol, and the laurel leaves next to the star of Commander in Chief on his epaulettes; his salt-and-pepper beard was something none of his legendary heroes from the past could boast of. How different Fidel seemed to me now from the man I met when I was young, during that far-off time spent at the Varadero beach and during the electoral campaign in which he harangued the people with that inflection that was a mixture of Eddy Chibás and Pardo Llada, standing on a podium or shouting from the back of a truck, in his sloppy dress, in shirt sleeves, sweating profusely.

Why hadn't he been "hard, inflexible and severe" in my case? He let Pedro Luis Boitel die in prison during a hunger strike; Paco Chavarri, who had been Vice Minister of Foreign Relations and a militant in the 26th of July Movement, was sent off to prison because of Fidel's rage over his criticism. Jorge Valls was sentenced to twenty years for having testified in favor of Marcos Rodríguez in the trial which sought to implicate the militants of the old CP. I, on the other hand, had expressed my ideas in a book of poems, *Fuera del juego*, and in a novel, but I spent only thirty-seven days in the custody of State Security and as a patient in the Military Hospital. The cells where Boitel, Martha Frayde, Jorge Valls, and Chavarri were imprisoned were the worst anyone in Cuba could have been in at that time. Fidel describes the one he was held in in March of 1954:

> Can you possibly imagine the solitude of this cell? Since I am a good cook, once in a while I entertain myself fixing up something. A few days ago, my sister sent me from Oriente Province a small ham; I fried up a slab of it with guava jelly. But that's nothing; today the boys sent me a little pot of stew with pignoli nuts in syrup. I'm telling you I'll conjure up these things for you by thought alone! Tomorrow I'll have more ham. What do you think? I also do spaghetti sometimes with different sauces or sometimes a tortilla. They are really good. Of course, the repertory is not limited to that. I brew luscious coffee, too. No problem about tobacco—I have a box of Upmanns thanks to Dr. Miró Cardona, and two boxes from my brother Ramón, a bunch from another friend, and even a little box of small ones which came along with some books, one of which I am lighting right now . . .

That was the cell which General Fulgencio Batista reserved for his principal adversary after the assault on the Moncada Barracks.

Fidel asked me suddenly: "How are your relations with Gabriel García Márquez?"

"I saw him a year ago."

"But I know that Belkis has been in touch with him."

True, she had called him many times at his home in Mexico to ask him to keep up the pressure for my release. In all the letters which she sent me during the year we were separated from each other, she would allude to conversations with García Márquez. At his insistence, a motion pending in the Venezuelan senate concerning my case had been quashed, García Márquez having assured her that if it could be stopped, he would be able to obtain permission for me to leave immediately.

Before going on, Fidel asked Chomi for coffee and water for the three of us.

"I know that García Márquez has worried a lot about your case. Besides, he is someone who says exactly what is on his mind. As far as you are concerned, your wife has been told right here in this office to let us know how we could improve your living conditions, that you should ask for anything you needed. But she answered by saying that your only wish was to leave Cuba. Some excesses were committed by us in your case, but I do not believe that is the true reason why you want to leave. I think that you still feel the way you did before. Your friend Alberto Mora blew his brains out, but you prefer to flee the country."

Then, driven to ask a question that he must have wanted to ask me for a long time, he shouted out, "Isn't there anything in the cultural sector of the Revolution that you find admirable?"

He waited impatiently for my answer.

"All the state publishing houses that have been created are admirable," I said.

"Nothing more?"

"The film industry also. Cuba now has its own films, and some of them have been excellent."

He waxed enthusiastic over what I had just said. He felt the same way, he told me. He thought that the success of the ICAIC was the result of teamwork. A film was not the work of one person alone. It was a collaboration between artists, writers, technicians, and manual laborers and required effective political oversight. The filming of *The Brothers Karamazov* had been a joyful task for the Soviet artists who took part in it, whereas the novel cost Dostoevsky untold suffering, since he had to write it within a system of exploitation. Fidel told me that, politically, the cultural arena was an extremely delicate subject for any leader. The conflicts that arose came out of rivalries that were inherent to culture.

Fidel paused, but I said nothing.

"And then you have the case of Jorge Edwards," he went on. "He did praise your thorny, even capricious personality, but still believed you to be a revolutionary. Afterwards, he wrote that book where he stated in so many words that State Security was right; it was more generous to you and to others than he had been. That is a phenomenon typical of all writers. None of the journalists or professors who have interviewed me until now has literally reproduced on the printed page what I have said to them. They invent everything, twist everything, even when they want to make you look better. I remember an answer which Jean-Paul Sartre attributed to me when in fact the question was just as imaginary:

" 'And if the people were to ask you for the moon, what would you do?'

" 'I would give it to them, because I am sure that they would be in need of it.'

"That's not bad, but if all famous phrases have the authenticity of that one, we'll have to find the third party who invents them. Same for historians. The books of Hugh Thomas on the Spanish Civil War and on the Cuban Revolution are loaded with errors."

He drew closer as if to confide a secret. "For a long time now, I have been recording all my conversations with journalists and diplomats. When I get around to writing my memoirs, I will do a separate chapter entitled 'Versions.' I think that it will be an excellent contribution to history."

An hour had passed, but he did not seem tired. He said to Chomi, "What happened to the coffee and the water?"

Suddenly the door opened to reveal a young man dressed in white, standing at attention next to a cart with the coffee and the water. He hadn't dared to knock at the door; the coffee was cold.

Fidel got up. "If you ever describe this conversation in the future, remember that I've got it on tape. Look, what I didn't do with Edwards I will do with you. Your version will have to compete with mine."

Before leaving, he said, "That Chilean diplomat gradually convinced himself that the good days of the Cuban Revolution had ended. The one who ended was poor Allende, who died with a courage that none of his enemies possessed. But when they ask you abroad about this revolution, tell them it will keep on going, and that other revolutions will break out throughout Latin America, because that is where the exploitation and the hunger are. Even though you will never admit it publicly, I know that this revolution will grow in your memory, and you will find out that the best years of your life were lived when you were supporting it, before you got sick and embittered." And Fidel turned his back on me and disappeared into the adjoining office.

Out in the noonday sun, I walked along the street dumbfounded, as if I had just come out of a chapter from a novel. The brisk March air intensified my rapture, but what I was feeling was not really joy but a nervous current coursing through my body. I went over to Alberto Martínez's apartment; *he* showed real joy.

At midnight Belkis called to tell me that Jan Kalicki, an aide to Senator Edward Kennedy, had called to tell her that the Cuban representatives in Washington had told the senator that I had been given permission to leave Cuba. García Márquez called later to say that he was about to arrive in Cuba and that he wanted to talk to me before I left.

The next morning, he called to arrange a meeting in the cafeteria of the Havana Riviera. He said he was delighted that my wishes were being fulfilled, although he was not in favor of any Cuban leaving his own country. He wanted to ask me one question, "because I cannot hide from you the fact that it is annoying to be always walking around with a list of names for me to bring up when I see Fidel. One day he'll get sick of me; but my question is this, Heberto: Why do you think it is that the Cuban government has the same problems with writers that the Soviet Union had in the past?"

I was surprised by the question. I thought he had already answered it a long time ago in his probing articles written during his visits to the Eastern bloc countries and to the Soviet Union.

He noticed my surprise. "I can assure you that I will keep whatever you say confidential. I know how to keep a secret."

"But, Gabriel, those words of yours are already a part of the answer."

Smiling, he said, "I guess that for a time these dilemmas will not be resolved in any socialist country. The Soviet Union has not found a solution in sixty years."

He crossed his legs and I noted that he had on the same maroon boots I had seen him in the year before. We would have the opportunity, he said, of speaking about this matter somewhere else when I would feel less ill at ease.

We shook hands in the lobby of the hotel. This time I didn't see Gustavo Castañeda, the agent from State Security, nor did

I care if he was checking on us. I took a taxi to the old American embassy, where Pablo Armando Fernández was waiting for me. He introduced me to Wayne Smith, the head of the U.S. Interest Section in Havana. Just then the telephone rang and Smith picked it up. It was Jan Kalicki from Senator Kennedy's office, informing him that the State Department had approved my departure for the United States, via Canada.

"Everything is all set," Smith told me. "Kalicki suggests that you go through Montreal. He will be waiting for you at Kennedy with an overcoat and some cash which Bob Silvers wants you to have when you arrive."

With the help of a now cooperative Castañeda, all the paperwork and arrangements for the flight were taken care of in three days. I was exhausted. The afternoon before I left, I went to the beach as if performing an obligatory ritual, and swam out toward the horizon, floating as I contemplated the fiery sky with the sun about to set. All the tension that had built up in recent days vanished mysteriously as I swam. Then I walked up the beach and over to a club where I used to take Belkis and the children. The bar was about to open. I asked for a beer and sat down on the terrace for the last time.

Once again I heard the words Fidel Castro had spoken to me: ". . . Even though you will never admit it publicly, I know that this revolution will grow in your memory . . ." And, in fact, a month after I left I found the Revolution growing in my memory, but in a horrific way. More than 100,000 Cubans, taking advantage of a flukish happenstance, sought asylum in the Peruvian embassy in Havana, and a while later 120,000 were able to leave the island. The streets were full of police swinging iron clubs with orders to pummel and kill anyone who "got in the way." The fervent disciple of Robespierre once again learned his lesson: "We must be hard, inflexible, severe; sin by excess, never by default."

Fidel is an old man now, gray hair and beard, thick glasses, and constantly darting eyes. He is the grandfather of that young man who wrote from Batista's prison a few sentences that might well be taken as his epitaph:

> There is a year in a man's life which he should never go beyond, and that is the year when his life begins to decline, when the flame which lit his most luminous moments goes out, when the physical powers which drove his steps along in his maturity begin to wane—then you see such survivors whimpering and repentant like renegades, sinking into the quicksand of abjection.

*   *   *

At the airport, the last copy of my novel—the original, in fact—was saved by a miracle. Five copies of the manuscript had been discovered by State Security, but this one remained unscathed in a wicker satchel, invisible among toys, letters, and bric-a-brac. The customs inspector's hand was suspended in midair (just as in a detective novel) when his superior, satisfied with the plunder recovered, ordered an end to the inspection of my possessions.

I had brought the manuscript to the airport concealed in that satchel, which contained the hundreds of letters my wife had sent me from the United States during our year of separation. I showed Gustavo the satchel, saying that I wanted to keep the letters with me. Of all the people who were seeing me off at the airport, only my friend Alberto Martínez Herrera knew exactly where the last copy of the manuscript was hidden. He was tense and pale, and he seemed to grow more and more anxious with every passing second. The plane for Montreal was unusually late. I paced up and down the waiting room under Gustavo's watchful eye. His blue safari jacket only barely concealed his pistol. I had the impression that he was still looking at my luggage with marked interest, but Fidel Castro had given the order to let me go. What would he accomplish by searching it again?

In an effort to ease the tension of the wait, I remarked to him on the items the tourists—mostly French-speaking Canadian girls—were buying. I saw the rum bottles lined up for sale, and I said to Gustavo that I was going to buy one, but the cashier told me that they could be bought only with dollars. Gustavo heard this and turned pale. He said he was going to the washroom, and when he came back, he offered to buy me a beer. Minutes afterwards, from a corner of the waiting room, someone signaled him. I pretended that I hadn't noticed; I went to the washroom myself. The plan was to leave in a few minutes, and I would be the first person on board, I had been told. Gustavo led me through a side door and we walked across the tarmac toward the boarding steps already nudged up against the plane with its door wide open. I saw a man approaching us with a package; it was a bottle of rum.

"Our gift to you. Send us a picture when you drink a toast in the United States," Gustavo said. "No hard feelings, I hope." As a matter of fact, I had none. He was my natural enemy, he had orders to be just that—to dog my steps, to learn my thoughts, to make veiled threats over the telephone whenever a foreign visitor expressed an interest in seeing me. In retrospect, his impassivity whenever I screamed at him to his face now seems admirable. He never lost his composure, not even when he tried to prevent García Márquez from speaking to me.

He was a short man with a pale complexion, lank blond hair, and light eyes. Sometimes he weighed a lot, sometimes not, depending on the ups and downs of his kidney disease; that last time I saw him, he was in a bad way. He had been divorced and remarried, and was trying to make a more pleasant life for two little girls, his own child and his new wife's. His brother had committed suicide in his office at the Department of Philosophy at the university. But Gustavo loved his job, took enormous pride in what he was doing, and indeed the truly great tragedy of his life was not being able to show off at the Ministry of Culture or the Writers' Union the major's uniform that was his glory.

I got on the plane and sat next to a window. I could see the airport I had freely passed through to go in and out of Cuba for so many years, and which, on a certain day, had been forbidden me on the decision of one man. Now, thirteen years later, that same man had decided to open it for me again. The observation deck was full of people waving goodbye to those who, like me, had been set free. I saw it all with a sensation of growing unreality. Still standing a few yards from the plane, Gustavo contemplated the scene. I saw him for the first time not from a moral but from a physical height; he was below, down there, like the now dead time of my past troubles.

And in the plane I thought again of wretched Gustavo, whose shouts I was beginning to miss, as the silence of solitude heightened my desolation. I was about to leave all that back there, where he was standing. I held on to the satchel with Belkis's letters and my manuscript. The plane's engines began to sputter. At last we were rolling down the runway, and Gustavo disappeared from view. The plane took off. I heard the stewardess telling us to continue observing the "No Smoking" sign. The plane climbed and leveled off. I looked out the window at the great brilliant expanse—that vivid frieze of greenness and luminosity that is Cuba.